Thomas De Witt Talmage

**Old wells dug out**

Being a third series of sermons

Thomas De Witt Talmage

**Old wells dug out**

*Being a third series of sermons*

ISBN/EAN: 9783337264741

Printed in Europe, USA, Canada, Australia, Japan

Cover: Foto ©Lupo / pixelio.de

More available books at **www.hansebooks.com**

# OLD WELLS DUG OUT:

*BEING A THIRD SERIES OF SERMONS.*

BY

## T. DE WITT TALMAGE,

AUTHOR OF

"CRUMBS SWEPT UP," "THE ABOMINATIONS OF MODERN SOCIETY," "FIRST SERIES OF SERMONS," "SECOND SERIES OF SERMONS," ETC.

PHONOGRAPHICALLY REPORTED AND REVISED.

NEW YORK:
FUNK & WAGNALLS,
10 AND 12 DEY STREET.
1886.

Entered, according to Act of Congress, in the year 1886, by
FUNK & WAGNALLS,
In the Office of the Librarian of Congress at Washington, D. C.

# PREFACE.

This book takes its title not more from the first sermon than from the fact that it is an attempt to re-open the old fountains of the Gospel, which have of late years been partially filled up. For that reason we call the book "Old Wells Dug Out."

Some of these discourses were preached in the Brooklyn Tabernacle, and others in the Academy of Music, while our new church was being built.

As word comes to us from all directions that the previous volumes have been the means of comfort and salvation to very many on both sides the Atlantic, we send this book out, hoping it may do a similar work. These sermons, like their predecessors, were taken down by phonographers, and are left as they were uttered in extemporaneous delivery, without any material changes, because I have not had time to reconstruct them.

They are part of my life. With me the lecturing platform and the literary column are episodes; but the preaching of the Gospel of the Son of God is my chief employment and my indescribable delight. The Christian printing-press is only the pulpit on cylinders. May this attempt to preach through the printed page harvest many sheaves for the Lord's garner!

T. De Witt Talmage.

# CONTENTS.

|  | PAGE |
|---|---|
| OLD WELLS DUG OUT | 13 |
| CHRIST EVERY THING | 28 |
| THE KING'S WAGONS | 39 |
| THE UPPER AND NETHER SPRINGS | 51 |
| THE "VILLE DU HAVRE" | 62 |
| GRACE IN CRYSTALS | 75 |
| GOSPEL ARCHERY | 85 |
| THE BEST WE HAVE | 97 |
| WASTED AROMA | 109 |
| THINGS NOT BURNED UP | 120 |
| WICKEDNESS IN HIGH PLACES | 133 |
| FOURTH ANNIVERSARY | 147 |
| MIGRATION HEAVENWARD | 162 |
| THE LAVER OF LOOKING-GLASSES | 174 |
| CRUMBS UNDER THE TABLE | 187 |
| ORDERED BACK TO THE GUARD-ROOM | 201 |
| FREE CHURCHES ADVOCATED | 213 |
| OBJECTIONS TO FREE CHURCHES ANSWERED | 227 |
| WOMAN'S WAR AGAINST THE BOTTLE | 242 |
| THE PROUD RIDER UNHORSED | 257 |
| THE CHRISTIAN NEEDLE-WOMAN | 269 |
| HORACE GREELEY, LIVING AND DEAD | 280 |
| ARRIVAL OF AUTUMN | 292 |
| BLEATING SHEEP AND LOWING OXEN | 305 |
| DIFFICULT ROWING | 316 |
| THE BURNING OF THE BROOKLYN TABERNACLE | 329 |

|   | PAGE |
|---|---|
| THE BRIGHTEST OF DAYS | 340 |
| THE WORLD GOING | 356 |
| WEAPONS CAPTURED | 365 |
| THE PILE OF STONES SPEAKING | 376 |
| CHRIST OUR SONG | 387 |
| THE WELL BY THE GATE | 401 |
| CESSATION OF EXPERIMENT | 415 |

# OLD WELLS DUG OUT.

## OLD WELLS DUG OUT.

"And Isaac digged again the wells of water, which they had digged in the days of Abraham his father; for the Philistines had stopped them after the death of Abraham: and he called their names after the names by which his father had called them."—*Genesis* xxvi., 18.

IN Oriental lands a well of water is a fortune. If a king dug one, he became as famous as though he had built a pyramid or conquered a province. Great battles were fought for the conquest or defense of wells of water; castles and towers were erected to secure permanent possession of them. The traveler to-day finds the well of Jacob dug one hundred feet through a solid rock of limestone. These ancient wells of water were surrounded by walls of rock. This wall of rock was covered up with a great slab. In the centre of the slab there was a hole through which the leathern bottle or earthen jar was let down. This opening was covered by a stone. When Jacob, a young man of seventy years, was courting Rachel, he won her favor, the Bible says, by removing the stone from the opening of the well. He liked *her* because she was industrious enough to come down and water the camels. She liked *him* because he was clever enough to lay hold and give a lift to one who needed it.

It was considered one of the greatest calamities that could happen a nation when these wells of water were stopped. Isaac, you see in the text, found out that the wells of water, that had been dug out by his father Abraham at great expense and care, had been filled up by the spiteful Philistines. Immediately Isaac orders them all opened again. I see the spades plunging, and the earth tossing, and the water starting, until the old wells are entirely restored; and the cattle come down to the trough and thrust their nostrils in the water, their bodies quaking at every swallow, until they lift up their heads and look around and take a long breath, the water from the sides of their mouths dripping in sparkles down into the trough. I never tasted such water in my life as in my boyhood I drank out of the moss-covered bucket that swung up on the chains of the old well-sweep; and I think when Isaac leaned over the curb of these restored wells, he felt within himself that it was a beverage worthy of God's brewing. He was very careful to call all the wells by the same names which his father had called them by; and if this well was called "The Well in the Valley," or "The Well by the Rock," or "The Well of Bubbles," Isaac baptized it with the same nomenclature.

You have noticed, my Christian friends, that many of the old Gospel wells that our fathers dug have been filled up by the modern Philistines. They have thrown in their skepticisms and their philosophies, until the well is almost filled up, and it is nigh impossible to get one drop of the clear water. These men tell us that you ought to put the Bible on the same shelf with the Koran and the old Persian manuscripts, and to read it with the same spirit; and there is not a day but somebody comes along and drops a brick or a stone or a carcass in this old Gospel well. We are told that all the world wants is development, forgetful of the fact that without the Gospel the world always develops downward, and that if you should take the religion of Christ out of this world, in one hundred years it would develop into the "Five Points" of the universe. Yet there are a great many men and there are a great many rostrums whose whole work it is to fill up these Christian wells.

You will not think it strange, then, if the Isaac who speaks to you this morning tries to dig open some of the old wells made by Abraham, his father, nor will you be surprised if he calls them by the same old names.

Bring your shovel and pickaxe and crow-bar, and the first well we will open is the glorious well of *the Atonement*. It is nearly filled up with the chips and *débris* of old philosophies that were worn out in the time of Confucius and Zeno, but which smart men in our day unwrap from their mummy-bandages, and try to make us believe are original with themselves. I plunge the shovel to the very bottom of the well, and I find the clear water starting. Glorious well of the Atonement! Perhaps there are people here who do not know what "atonement" means, it is so long since you have heard the definition. The word itself, if you give it a peculiar pronunciation, will show you the meaning—*at-one-ment*. Man is a sinner, and deserves to die. Jesus comes in and bears his punishments and weeps his griefs. I was lost once, but now I am found. I deserved to die, but Jesus took the lances into his own heart until his face grew pale and his chin dropped on his chest, and he had strength only to say, "It is finished!" The boat swung round into the trough of the sea, and would have been swamped, but Jesus took hold of the oar. I was set in the battle, and must have been cut to pieces had not, at night-fall, he who rideth on the white horse come into the fray. That which must have been the Waterloo of my defeat now becomes the Waterloo of my triumph, because Blucher has come up to save. Expiation! expiation! The law tried me for high treason against God, and found me guilty. The angels of God were the jurors impaneled in the case, and they found me guilty. I was asked what I had to say why sentence of eternal death should not be pronounced upon me, and I had nothing to say. I stood on the scaffold of God's justice; the black cap of eternal death was about to be drawn over my eyes, when from the hill of Calvary One came. He dashed through the ranks of earth and heaven and hell. He rode swiftly. His garments were dyed with blood, his face was bleeding, his feet were dabbled with gore, and he cried out, "Save that man from going down to the pit. I am the ransom." And he threw back the coat from his heart, and that heart burst into a crimson fountain, and he dropped dead at my feet; and I felt of his hands, and they were stiff; and I felt of his feet, and they were cold; and I felt of his heart, and it was pulseless; and I cried, "Dead!" And angels with excited wings flew upward, amidst the the thrones, crying, "Dead!" and spirits lost in black brood wheeled down amidst the caverns, crying, "Dead!" Expiation! expiation!

Cowper, overborne with his sin, threw himself into a chair by the window, picked up a New Testament, and his eye lighted upon this, "Whom God hath set forth as a propitiation through faith in his blood;" and instantly he was free! Unless Christ pays our debt, we go to eternal jail. Unless our Joseph opens the king's corn-crib, we die of famine. One sacrifice for all.

A heathen got worried about his sins, and came to a priest and asked how he might be cured. The priest said, "If you will drive spikes in your shoes and walk five hundred miles, you will get over it." So he drove spikes in his shoes and began the pilgrimage, trembling, tottering, agonizing on the way, until he came about twenty miles, and sat down under a tree, exhausted. Near by a missionary was preaching Christ, the Saviour of all men. When the heathen heard it, he pulled off his sandals, threw them as far as he could, and cried, "That's what I want; give me Jesus! give me Jesus!" Oh, ye who have been convicted and worn of sin, trudging on all your days to reap eternal woe, will you not, this morning, at the announcement of a full and glorious atonement, throw your torturing transgressions to the winds? "The blood of Jesus Christ cleanseth from all sin;" that was the very passage that came to the tent of Hedley Vicars, the brave English soldier, and changed him into a hero for the Lord.

Around this great well of the Atonement the chief battles of Christianity are to be fought. Ye Bedouins of infidelity, take the other wells, but do not touch this. I call it by the same name that our father Abraham gave it—*the Atonement*. Here is where he stood, his staff against the well-curb. Here is where he walked, the track of his feet all around about the well. This is the very water that with trembling hand, in his dying moment, he put to his lips. Oh, ye sun-struck, desert-worn pilgrims, drive up your camels, and dismount! A pitcher of water for each one of you, and I will fill the trough for the camels. See the bucket tumble and dash into the depths; but I bring it up again, hand over hand, crying, "Ho, every one that thirsteth, come ye to the waters!"

Now, bring your shovels and your pickaxes, and we will try to open another well. I call it *the well of Christian comfort.* You have noticed that there are a good many new ways of comforting. Your father dies. Your neighbor comes in, and he says, "It is only a natural law that your father should die. The machinery is merely worn out;" and before he leaves you, he makes some other excellent remarks about the coagulation of blood, and the difference between respiratory and nitrogenized food. Your child dies, and your philosophic neighbor comes, and for your soothing tells you that it was impossible the child should live with such a state of mucous membrane! Out! with your chemistry and physiology when I have trouble, and give me a plain New Testament! I would rather have an illiterate man from the backwoods who knows Christ, talk with me, when I am in trouble, than the profoundest worldling who does not know him. The Gospel, without telling you any thing about mucous membrane or gastric juice or hydrochloric ac'd, comes and says, "All things together work for good to those who love God," and that if your child is gone, it is only because Jesus has folded it in his arms, and that the Judgment-day will explain things that are now inexplicable. Oh! let us dig out this Gospel well of comfort. Take away the stoicism and fatality with which you have been trying to fill it. Drive up the great herd of your cares and anxieties, and stop their bleating in this cool fountain! To this well David came when he lost Absalom; and Paul, when his back was red and raw with the scourge; and Dr. Young, when his daughter died; and Latimer, when the flames of martyrdom leaped on his track; and M'Kail, when he heard the knife sharpening for his beheading; and all God's sheep in all the ages.

After one of Napoleon's battles, it was found that the fight had been so terrific that, when the muster-roll was called of one regiment, there were only three privates and one drummer-boy that answered. An awful fight that! Oh! that Christ to-day might come so mightily for the slaying of your troubles and sorrows that when you go home and call the muster-roll of the terrible troop, not one—*not one*—shall answer, Christ having quelched every annoyance, and salved every gash, and wiped every tear, and made complete extermination.

Now bring your shovels and pickaxes, and we will dig out another well—a well opened by our father Abraham, but which the Philistines have filled up. It is the *well of Gospel Invitation*. I suppose you have noticed that religious address in this day, for the most part, has gone into the abstract and essayic. You know the word "sinner" is almost dropped out of the Christian vocabulary; it is not thought polite to use that word now. It is methodistic or old-fashioned. If you want to tell men that they are sinners, you must say they are spiritually erratic, or have moral deficits, or they have not had a proper spiritual development; and I have not heard in twenty years that old hymn,

"Come, ye sinners, poor and needy."

In the first place, they are not sinners, and in the second place, they are neither poor nor needy! I have heard Christian men in prayer-meetings and elsewhere talk as though there were no very great radical change before a man becomes a Christian. All he has got to do is to stop swearing, clear his throat a few times, take a good wash, and he is ready for heaven! My friends, if every man has not gone astray, and if the whole race is not plunged in sin and ruin, then that Bible is the greatest fraud ever enacted; for, from beginning to end, it sets forth that they are. Now, my brothers and sisters, if a man must be born again in order to see the kingdom of God, and if a man is absolutely ruined unless Christ check his course, why not proclaim it? There must be an infinite and radical change in every man's heart, or he can not come within ten thousand miles of heaven. There must be an earthquake in his soul, shaking down his sins, and there must be the trumpet-blast of Christ's resurrection bringing him up from the depths of sin and darkness into the glorious life of the Gospel. Do you know why more men do not come to Christ? It is because men are not invited that they do not come. You get a general invitation from your friend: "Come round some time to my house and dine with me." You do not go. But he says, "Come around to-day at four o'clock, and bring your family, and we'll dine together." And you say, "I don't know as I have any engagement: I will come." "I expect you at four o'clock." And you go. The world feels it is a general invitation to come around some time and sit at the great Gospel feast, and men do not come because they are not specially invited. It is because you do not take hold of them and say, "My brother, come to Christ; come now—come now!" How was it that in the days of Daniel Baker and Truman Osborne, and Nettleton, so many thousands came to Jesus? Because those men did nothing else but invite them to come. They spent their lifetime uttering invitations, and they did not mince matters either? Where did John Bunyan's pilgrim start from? Did he start from some easy, quiet, cozy place? No; if you have read John Bunyan's "Pilgrim's Progress," you know where he started from, and that was the *City of Destruction*, where every sinner starts from. Do you know what Livingstone, the Scotch minister, was preaching about in Scotland when three hundred souls under one sermon came to Christ? He was preaching about the human heart as unclean, and hard, and stony. Do you know what George Whitefield was preaching about in his first sermon, when fifteen souls saw the salvation of God? It was this: "Ye must be born again." Do you know what is the last subject he ever preached upon? "Flee the wrath to come." Oh! that the Lord God would come into our pulpits, and prayer-meetings, and Christian circles, and bring us from our fine rhetoric and profound metaphysics, and our elegant hair-splitting, to the old-fashioned well of Gospel Invitation. There are enough sinners in this house this morning, if they should come to God, to make joy enough in heaven to keep jubilee a thousand years. Why not come? Have you never had a special invitation to come? If not, I give it now: you, you, you, come now to Jesus! Why do you try to cover up that cancer with a piece of court-plaster, when Christ, the surgeon, with his scalpel, would take it all away, and it would never come again? Do you know that your nature is all wrong unless it has been changed by the grace of God? Do you not know that God can not be pleased with you, my dear brother, in your present state? Do you know that your sinful condition excites the wrath of God? "God is angry with the wicked every day." Do you not know that you have made war upon God? Do you not know that you have plunged your spear into the Saviour's side, and that you have punctured his temples, and spiked his feet, and that you have broken his heart?

Oh! is this what he deserves, you blood-bought soul? Is this the price you pay him for his long, earthly tramp, and his shelterless nights, and his dying prayer, and the groan that made creation shiver? Do you want to drive another nail into him? Do you want to stick him with another thorn? Do you want to join the mob that with bloody hands smote him on the cheek, crying, "His blood be on us and our children forever!" Oh, your sins! And when I say that, I do not pick out some man who may not have been in a house of worship for forty years, but I pick out any man you choose, whose heart has not been changed by the grace of God. Oh, your sins! I press them on your attention—the sins of your lifetime. What a record for a death-pillow! What *data* for the Judgment-day! What a cup of gall for your lips! Look at all the sins of your childhood and riper years, with their forked tongues and adder stings and deathless poignancy, unless Jesus with his heel shall crush the serpents. You have sinned against your God; you have sinned against your Jesus; you have sinned against your grave—ay, you have sinned against the little resting-place of your darling child, for you will never see her again unless you repent. How can you go to the good place, the pure place where she is, your heart unpardoned? You have sinned against a Christian father's counsel and a dying mother's prayer.

I saw an account the other day of a little boy who was to be taken by a city missionary, with some other boys, to the country to find homes. He was well clad, and had a new hat given him; but while the missionary was getting the other children ready to go, this boy went into a corner and took the hat he had thrown off, and tore the lining out of it. The missionary said, "What are you doing with that hat? You don't want it. What are you tearing the lining out of it for?" "Ah!" said the boy, "that was made out of mother's dress. She loved me very much before she died, and I have nothing to remember her by but the lining." And so the boy tore it out and put it in his bosom. Oh! would you not like to have one shred of your mother's religion to remember her by? Do not her prayers clamor for an answer this morning? Do you not see her hold her withered hands stretched out from the death-bed, begging you to come to God and be at peace with him? Would you not like to have the purity of your mother? Would you not like to have the comfort she felt in dark days? Would you not like to have some of that peace which she had in her last moments, when she looked up through her spectacles at you, and said she must go away, for Jesus called her, and you said, "Mother, we can't spare you;" and the outcry of grief was answered by a long breath that told you it was all over? Oh, my God! let not mother be on one side and father on the same side, and loved ones on the same side of the throne, and

I be on the other side. If we are this morning on the wrong side, let us cross over — let us cross over now. Blessed Jesus, we come, bruised with sin, and throw ourselves in the arms of thy compassion! None ever wanted thee more than we. Oh! turn on us thy benediction! Whatever else we lose or get, we must win heaven. "Lord, save us—we perish!"

Let us come around the old Gospel well. A good many of you came in these doors this morning carrying a very heavy burden. I do not know what it is—I can not guess what it is; but I noticed some of you, when you came in this morning, looked sad. It may be a home trouble you can not tell any body. How many have burdens on your shoulders and on your hearts! Come to the well; put down the pack right beside the well. Jacob's well was one hundred feet deep, and cut through the rock; but this Gospel well is deep as eternity, and it is cut right down through the heart of the Son of God. Shovels opened that other well; spears opened this. You remember the old well-sweep in the country was made out of two pieces—one planted in the ground, and on it was swung a long beam, which we laid hold of in our boyhood and brought downward, and the bucket dipped into the water and came up full. So the cross of Jesus is made out of two pieces. I take one piece and plant it close by this good old well, and then swing on it the long piece, and I lay hold of it with my prayer, and I pull it down until the bucket strikes the bottom of the Saviour's groans and the Saviour's tears, and then I fetch it up, bubbling, foaming, brimming, sparkling, with the water of which, if a man drink, he shall never thirst.

"To the dear fountain of thy blood,
 Incarnate God! I fly:
Here let me wash my spotted soul
 From crimes of deepest dye.

"A guilty, weak, and helpless worm,
 On thy kind arms I fall;
Be thou my strength and righteousness,
 My Jesus and my all."

## CHRIST EVERY THING.

"Christ is all and in all."—*Colossians* iii., 11.

EVERY age of the world has had its historians, its philosophers, its artists, its thinkers, and its teachers. Were there histories to be written, there has always been a Moses, or a Herodotus, or a Xenophon, or a Josephus to write them. Were there poems to be constructed, there has always been a Job or a Homer to construct them. Were there thrones, lustrous and powerful, to be lifted, there has always been a David or a Cæsar to raise them. Were there teachers demanded for the intellect and the hearts, there has been a Socrates, and a Zeno, and a Cleanthes, and a Marcus Antoninus coming forth on the grand and glorious mission. Every age of the world has had its triumphs of reason and morality. There has not been a single age of the world which has not had some decided system of religion. The Platonism, Orientalism, Stoicism, Brahmanism, and Buddhism, considering the ages in which they were established, were not lacking in ingenuity and force. Now, in this line of beneficent institutions and of noble men, there appeared a personage more wonderful than any predecessor. He came from a family without any royal or aristocratic pretension. He became a Galilean mechanic. He had no advantage from the schools. There were people beside him day after day who had no idea that he was going to be any thing remarkable or do any thing remarkable. Yet, notwithstanding all this, and without any title, or scholarly profession, or flaming rhetoric, he startled the world with the strangest announcements, ran in collision with solemn priest and proud ruler, and with a voice that rang through temple, and palace, and over ship's deck, and mountain top, exclaimed, "I am the light of the world!" Men were taken all aback at the idea that that hand, yet hard from the use of the axe, and saw, and adze, and hatchet, should wave the sceptre of authority, and that upon that brow, from which they had so often seen him wipe the sweat of toil, there would yet come the crown of unparalleled splendor and of universal dominion. We all know how difficult it is to think that any body who was at school with us in boyhood has got to be any thing great or famous; and no wonder that those who had been boys with Christ in the streets of Nazareth, and seen him in after-years in the days of his complete obscurity, should have been very slow to acknowledge Christ's wonderful mission.

From this humble point the stream of life flowed out. At first it was just a faint rill, hardly able to find its way down the rock; but the tears of a weeping Christ added to its volume; and it flowed on until, by the beauty and greenness of the banks, you might know the path the crystal stream was taking. On and on, until the lepers were brought down and washed off their leprosy, and the dead were lifted into the water that they might have life, and pearls of joy and promise were gathered from the brink, and innumerable churches gathered on either bank, and the tide flows on deeper, and stronger, and wider, until it rolls into the river from under the throne of God, mingling billow with billow, and brightness with brightness, and joy with joy, and hosanna with hosanna!

I was looking a few days ago at some of the paintings of the late artist, Mr. Kensett. I saw some pictures that were just faint outlines; in some places you would see only the branches of a tree and no trunk; and in another case the trunk and no branches. He had not finished the work. It would have taken him days and months, perhaps, to have completed it. Well, my friends, in this world we get only the faintest outline of what Christ is. It will take all eternity to fill up the picture—so loving, so kind, so merciful, so great! Paul does not, in this chapter, say of Christ he is good, or he is loving, or he is patient, or he is kind; but in his exclamation of the text he embraces every thing when he says, "Christ is all and in all."

I remark, in the first place, Christ is *every thing in the Bible*. I do not care where I open the Bible, I find Jesus. In whatever path I start, I come, after a while, to the Bethlehem manger. I go back to the old dispensation, and see a lamb on the altar, and say, "Behold the Lamb of God which taketh away the sin of the world!" Then I go and see the manna provided for the Israelites in the wilderness, and I say, "Jesus, the bread of life." Then I look at the rock which was smitten by the prophet's rod, and, as the water gushes out, I say, "It is Jesus, the fountain opened for sin and for uncleanness." I go back and look at the writings of Job, and hear him exclaim, "I know that my Redeemer liveth." Then I go to Ezekiel, and I find Christ presented there as "a plant of renown;" and then I turn over to Isaiah, and Christ is spoken of "as a sheep before her shearers." It is Jesus all the way between Genesis and Malachi. Then I turn over to the New Testament, and it is Christ in the parable, it is Christ in the miracle, it is Christ in the evangelists' story, it is Christ in the apostles' epistles, and it is Christ in the trumpet peal of the Apocalypse. I know there are a great many people who *do not find Christ* in the Bible. Here is a man who studies the Bible *as a historian*. Well, if you come as a historian, you will find in this book how the world was made, how the seas fled to their places, how empires were established, how nation fought with nation, javelin ringing against harbegeon, until the earth was ghastly with the dead. You will see the coronation of princes, the triumph of conquerors, and the world turned upside down and back again and down again, cleft and scarred with great agonies of earthquake, and tempest, and battle. It is a wonderful history, putting to the blush all others in the accuracy of its recital, and in the stupendous events it records. Homer, and Thucydides, and Gibbon could make great stories out of little events; but it took a Moses to tell how the heavens and the earth were made in one chapter, and to give the history of thousands of years upon two leaves.

There are others who come to the Bible merely *as antiquarians*. If you come as an antiquarian you will find a great many odd things in the Bible: peculiarities of manner and custom, marriage and burial; peculiarities of dress, tunics, sandals, crisping-pins, amulets and girdles, and tinkling ornaments. If you come to look at military arrangements, you will find coats of mail, and javelins, and engines of war, and circumvallation, and encampments. If you look for peculiar musical instruments, you will find psalteries, and shigionoths, and ram's horns. The antiquarian will find in the Bible curiosities in agriculture, and in commerce, and in art, and in religion, that will keep him absorbed a great while. There are those who come to this Bible as you would to a cabinet of curiosities, and you pick up this and say, "What a strange sword that is!" and "What a peculiar hat this is!" and "What an unlooked-for lamp that is!" and the Bible to such becomes a British Museum.

Then there are others who find nothing in the Bible but *the poetry*. Well, if you come as a poet, you will find in this book faultless rhythm, and bold imagery, and startling antithesis, and rapturous lyric, and sweet pastoral, and instructive narrative, and devotional psalm: thoughts expressed in a style more solemn than that of Montgomery, more bold than that of Milton, more terrible than that of Dante, more natural than that of Wordsworth, more impassioned than that of Pollock, more tender than that of Cowper, more weird than that of Spenser. This great poem brings all the gems of the earth into its coronet, and it weaves the flames of judgment in its garland, and pours eternal harmonies in its rhythm. Every thing this book touches it makes beautiful, from the plain stones of the summer threshing-floor, and the daughters of Nahor filling the trough for the camels, and the fish-pools of Heshbon, up to the Psalmist praising God with diapason of storm and whirlwind, and Job leading forth Orion, Arcturus, and the Pleiades. It is a wonderful poem; and a great many people read it as they do Thomas Moore's "Lalla Rookh," and Walter

Scott's "Lady of the Lake," and Southey's "Curse of Gehenna." They sit down, and are so absorbed in looking at the shells on the shore that they forget to look off on the great ocean of God's mercy and salvation.

Then there are others who come to this book *as skeptics*. They marshal passage against passage, and try to get Matthew and Luke in a quarrel, and would have a discrepancy between what Paul and James say about faith and works; and they try the account of Moses concerning the Creation by modern decisions in science, and resolve that in all questions between the scientific explorer and the inspired writer they will give the preference to the geologist. These men—these spiders, I will say—suck poison out of the sweetest flowers. They fatten their infidelity upon the truths which have led thousands to heaven, and in their distorted vision prophet seems to war with prophet, and evangelist with evangelist, and apostle with apostle; and if they can find some bad trait of character in a man of God mentioned in that Bible, these carrion crows caw and flap their wings over the carcass. Because they can not understand how the whale swallowed Jonah, they attempt the more wonderful feat of swallowing the monster whale of modern skepticism. They do not believe it possible that the Bible story should be true which says that the dumb ass spake, while they themselves prove the thing possible by their own utterances. I am amused beyond bounds when I hear one of these men talking about a future life. Just ask a man who rejects that Bible what heaven is, and hear him befog your soul. He will tell you that heaven is merely the development of the internal resources of a man; it is an efflorescence of the dynamic forces into a state of ethereal and transcendental lucubration, in close juxtaposition to the ever-present "was," and the great "to be," and the everlasting "No." Considering themselves wise, they are fools for time, fools for eternity.

Then there is another class of persons who come to the Bible *as controversialists*. They are enormous Presbyterians, or fierce Baptists, or violent Methodists. They cut the Bible to suit their creed, instead of cutting their creed to suit the Bible. If the Scriptures think as they do, well; if not, so much the worse for the Scriptures. The Bible is merely the whetstone on which they sharpen the dissecting-knife of controversy. They come to it as a Government in time of war comes to armories or arsenals for weapons and munitions. They have declared everlasting war against all other sects, and they want so many broadswords, so many muskets, so many howitzers, so many columbiads, so much grape and canister, so many field-pieces with which to rake the field of dispute; for they mean to get the victory, though the heavens be darkened with the smoke and the earth rent with the thunder. What do they care about the religion of the Lord Jesus Christ? I have seen some such men come back from an ecclesiastical massacre as proud of their achievements as an Indian warrior boasting of the number of scalps he has taken. I have more admiration for a man who goes forth with his fists to get the championship—for a Heenan or a Morrissey—than I have for these theological pugilists who make our theological magazines ring with their horrible war-cry. There are men who seem to think the only use of the sword of truth is to stick somebody. There is one passage of the Scriptures that they like better than all others, and that is this: "Blessed be the Lord which teacheth my hands to war, and my fingers to fight." Woe to us if we come to God's word as controversialists, or as skeptics, or as *connoisseurs*, or as fault-finders, or merely as poets!

Those only get into the heart of God's truth who come seeking for Christ. Welcome all such! They will find him coming out from behind the curtain of prophecy, until he stands, in the full light of New Testament disclosure, Jesus the Son of God, the Saviour of the world. They will find him in genealogical table and in chronological calculation, in poetic stanza and in historical narrative, in profound parable and in startling miracle. They will see his foot on every sea, and his tears in the drops of dew on Hermon, and hear his voice in the wind, and behold his words all abloom in the valley between Mount Olivet and Jerusalem. There are some men who come and walk around the Temple of Truth, and merely see the outside. There are others who walk into the porch, and then go away. There are others who come in and look at the pictures, but they know nothing about the chief attractions of the Bible. It is only the man who comes and knocks at the gate, saying, "I would see Jesus." For him the glories of that book open, and he goes in and finds Christ, and with him peace, pardon, life, comfort, and heaven. "All in all is Jesus" in the Bible.

I remark again that Christ is every thing in the great *plan of redemption*. We are slaves; Christ gives deliverance to the captive. We are thirsty; Christ is the river of salvation to slake our thirst. We are hungry; Jesus says, "I am the bread of life." We are condemned to die; Christ says, "Save that man from going down to the pit; I am the ransom." We are tossed on a sea of troubles; Jesus comes over it, saying, "It is I, be not afraid." We are in darkness; Jesus says, "I am the bright and the morning-star." We are sick; Jesus is the balm of Gilead. We are dead; hear the shrouds rend and the grave hillocks heave as he cries, "I am the resurrection and the life; he that believeth in me, though he were dead, yet shall he live." We want justification; "Being justified by faith, we have peace with God *through our Lord Jesus Christ.*" We want to exercise faith; "Believe in the Lord Jesus Christ, and thou shalt be saved." I want to get from under condemnation; "There is now, therefore, no condemnation to them who are in Christ Jesus." The cross—he carried it. The flames of hell—he suffered them. The shame—he endured it. The crown—he won it. Heights of heaven sing it, and worlds of light to worlds of light all round the heavens cry, "Glory, glory!"

Let us go forth and gather the trophies for Jesus. From Golconda mines we gather the diamonds, from Ceylon banks we gather the pearls, from all lands and kingdoms we gather precious stones, and we bring the glittering burdens and put them down at the feet of Jesus, and say, "All these are thine. Thou art worthy." We go forth again for more trophies, and into one sheaf we gather all the sceptres of the Cæsars, and the Alexanders, and the Czars, and the Sultans, of all royalties and dominions, and then we bring the sheaf of sceptres and put it down at the feet of Jesus, and say, "Thou art King of kings, and these thou hast conquered." And then we go forth again to gather more trophies, and we bid the redeemed of all ages, the sons and daughters of the Lord Almighty, to come. We ask them to come and offer their thanksgivings, and the hosts of heaven bring crown, and palm, and sceptre, and here by these bleeding feet and by this riven side, and by this wounded heart, cry, "Blessing, and honor, and glory, and power be unto him that sitteth upon the throne and unto the Lamb forever and forever!" Tell me of a tear that he did not weep, of a burden that he did not carry, of a battle that he did not fight, of a victory that he did not achieve. "All in all is Jesus" in the great plan of redemption.

I remark again, Christ is every thing to the Christian *in time of trouble.* Who has escaped trouble? We must all stoop down and drink out of the bitter lake. The moss has no time to grow on the buckets that come up out of the heart's well, dripping with tears. Great trials are upon our track as certain as greyhound pack on the scent of deer. From our hearts in every direction there are a thousand chords reaching out binding us to loved ones, and ever and anon some of these tendrils snap. The winds that cross this sea of life are not all abaft. The clouds that cross our sky are not feathery and afar, straying like flocks of sheep on heavenly pastures; but wrathful and sombre, and gleaming with terror, they wrap the mountains in fire, and come down baying with their thunders through every gorge. The richest fruits of blessing have a prickly shell. Life here is not lying at anchor; it is weathering a gale. It is not sleeping in a soldier's tent with our arms stacked; it is a bayonet-charge. We stumble over grave-stones, and we drive on with our wheel deep in the old rut of graves. Trouble has wrinkled your brow, and it has frosted your head.

Falling in this battle of life, is there no angel of mercy to bind our wounds? Hath God made this world with so many things to hurt and none to heal? For this snake-bite of sorrow, is there no herb growing by all the brooks to heal the poison? Blessed be God that in the Gospel we find the antidote! Christ has bottled an ocean of tears. How many thorns he hath plucked out of human agony! Oh! he knows too well what it is to carry a cross, not to help us carry ours. He knows too well what it is to climb the mountain, not to help us up the steep. He knows too well what it is to be persecuted, not to help those who are imposed upon. He knows too well what it is to be sick, not to help those who suffer. Ay, he knows too well what it is to die, not to help us in our last extremity. Blessed Jesus, thou knowest it all. Seeing thy wounded side, and thy wounded hand, and thy wounded feet, and thy wounded brow, we are sure thou knowest it all. Oh! when those into whose bosom we used to breathe our sorrows are snatched from us, blessed be God the heart of Jesus still beats; and when all other lights go out and the world gets dark, then we see coming out from behind a cloud something so bright and cheering, we know it to be the morning-star of the soul's deliverance. The hand of care may make you stagger, or the hand of persecution may beat you down, or the hand of disappointment may beat you back; but there is a Hand, and it is so kind, and it is so gentle, that it wipeth all tears from all faces.

## THE KING'S WAGONS.

"And when he saw the wagons which Joseph had sent to carry him, the spirit of Jacob, their father, revived."—*Genesis* xlv., 27.

THE Egyptian capital was the focus of the world's wealth. In ships and barges, there had been brought to it from India frankincense, and cinnamon, and ivory, and diamonds; from the North, marble and iron; from Syria, purple and silk; from Greece, some of the finest horses of the world, and some of the most brilliant chariots; and from all the earth that which could best please the eye, and charm the ear, and gratify the taste. There were temples aflame with red sandstone, entered by gate-ways that were guarded by pillars bewildering with hieroglyphics, and wound with brazen serpents, and adorned with winged creatures—their eyes, and beaks, and pinions glittering with precious stones. There were marble columns blooming into white flower-buds; there were stone pillars, at the top bursting into the shape of the lotus when in full bloom. Along the avenues, lined with sphinx, and fane, and obelisk, there were princes who came in gorgeously-upholstered palanquin, carried by servants in scarlet, or elsewhere drawn by vehicles, the snow-white horses, golden-bitted, and six abreast, dashing at full run. There were fountains from stone-wreathed vases climbing the ladders of the light. You would hear a bolt shove, and a door of brass would open like a flash of the sun. The surrounding gardens were saturated with odors that mounted the terrace, and dripped from the arbors, and burned their incense in the Egyptian noon. On floors of mosaic the glories of Pharaoh were spelled out in letters of porphyry, and beryl, and flame. There were ornaments twisted from the wood of the tamarisk, embossed with silver breaking into foam. There were footstools made out of a single precious stone. There were beds fashioned out of a crouched lion in bronze. There were chairs spotted with the sleek hide of leopards. There were sofas footed with the claws of wild beasts, and armed with the beaks of birds. As you stand on the level beach of the sea on a summer-day, and look either way, and there are miles of breakers, white with the ocean foam, dashing shoreward; so it seemed as if the sea of the world's pomp and wealth in the Egyptian capital for miles and miles flung itself up into white breakers of marble temple, mausoleum, and obelisk.

This was the place where Joseph, the shepherd-boy, was called to stand next to Pharaoh in honor. What a contrast between this scene and his humble starting, and the pit into which his brothers threw him! Yet he was not forgetful of his early home; he was not ashamed of where he came from. The Bishop of Mentz, descended from a wheelwright, covered his house with spokes, and hammers, and wheels; and the King of Sicily, in honor of his father, who was a potter, refused to drink out of any thing but an earthen vessel. So Joseph was not ashamed of his early surroundings, or of his old-time father, or of his brothers. When they came up from the famine-stricken land to get corn from the king's corn-crib, Joseph, instead of chiding them for the way they had maltreated and abused him, sent them back with wagons, which Pharaoh furnished, laden with corn; and old Jacob, the father, in the very same wagons, was brought back, that Joseph, the son, might see him, and give him a comfortable home all the rest of his days.

Well, I hear the wagons, the king's wagons, rumbling down in front of the palace. On the outside of the palace, to see the wagons go off, stands Pharaoh in royal robes; and beside him prime-minister Joseph, with a chain of gold around his neck, and on his hand a ring given by Pharaoh to him, so that any time he wanted to stamp the royal seal upon a document he could do so. Wagon after wagon rolls on down from the palace, laden with corn, and meat, and changes of raiment, and every thing that could help a famine-struck people. One day I see aged Jacob seated in the front of his house. He is possibly thinking of his absent boys (sons, however old they get, are never to a father any more than boys); and while he is seated there, he sees dust arising, and he hears wagons rumbling, and he wonders what is coming now, for the whole land had been smitten with the famine, and was in silence. But after a while the wagons have come near enough, and he sees his sons on the wagons, and before they come quite up, they shout, "Joseph is yet alive!" The old man faints dead away. I do not wonder at it. The boys tell the story how that the boy, the long-absent Joseph, has got to be the first man in the Egyptian palace. While they unload the wagons, the wan and wasted creatures in the neighborhood come up and ask for a handful of corn, and they are satisfied.

One day the wagons are brought up for Jacob, the old father, is about to go to see Joseph in the Egyptian palace. You know it is not a very easy thing to transplant an old tree, and Jacob has hard work to get away from the place where he has lived so long. He bids good-bye to the old place, and leaves his blessing with the neighbors, and then his sons steady him, while he, determined to help himself, gets into the wagon, stiff, old, and decrepit. Yonder they go, Jacob and his sons, and their wives, and their children, eighty-two in all, followed by herds and flocks, which the herdsmen drive along. They are going out from famine to luxuriance; they are going from a plain country home to the finest palace under the sun. Joseph, the prime minister, gets in his chariot, and drives down to meet the old man. Joseph's charioteer holds up the horses on the one side —the dust-covered wagons of the emigrants stop on the other. Joseph, instead of waiting for his father to come, leaps out of the chariot and jumps into the emigrants' wagon, throws his arms around the old man, and weeps aloud for past memories and present joy. The father, Jacob, can hardly think it is his boy. Why, the smooth brow of childhood has become a wrinkled brow, wrinkled with the cares of state, and the garb of the shepherd-boy has become a robe royally bedizened! But as the old man finds out it is actually Joseph, I see the thin lip quiver against the toothless gum as he cries out, "Now let me die, since I have seen thy face; behold, Joseph is yet alive!" The wagons roll up in front of the palace. Help out the grandchildren, and take them in out of the hot Egyptian sun. Help old Jacob out of the wagon. Send word to Pharaoh that the old shepherd has come. In the royal apartment Pharaoh and Jacob meet—dignity and rusticity—the gracefulness of the court and the plain manners of the field. The king, wanting to make the old countryman at ease, and seeing how white his beard is, and how feeble his step, looks familiarly into his face, and says to the aged man, "How old art thou?" Give the old man a seat. Unload the wagons; drive out the cattle toward the pastures of Goshen. Let the slaves in scarlet kneel and wash the feet of the newly-arrived, wiping them on the finest linen of the palace. From vases of perfume let the newly-arrived be sprinkled and refreshed; let minstrels come in with sandals of crimson, and thrum the harps, and clap the cymbals, and jingle the tambourines, while we sit down, at this great distance of time and space, and learn *the lesson of the king's wagons.*

My friends, we are in a world by sin famine-struck; but the King is in constant communication with us, his wagons coming and going perpetually; and in the rest of my discourse I will show you what the wagons bring and what they take back.

In the first place, like those that came from the Egyptian palace, the King's wagons now bring us *corn and meat, and many changes of raiment.* We are apt to think of the fields and the orchards as feeding us; but who makes the flax grow for the linen, and the wheat for the bread, and the wool on the sheep's back? Oh, I wish we could see through every grain-field, by every sheep-fold, under the trees of every orchard, the King's wagons! They drive up three times a day—morning, noon, and night. They bring furs from the arctic, they bring fruits from the tropic, they bring bread from the temperate zone. The King looks out, and he says, "There are twelve hundred millions of people to be fed and clothed.

So many pounds of meat, so many barrels of flour, so many yards of cloth and linen and flannel, so many hats, so many socks, so many shoes;" enough for all, save that we who are greedy get more shoes than belong to us, and others go barefooted. None but a God could feed and clothe the world. None but a king's corn-crib could appease the world's famine. None but a king could tell how many wagons to send, and how heavily to load them, and when they are to start. They are coming over the frozen ground to-day. Do you not hear their rumbling? They will stop at noon at your table. Oh, if for a little while they should cease, hunger would come into the nations, as to Utica when Hamilcar besieged it, and as in Jerusalem when Vespasian surrounded it; and the nations would be hollow-eyed, and fall upon each other in universal cannibalism; and skeleton would drop upon skeleton; and there would be no one to bury the dead; and the earth would be a field of bleached skeletons; and the birds of prey would fall dead, flock after flock, without any carcasses to devour; and the earth in silence would wheel around, one great black hearse! All life stopped because the King's wagons are stopped. Oh, thank God for bread—*for bread!*

I remark again, that, like those that came from the Egyptian palace, the King's wagons bring us *good news*. Jacob had not heard from his boy for a great many years. He never thought of him but with a heart-ache. There was in Jacob's heart a room where lay the corpse of his unburied Joseph; and when the wagons came, the king's wagons, and told him that Joseph was yet alive, he faints dead away. Good news for Jacob! good news for us! The King's wagons come down and tell us that our Joseph-Jesus is yet alive; that he has forgiven us because we threw him into the pit of suffering and the dungeon of shame. He has risen from thence to stand in a palace. The Bethlehem shepherds were awakened at midnight by the rattling of the wagons that brought the tidings. Our Joseph-Jesus sends us a message of pardon, of life, of heaven; corn for our hunger, raiment for our nakedness. Joseph-Jesus is yet alive!

I go to hunt up Jesus. I go to the village of Bethany, and say, "Where does Mary live?" They say, "Yonder Mary lives." I go in. I see where she sat in the sitting-room. I go out where Martha worked in the kitchen, but I find no Jesus. I go into Pilate's court-room, and I find the judges and the police and the prisoner's box, but no Jesus. I go into the Arimathean cemetery; but the door is gone, and the shroud is gone, and Jesus is gone. By faith I look up to the King's palace; and behold I have found him! Joseph-Jesus is still alive! Glorious religion, a religion made not out of deaths'-heads, and cross-bones, and undertaker's screw-driver, but one bounding with life, and sympathy, and gladness. Joseph is yet alive!

> "I know that my Redeemer lives.
> What comfort this sweet sentence gives!
> He lives, He lives, who once was dead,
> He lives, my ever-living Head!
>
> "He lives to grant me daily breath,
> He lives, and I shall conquer death.
> He lives my mansion to prepare,
> He lives to bring me safely there.
>
> "He lives, all glory to His name;
> He lives, my Jesus still the same.
> Oh, the sweet joy this sentence gives,
> I know that my Redeemer lives!"

The King's wagons will after a while unload, and they will turn around, and they will go back to the palace, and I really think that you and I will go with them. The King will not leave us in this famine-struck world. The King has ordered that we be lifted into the wagons, and that we go over into Goshen, where there shall be pasturage for our largest flock of joy, and then we will drive up to the palace, where there are glories awaiting us which will melt all the snow of Egyptian marble into forgetfulness.

I think that the King's wagons will take us up *to see our lost friends*. Jacob's chief anticipation was not seeing the Nile, nor of seeing the long colonnades of architectural beauty, nor of seeing the throne-room. There was a focus to all his journeyings, to all his anticipations; and that was Joseph. Well, my friends, I do not think heaven would be worth much if our brother Jesus was not there. If there were two heavens, the one with all the pomp and paraphernalia of an eternal monarchy, but no Christ, and the other were a plain heaven, humbly thatched, with a few daisies in the yard, and Christ were there, I would say, "Let the King's wagons take me up to the old farm-house."

If Jesus were not in heaven, there would be no music there; there would be but very few people there; they would be off looking for the lost Christ, crying through the universe, "Where is Jesus? where is Jesus?" and after they had found him, with loving violence they would take him and bear him through the gates; and it would be the greatest day known in heaven within the memory of the oldest inhabitant. Jesus never went off from heaven but once, and he was so badly treated on that excursion they will never let him go again.

Oh, the joy of meeting our brother, Joseph-Jesus! After we have talked about him for ten, or fifty, or seventy years, to talk *with* him, and to clasp hands with the hero of the ages; not crouching as underlings in his presence, but, as Jacob and Joseph, hug each other. We will want some new term by which to address him. On earth we call him Saviour, or Redeemer, or friend; but when we throw our arms around him in everlasting embrace, we will want some new name of endearment. I can think of what we shall do through the long ages of eternity; but what we shall do the first minute I can not guess. In the first flash of his countenance, in the first rush of our emotions, what we shall do I can not imagine. Oh the overwhelming glory of the first sixty seconds in heaven! Methinks we will just stand, and look and look and look.

The king's wagons took Jacob up to see his lost boy, and so I really think that the King's wagons will take us up to see our lost kindred. How long is it since Joseph went out of your household? How many years is it now last Christmas, or the fourteenth of next month? It was a dark night when he died, and a stormy day it was at the burial; and the clouds wept with you, and the winds sighed for the dead. The bell at Greenwood's gate rang only a few moments, but your heart has been tolling, tolling, ever since. You have been under a delusion, like Jacob of old. You have thought that Joseph was dead. You put his name first in the birth-record of the family Bible, and then you put it in the death-record of the family Bible, and you have been deceived. *Joseph is yet alive.* He is more alive than you are. Of all the sixteen thousand millions of children that statisticians say have gone into the future world, there is not one of them dead, and the King's wagons will take you up to see them. You often think how glad you will be to see them. Have you never thought, my brother, my sister, how glad they will be to see you? Jacob was no more glad to see Joseph than Joseph was to see Jacob. Every time the door in heaven opens, they look to see if it is you coming in. Joseph, once standing in the palace, burst out crying when he thought of Jacob—afar off. And the heaven of your little ones will not be fairly begun until you get there. All the kindnesses shown them by immortals will not make them forget you. There they are, the radiant throngs that went out from your homes! I throw a kiss to the sweet darlings. They are all well now in the palace. The crippled child has a sound foot now. A little lame child says, "Ma, will I be lame in heaven?" "No, my darling you won't be lame in heaven." A little sick child says, "Ma, will I be sick in heaven?" "No, my dear, you won't be sick in heaven." A little blind child says, "Ma, will I be blind in heaven?" "No, my dear, you won't be blind in heaven." They are all well there.

In my boyhood, for some time we lived three miles from church, and on stormy days the children staid at home, but father and mother always went to church: that was a habit they had. On those stormy Sabbaths when we staid at home, the absence of our parents seemed very much protracted; for the roads were very bad, and they could not get on very fast. So we would go to the window at twelve o'clock to see if they were coming, and then we would go at half-past twelve to see if they were coming, and at a quarter to one, and then at one o'clock. After a while, Mary, or David, or De Witt would shout, "The wagon's coming!" and then we would see it winding out of the woods, and over the brook, and through the lane, and up in front of the old farm-house; and then we would rush out, leaving the doors wide open, with many things to tell them, asking them many questions.  Well, my dear brethren, I think we are many of us in the King's wagons, and we are on the way home.  The road is very bad, and we get on slowly; but after a while we will come winding out of the woods, and through the brook of death, and up in front of the old heavenly homestead; and our departed kindred, who have been waiting and watching for us, will rush out through the doors and over the lawn, crying, "The wagons are coming! the King's wagons are coming!"  Hark! the bell of the City Hall strikes twelve.  Twelve o'clock on earth, and likewise it is high noon in heaven.

During the past week some of God's wagons have come to us, and a loved one is gone: John R. Lansing, an elder of this church, loved by me, loved by you all—one of those pure spirits that we sometimes see early ripening for heaven.  I never heard a young man pray as Lansing did.  He talked with God like an old Christian.  Last Thursday morning the King's wagon halted at his pillow.  There was no one present to see him go.  Yes there was; Jesus was there.  I went around afterward where he dwelt, and they had nothing but words of praise to say of him—so kind he was, so gentle he was, so pure he was, so upright he was!  We picked him out of our large congregation as especially qualified for the service of the eldership.  I have always been glad since, we did.  He was a young man to be called an elder; but he was worthy of his office, and he honored it.  If I knew of any better words of eulogium, honest eulogium, than those I have already uttered, I would say them. Joy to him! No more asthma or heart disease for him. He is well now. He will never cough again. Joy, joy! But ours is the grief, in the elders' board, in the Sabbath-school, in the prayer-meeting—ours is the grief. "Let me die the death of the righteous, and let my last end be like his." May God comfort those that mourn, especially that aged mother, too feeble to hear of such tidings. I do not know but that the King's wagon will take them both side by side through the gates into the city.

Does not the subject of the morning take the gloom out of the thoughts that would otherwise be struck through with midnight? We used to think that when we died we would have to go afoot, sagging down in the mire, and the hounds of terror might get after us, and that if we got through into heaven at all, we would come in torn, and wounded, and bleeding. I remember when my teeth chattered and my knees knocked together when I heard any body talk about death; but I have come to think that the grave will be the softest bed I ever slept in, and the bottom of my feet will not be wet with the passage of the Jordan. "Them that sleep in Jesus will God bring with him."

I was reading a day or two ago of Robert Southey, who said he wished he could die far away from his friends—like a dog, crawling into a corner and dying unobserved. Those were his words. Be it ours to die on a couch surrounded by loved ones, so that they with us may hear the glad, sweet, jubilant announcement, "The King's wagons are coming." Hark! I near them now. Are they coming for you or me?

## THE UPPER AND NETHER SPRINGS.

"Thou hast given me a south land; give me also springs of water. And he gave her the upper springs and the nether springs."—*Joshua* xv., 19.

THE city of Debir was the Boston of antiquity—a great place for brain and books. Caleb wanted it, and he offered his daughter Achsah as a prize to any one who would capture that city. It was a strange thing for Caleb to do; and yet the man that could take the city would have, at any rate, two elements of manhood—bravery and patriotism. Besides, I do not think that Caleb was as foolish in offering his daughter to the conqueror of Debir, as thousands in this day who seek alliances for their children with those who have large means, without any reference to moral or mental acquirements. Of two evils, I would rather measure happiness by the length of the sword than by the length of the pocket-book. In one case there is sure to be one good element of character; in the other there may be none at all. With Caleb's daughter as a prize to fight for, General Othniel rode into the battle. The gates of Debir were thundered into the dust, and the city of books lay at the feet of the conquerors. The work done, Othniel comes back to claim his bride. Having conquered the city, it is no great job for him to conquer the girl's heart; for however faint-hearted a woman herself may be, she always loves courage in a man. I never saw an exception to that. . The wedding festivity having gone by, Othniel and Achsah are about to go to their new home. However loudly the cymbals may clash and the laughter ring, parents are always sad when a fondly-cherished daughter goes off to stay; and Achsah, the daughter of Caleb, knows that now is the time to ask almost any thing she wants of her father. It seems that Caleb, the good old man, had given as a wedding-present to his daughter a piece of land that was mountainous, and sloping southward toward the deserts of Arabia, swept with some very hot winds. It was called "a south land." But Achsah wants an addition of property; she wants a piece of land that is well watered and fertile. Now it is no wonder that Caleb, standing amidst the bridal party, his eyes so full of tears because she was going away that he could hardly see her at all, gives her more than she asks. She said to him, "Thou hast given me a south land; give me also springs of water. And he gave her the upper springs, and the nether springs."

I never saw that passage until a little while ago; and as I came upon it I said, if God will give me grace, I shall preach a sermon upon that before long. The fact is, that as Caleb, the father, gave Achsah, the daughter, a south land, so God gives to us his world. I am very thankful he has given it to us. But I am like Achsah in the fact that I am not satisfied with the portion. Trees, and flowers, and grass, and blue skies are very well in their places; but he who has nothing but this world for a portion has no portion at all. It is a mountainous land, sloping off toward the desert of sorrow, swept by fiery siroccos; it is "a south land," a poor portion for any man that tries to put his trust in it. What has been your experience? What has been the experience of every man, of every woman that has tried this world for a portion? Queen Elizabeth, amidst the surroundings of pomp, is unhappy because the painter sketches too minutely the wrinkles on her face, and she indignantly cries out, "You must strike off my likeness without any shadows!" Hogarth, at the very height of his artistic triumph, is stung almost to death with chagrin because the painting he had dedicated to the king does not seem to be acceptable; for George II. cries out, "Who is this Hogarth? Take his trumpery out of my presence." Brinsley Sheridan thrilled the earth with his eloquence, but had for his last words, "I am absolutely undone." Walter Scott, fumbling around the inkstand, trying to write, says to his daughter, "Oh, take me back to my room; there is no rest for Sir Walter but in the grave!" Stephen Girard, the wealthiest man in his day, or, at any rate, only second in wealth, says, "I live the life of a galley-slave: when I arise in the morning my one effort is to work so hard that I can sleep when it gets to be night." Charles Lamb, applauded of all the world, in the very midst of his literary triumph, says, "Do you remember, Bridget, when we used to laugh from the shilling gallery at the play? There are now no good plays to laugh at from the boxes." But why go so far as that? I need to go no farther than your street to find an illustration of what I am saying.

Pick me out ten successful worldlings—and you know what I mean by thoroughly successful worldlings—pick me out ten successful worldlings, and you can not find more than one that looks happy. Care drags him across the ferry; care drags him back. Take your stand at two o'clock at the corner of Nassau and Wall streets, or at the corner of Canal Street and Broadway, and see the agonized physiognomies. Your bankers, your insurance men, your importers, your wholesalers, and your retailers, as a class—as a class, are they happy? No. Care dogs their steps; and, making no appeal to God for help or comfort, they are tossed everywhither, while Jay Gould makes New York quake from Central Park to the Battery. How has it been with you, my hearer? Are you more contented in the house of fourteen rooms than you were in the two rooms you had in a house when you started? Have you not had more care and worriment since you won that fifty thousand dollars than you did before? Some of the poorest men I have ever known have been those of great fortune. A man of small means may be put in great business straits, but the ghastliest of all embarrassments is that of the man who has large estates. The men who commit suicide because of monetary losses are those who can not bear the burden any more, because they have only fifty thousand dollars left.

On Bowling Green, New York, there is a house where Talleyrand used to go. He was a favorite man. All the world knew him, and he had wealth almost unlimited; yet at the close of his life he says, "Behold, eighty-three years have passed without any practical result, save fatigue of body and fatigue of mind, great discouragement for the future, and great disgust for the past." Oh, my friends, this is "a south land," and it slopes off toward deserts of sorrows; and the prayer which Achsah made to her father Caleb we make this day to our Father God: "Thou hast given me a south land; give me also springs of water. And he gave them the upper springs, and the nether springs."

Blessed be God! we have more advantages given us than we can really appreciate. We have spiritual blessings offered us in this world which I shall call the nether springs, and glories in the world to come which I shall call the upper springs.

Where shall I find words enough threaded with light to set forth the pleasure of religion? David, unable to describe it in words, played it on a harp. Mrs. Hemans, not finding enough power in prose, sings that praise in a canto. Christopher Wren, unable to describe it in language, sprung it into the arches of St. Paul's. John Bunyan, unable to present it in ordinary phraseology, takes all the fascination of allegory. Handel, with ordinary music unable to reach the height of the theme, rouses it up in an oratorio. Oh, there is no life on earth so happy as a really Christian life! I do not mean a sham Christian life, but a real Christian life. Where there is a thorn, there is a whole garland of roses. Where there is one groan, there are three doxologies. Where there is one day of cloud, there is a whole season of sunshine. Take the humblest Christian man that you know—angels of God canopy him with their white wings; the lightnings of heaven are his armed allies; the Lord is his Shepherd, picking out for him green pastures by still waters; if he walk forth, heaven is his body-guard; if he lie down to sleep, ladders of light, angel-blossoming, are let into his dreams; if he be thirsty, the potentates of heaven are his cup-bearers; if he sit down to food, his plain table blooms into the King's banquet. Men say, "Look at that old fellow with the worn-out coat;" the angels of God cry, "Lift up your heads, ye everlasting gates, and let him come in!" Fastidious people cry, "Get off my front steps!" the door-keepers of heaven cry, "Come you, blessed of my Father, inherit the kingdom!" When he comes to die, though he may be carried out in a pine box to the potter's field, to that potter's field the chariots of Christ will come down, and the cavalcade will crowd all the boulevards of heaven.

I bless Christ for the present satisfaction of religion. It makes a man all right with reference to the past; it makes a man all right with reference to the future. Oh these nether springs of comfort! They are perennial. The foundation of God standeth sure having this seal, "The Lord knoweth them that are his." "The mountains shall depart and the hills be removed, but my kindness shall not depart from thee, neither shall the covenant of my peace be removed, saith the Lord, who hath mercy upon them." Oh, cluster of diamonds set in burnished gold! Oh, nether springs of comfort bursting through all the valleys of trial and tribulation! When you see, you of the world, what satisfaction there is on earth in religion, do you not thirst after it as the daughter of Caleb thirsted after the water-springs? It is no stagnant pond, scummed over with malaria, but springs of water leaping from the Rock of Ages! Take up one cup of that spring-water, and across the top of the chalice will float the delicate shadows of the heavenly wall, the yellow of jasper, the green of emerald, the blue of sardonyx, the fire of jacinth.

I wish I could make you understand the joy religion is to some of us. It makes a man happy while he lives, and glad when he dies. With two feet upon a chair and bursting with dropsies, I heard an old man in the poor-house cry out, "Bless the Lord, oh my soul!" I looked around and said, "What has this man got to thank God for?" It makes the lame man leap as a hart, and the dumb sing. They say that the old Puritan religion is a juiceless and joyless religion; but I remember reading of Dr. Goodwin, the celebrated Puritan, who in his last moment said, "Is this dying? Why, my bow abides in strength! I am swallowed up in God!" "Her ways are ways of pleasantness, and all her paths are peace." Oh, you who have been trying to satisfy yourselves with the "south land" of this world, do you not feel that you would, this morning, like to have access to the nether springs of spiritual comfort? Would you not like to have Jesus Christ bend over your cradle and bless your table and heal your wounds, and strew flowers of consolation all up and down the graves of your dead?

> "'Tis religion that can give
> Sweetest pleasures while we live:
> 'Tis religion can supply
> Sweetest comfort when we die."

But I have something better to tell you, suggested by this text. It seems that old Father Caleb on the wedding-day of his daughter wanted to make her just as happy as possible. Though Othniel was taking her away, and his heart was almost broken because she was going, yet he gives her a "south land;" not only that, but the *nether* springs; not only that, but the *upper* springs. O God! my Father, I thank thee that thou hast given me a "south land" in this world, and the nether springs of spiritual comfort in this world; but, more than all, I thank thee for the upper springs in heaven.

It is very fortunate that we can not see heaven until we get into it. Oh, Christian man, if you could see what a place it is, we would never get you back again to the office or store or shop, and the duties you ought to perform would go neglected. I am glad I shall not see that world until I enter it. Suppose we were allowed to go on an excursion into that good land with the idea of returning. When we got there, and heard the song, and looked at their raptured faces, and mingled in the supernal society, we would cry out, "Let us stay! We are coming here anyhow. Why take the trouble of going back again to that old world? We are here now; let us stay." And it would take angelic violence to put us out of that world, if once we got there. But as people who can not afford to pay for an entertainment sometimes come around it and look through the door ajar, or through the openings in the fence, so we come and look through the crevices into that good land which God has provided for us. We can just catch a glimpse of it. We come near enough to hear the rumbling of the eternal orchestra, though not near enough to know who blows the cornet or who fingers the harp. My soul spreads out both wings and claps them in triumph at the thought of those upper springs. One of them breaks from beneath the throne; another breaks forth from beneath the altar of the temple; another at the door of "the house of many mansions." Upper springs of gladness! upper springs of light! upper springs of love! It is no fancy of mine. "The Lamb which is in the midst of the throne shall lead them to living fountains of water." Oh, Saviour divine, roll in upon our souls one of those anticipated raptures! Pour around the roots of the parched tongue one drop of that liquid life! Toss before our vision those fountains of God, rainbowed with eternal victory. Hear it! They are never sick there; not so much as a headache, or twinge rheumatic, or thrust neuralgic. The inhabitant never says, "I am sick." They are never tired there. Flight to farthest world is only the play of a holiday. They never sin there. It is as easy for them to be holy as it is for us to sin. They never die there. You might go through all the outskirts of the great city and find not one place where the ground was broken for a grave. The eyesight of the redeemed is never blurred with tears. There is health in every cheek. There is spring in every foot. There is majesty on every brow. There is joy in every heart. There is hosanna on every lip. How they must pity us as they look over and look down and see us, and say, "Poor things away down in that world!" And when some Christian is hurled into a fatal accident, they cry, "Good, he is coming!" And when we stand around the couch of some loved one (whose strength is going away) and we shake our heads forebodingly, they cry, "I am glad he is worse; he has been down there long enough. There, he is dead! Come home! come home!" Oh, if we could only get our ideas about that future world untwisted, our thought of transfer from here to there would be as pleasant to us as it was to a little child that was dying. She said, "Papa, when will I go home?" And he said, "To-day, Florence." "To-day? so soon? I am so glad!"

I wish I could stimulate you with these thoughts, oh Christian man, to the highest possible exhilaration. The day of your deliverance is coming, is coming. It is rolling on with the shining wheels of the day, and the jet wheels of the night. Every thump of the heart is only a hammer-stroke striking off another chain of clay. Better scour the deck and coil the rope, for harbor is only six miles away. Jesus will come down in the "Narrows" to meet you. " Now is your salvation nearer than when you believed."

Unforgiven man, unpardoned man, will you not to-day make a choice between these two portions, between the "south land" of this world, which slopes to the desert, and this glorious land which thy Father offers thee, running with eternal water-courses? Why let your tongue be consumed of thirst when there are the nether springs and the upper springs: comfort here, and glory hereafter?

Let me tell you, my dear brother, that the silliest and wickedest thing a man ever does is to reject Jesus Christ. The loss of the soul is a mistake that can never be corrected. It is a downfall that knows no alleviation; it is a ruin that is remediless; it is a sickness that has no medicament; it is a grave into which a man goes but never comes out. Therefore, putting my hand on your shoulder, as one brother puts his hand on the shoulder of a brother, I say this day, be manly, and surrender your heart to Christ. You have been long enough serving the world; now begin to serve the Lord who bought you. You have tried long enough to carry these burdens; let Jesus Christ put his shoulder under your burdens. Do I hear any one in the audience say, "I mean to attend to that after a while; it is not just the time?" It is the time, for the simple reason that you are sure of no other; and God sent you into the Academy of Music this morning, and he sent me here to confront you

## THE UPPER AND NETHER SPRINGS. 61

with this message; and you must hear now that Christ died to save your soul, and that if you want to be saved you may be saved. "Whosoever will, let him come." You will never find any more convenient season than this. Some of you have been waiting ten, twenty, thirty, forty, fifty, and sixty years. On some of you the snow has fallen. I see it on your brow, and yet you have not attended to those duties which belong to the very springtime of life. It is September with you now, it is October with you, it is December with you. I am no alarmist. I simply know this: if a man does not repent in this world he never repents at all, and that now is the accepted time, and now is the day of salvation. Oh, put off this matter no longer. Do not turn your back on Jesus Christ who comes to save you, lest you should lose your soul.

Last Monday morning a friend of mine started from New York to celebrate her birthday with her daughter in Virginia. Yesterday morning, just after sunrise, I stood at the gate of Greenwood waiting for her silent form to come in. It was only a few weeks ago she sat out yonder in the gallery while I preached. It is a long journey to take in one week—from New York to Philadelphia, from Philadelphia to Baltimore, from Baltimore to Washington, from Washington to Virginia, from Virginia into the great Eternity! "What thy hand findeth to do, DO IT."

## WRECK OF THE "VILLE DU HAVRE."

"In perils of waters."—2 *Corinthians* xi., 26.

IT required courage either to be a sailor or a voyager in olden times, the ships were so small, so clumsy, so unmanageable—the islands, the rocks, the shores so poorly defined; no weather "probabilities," no signals hoisted, no light-houses. It was almost impossible to hail a vessel if in distress, because ships were seldom seen! Sailors might have cried, "Ship ahoy!" "Haul down the flying-jib!" or "Brace her cross-jack yards sharp aback!" Nobody would have noticed it. Only here and there a vessel traversing the deep; and a vessel might go on for days and weeks, and not hail a single sail. Yet I am not certain but there are as great perils now on the sea as there were then, notwithstanding our perfect sea-charts and our light-houses and our sextants and our iron-clads, and the fact that there are flags flying all along the coast telling sailors, "Beware, for the storm is coming." The danger arises now from the multiplicity of crafts. The captain in mid-Atlantic puts the sea-glass to his eye and sweeps the horizon, and perhaps in the distance sees a full-rigged brig, bark, ship, or steamer of the Cunard, White Star, Inman, and National lines. It is a fact that in one year in this country there were built over fifty sea-going steamers. Every year there are fishing-smacks along the Banks of Newfoundland run down in the fog; and the only report of it is that John and George come not back to their home, and the women weep, and the children starve. Last summer, in the thick night, I heard the fog-horns of the fishermen off Newfoundland within twenty yards of where our leviathan ship ran by. If Paul in his day, because of the imperfect sea equipment, could talk of "perils of waters," certainly we may in this day, because of the multiplicity of crafts and the danger of collision.

Only a few days ago the *Loch Earn*, a vessel of one thousand two hundred tons, bowsprit steel-plated, weighed anchor in English waters. Only a few days ago the *Ville du Havre* was ready to sail from New York. The usual warning was given on deck, "All ashore that's going!" Then the gangways were cleared and the planks hauled in, and the usual farewell waving, and, as though foreboding evil, a young man stands on deck and waves to his friends ashore, crying, "Good-bye; you will never see me again on this side the water!" It seemed almost impossible that two vessels starting from such distant ports should even hail each other on the sea. Nevertheless, they came on through day and night, and darkness and storm, and fog and sunshine, approximating, as though they had appointed a place and a time for meeting. The *Loch Earn* sometimes took a different tack, and the *Ville du Havre* changed sometimes its course, but nevertheless approximating all the while, the hour for their meeting coming very soon. It is twelve o'clock at night. The bells have sounded. It is one o'clock in the morning. It is two o'clock in the morning. Lights hung in the rigging. The helmsman at the wheel. The fireman down at the furnace. The watch pacing the lookout. The passengers asleep in the berths and cabins; when crash! came the *Loch Earn* midships the *Ville du Havre*. They who were around the gangway rushed to the decks, and mariners and passengers ran wild, and some stark mad, and there was a rush for the life-boats, and a cry to God and man for help. No time to put on life-preservers. No time to sound the minute-gun of distress across the sea. Here they kneel in prayer; yonder leap into the wave; there they stand white with horror. The thought of home and loved ones far away comes over them, and they feel as if they can not, must not die. But already the steamer has begun to sink. Pull away there in the life-boats, lest you be sucked down in the awful ingulfment! Pull away there in the life-boats! The mizzen mast crashes upon some of the life-boats and they are gone, and the steamer sinks. As it goes down toward the bottom of the sea, down lower, until the deck is even with the wave, the combined, the unearthly, the stupendous shriek of two hundred and twelve passengers rends the air of earth and heaven with the catastrophe.

I can not, as a minister of Christ and as a lover of humanity, let this solemn occurrence pass without learning for myself and teaching you three or four lessons.

And first I learn the *responsibility of those who hold the lives, or the property, or the souls of men in keeping*. I will leave to the marine authorities to say who were guilty; but it is certain that there is wickedness somewhere. No fog, no storm, clear starlight; and yet five hundred, perhaps one thousand families, in this country and in Europe, are whelmed in bereavement to-day. I will not say who is to blame, I do not know who is to blame; but the two continents have been impaneled as coroner's jury, and have rendered the verdict, "Appalling guilt somewhere!" The commanders of steamships, the engineers of locomotives, the conductors of rail-trains, the architects of buildings, the pilots of steamboats, have in their hands and on their shoulders very great responsibility. God will hold them to account for what they do with the lives and with the souls of men. It may have seemed a very insignificant thing connected with this disaster that there were thirty-four thousand bushels of wheat that went to the bottom of the sea; but I do not think it was at all insignificant when there are so many starving for bread. The world could not afford to waste thirty-four thousand bushels of wheat. The responsibility must rest somewhere. Pastors of churches, private Christians who hold in their hands the souls of people, had better look out what they do with them—all the time having a light hung out, keeping the helm up, ringing the bells of warning, standing on the lookout, obeying the injunction, watch!

I tell you plainly that I would rather have been Captain Williams running the *Atlantic* last spring on Mars Head Rock until five hundred people dropped into the wave, than be a "Christian" minister, yet by preaching a wrong theology conduct an audience of hundreds and thousands of immortal men and women into an eternal catastrophe. "When I say to the wicked, 'Thou shalt surely die,' and thou givest him no warning, nor speakest to warn the wicked from his wickedness—that same man shall die in his iniquity, but his blood will I require at thy hands."

> " 'Tis not a cause of small import,
> The pastor's care demands;
> But what might fill an angel's heart—
> It filled a Saviour's hand."

Oh, men who have under your charge the bodies, the property, the souls of immortal men, look out how you discharge your responsibility!

Again, I learn from this disaster at sea that, *when we part from our friends, reunion is uncertain.* A voyage to Europe is so common, a journey to any part of our country so common, that when we part from our friends we expect certainly to see them again. My counsel to you is that if you have any duty to perform toward your friends in regard to their eternal interests, you had better perform that duty before they take steamer or rail car. If there were any impenitent persons who perished in that wreck of the *Ville du Havre*, how do you suppose their unfaithful Christian friends feel about it now? They are saying this very day, "Oh, if on the 15th of November, when I stood on the steamer's deck or stood on the wharf, before that vessel sailed, I had just asked them to come to Christ and make preparations for eternity! But that was my last chance—it was my last chance!" If your friends have already gone from you on a voyage or journey, write to them to-morrow morning by the first mail, lest they die on their way back, and you have a harrowing of the soul for them because you did not do your duty toward them. I believe that there are thousands and hundreds of thousands of souls out of Christ to-day simply because Christian friends do not do their duty. Did you notice that one strangely thrilling telegram that came last week? A husband and father sent out a wife and daughter on their excursion. They took the *Ville du Havre.* The wife went down in the wreck; the daughter was rescued, and she telegraphed to her father in New York, "I am saved! *Alone!*" Oh, will that be the history of any family in this house to-day? Will you at last reach heaven, and the rest be lost? Having so many opportunities of bringing your friends and your families into the kingdom of God, will it be announced at the last that you are "saved! *Alone!*"

I further learn from this disaster at sea that *elegant surrounding is no security.* The most of people could not afford to take that line of steamers. The fare is higher on that line of steamers than on any that sail the sea. It was a vessel of five thousand four hundred tons. It had cost, in its building and in its repair, one million five hundred thousand dollars. The saloons were upholstered with crimson and gold; but iceberg and storm and darkness and collision can see no difference between magnificent mail steamship, and Nantucket whaler, with rusty bolts and greasy deck. The plush, the tapestry, the paintings, the cut glass, the statuary, went down with the passengers. Oh, my hearer, do not think that brilliant surroundings will keep off the last foe! Belshazzar, in the banqueting-hall; Napoleon III., in the mansion at Chiselhurst; the Prince of Wales, in Windsor Castle; the German emperor, now wheeled every day from table to bed, and from bed to table, in his serious illness; the passengers of the *Ville du Havre*, in gilded cabin and amidst brilliant companionship, are summoned away. The armed sentinel stands at the gate of the king's palace. A man comes up. However great he may be, the sentinel cries "Halt!" and the man has to halt. But Death comes to the gate and captures both gate and sentinel. If those people on this fated steamer could have exchanged their money for life, would not they have given it? Oh yes. One would have cried out, "Here are twenty thousand dollars for one day." Another would have cried out, "I'll give you one hundred thousand dollars for one hour." Another would have said, "Two hundred thousand dollars for five minutes more." Ah, Death can not be bribed! He comes with muddy feet, from walking amidst the upturned earth of new-made graves, and blunders over the finest carpets, and sets his spade against the head-board of rose-wood bedstead. "They that boast themselves in the multitude of their riches, none of them can by any means redeem his brother nor give to God a ransom for him, that he should not see corruption: the wise men die, likewise the fool and the brutish person, and leave their wealth to others." Do not think that brilliant companionship and gorgeous surrounding will defend you against the last foe.

Again, I learn from this accident at sea that there are some *Christians nearer to glory than they think*. To many of the passengers on that ship death was translation. They arrived at a better port than France could have afforded them. They did not know, when they went to sleep that night, that they were so near the jasper sea, so near the throne of Christ, so near reunion with the friends gone before, so near to the end of all pain, and struggle, and trial. If they had had any appreciation of the coming joy, they could not have slept a wink that night. They would have said, "In one hour I shall be with Christ in glory." Heaven was a surprise to them. I suppose, for the past few days they had been thinking about how their friends would look when they came down the gangway, as they arrived in port. Perhaps they were thinking how the mementoes would look that were packed away in their trunks—mementoes of American travel. But God had a better reunion for them, and a better gladness.

Some of them were ministers of the Gospel. I suppose that the same Jesus they had preached in Madrid, and Paris, and Geneva, stood by them on the parting deck. I suppose that when the *Loch Earn* crashed in on the one side, the Lord Jesus Christ walked the water on the other side. Some of those men of God worshiped with us in this building only a few Sabbaths ago. One of them sat in that very box. I sent word to a member of my family to stand, and to give the brother a seat. I did not know he was so near to glory, so near to the mansions of the skies, so near heaven. I did not realize it. It was my only opportunity of showing him any courtesy. I never came any nearer to him than that. Oh! my friends, those men of God on the sea did not know that they were going from one Evangelical Alliance to another. But the one here was nothing compared to that great one beyond, made up of the one hundred and forty and four thousand, "of all nations, and kindreds, and people, and tongues." It was two o'clock in the morning—two o'clock, Sabbath morning—when those men went up to God—a good morning in which to go to heaven.

The Sabbath is a good day in which to live or to die. Day of resurrection. Day of jubilee. Day of ascension to their soul. Yet how strange it did seem that, fifteen minutes before, those men down in the cabins heard not the trumpets before the throne, heard not the rush of the chariots of salvation, heard not the hallelujah of the redeemed! Oh, wake up, ye men of God, down in the cabins, within fifteen minutes of glory! The gates are opening, the hospitalities of heaven are preparing, the kings and queens of God are coming down to the gate to greet you. Wake up! men of God, down in the cabins of the *Ville du Havre.*

Some of you are nearer heaven than you believe. Some of you are spending your last Sabbath, singing your last song, giving your last salutations. There is a *Loch Earn* somewhere that is making toward you, and ere you are aware you will open your eyes on raptures eternal. I congratulate you. Your friends in heaven have been saying to Jesus, " Why not let our friends come up from earth? Why not let them come now, O Jesus? We await their coming. Let them come now." And Jesus, to please them, and to please you, will say to his angels, " Bring them home." And the clusters are already on the table, and the beakers are filled, and there is an excitement as of expected arrival, and you will soon be gone.

" Be with me when my feet
Are slipping over the brink,
For I may be nearer home,
Nearer now than I think."

Again, I learn from this disaster at sea that the world has *not yet been persuaded of the nonsense of prayer.* I suppose those people on that ship had all read, in English, or French, or in Spanish, or in German, that prayer is unscientific and entirely useless. Had they been persuaded? Oh no. The report comes to us that they all prayed; and there was one woman who seemed to be the chief apostle of the scene, who prayed aloud until, it was said, her words sounded like inspiration. I do not suppose that she had ever been ordained by conference or by presbytery; but we all feel that that woman had a right to pray in that public assemblage. How soothing her words must have been in that awful anguish! How strong it makes one feel to hear a woman pray! A wife praying for her husband. A sister praying for her wayward brother. A mother praying for her children. A shipwrecked woman praying for two hundred drowning! Oh! women of Christ, can you pray aloud? Can you pray aloud? You may never have to officiate as priestess of God, as that woman did, on the deck of a foundering ship, but there will be times when there will be dying souls who will want from you not so much silent prayer as audible supplication. Can you pray aloud? Are you ashamed to have your children hear you pray aloud? I have heard doctors of divinity pray, and I have heard learned bishops pray, but against all the prayers that I ever heard, I put, for tenderness and power, the uneducated prayer of my mother, now eleven years in glory. She did not have to go to an English hospital to have the "prayer test." She had it in her own home when she prayed that all her children might be brought to God; and they all were brought to God, five of them already with her in the land where God wipes away all tears from the eyes.

Had Tyndall been there, and all the skeptics and philosophers of the world, they would have prayed too; though I fear not with the calmness, and power, and unction of that woman who officiated on the deck. Have you been persuaded of the uselessness of prayer? I have not. Rather, I say, Oh, the omnipotence of prayer! Had you not better try it, ye who have sins to be pardoned, ye who have diseases to be healed, ye who have burdens to carry?

> "Restraining prayer, we cease to fight;
> Prayer makes the Christian's armor bright;
> And Satan trembles when he sees
> The weakest saint upon his knees.
>
> "Were half the breath that's vainly spent
> To heaven in supplication sent,
> Our cheerful song would oftener be:
> 'Hear what the Lord has done for me.'"

I learn, also, from this disaster, *the importance of always being ready for transition*. What an awful thing it must have been, at two o'clock in the morning, on that ship for those not ready! The longest time spoken of, between the collision and the plunge, was twelve minutes. Alas! for the impenitent people on board that vessel! Only twelve minutes to do the whole work of a lifetime, and make preparation for countless ages of eternity. Twelve minutes! Twelve minutes! I think they took ten of them in hoping that they could get off into the life-boats or on the *Loch Earn*, climbing down the mast. I think that ten minutes were taken in that way, hoping to get off. Then, there were only two minutes left; but even these two minutes must be split up; one minute to look over a wasted life, and the other minute to look forward to the great eternity. What a short time that is, you say, what a short time for preparation! But do you not realize the fact, my dear brother, that you may not be so fortunate as that? "Oh!" you say, "I will never venture on the sea." Perhaps you may never step on shipboard, but do you not know that men go out of life without twelve minutes warning, without one minute? When the Avondale explosion took place, how long did those men have time to prepare for eternity? Not half a second! Witness our railway disasters, how, in an instant, they hurl men and women into *an unending eternity.* "In such a day and in such an hour as ye think not, the Son of Man cometh." You have had friends leave the world—did they go at the time you expected, at the time they expected? Is it not almost always a surprise? It has been so with my friends. None of them went away at the time I thought they would. Though their sickness may have been long, though they may have been sick for three months, yet death was a surprise at the last. So it will be with you, in all probability, and so with me. "In such an hour as ye think not, the Son of Man cometh."

I can not realize that that steamer is gone. Did you ever see her? She was a beautiful vessel. I was on her deck one day (she was lying at the wharf) examining the marvels of her structure and the beauty of her cabins. She was the most beautiful steamer I ever saw; and now at the bottom of the Atlantic is that dead steamer. The furnaces all out. The pulsating machinery still. Passengers still in their berths, sleeping their last sleep! No hand on the helm. No foot pacing the lookout. Sea-monsters floating in and out the gashed side of the steamer. Along the gangway, on the stairs, and in the cabins, the bodies of men, and fair maidens, and beautiful children waiting for the resurrection. Oh! the dead steamer, buried in coffin of coral, under garlands of sea-weed, in the cemetery of dead ships, beside the *Arctic,* and the *Pacific,* and the *Cambria,* and the *President,* and the *City of Boston.* Toll all the cathedral bells of Madrid, and Paris, and Geneva, and New York.

But all those shipwrecked ones must come up. "The sea shall give up its dead," and all the cemeteries on the land must yield their trophies. What a time there will be in Greenwood, and in Laurel Hill, and in the village grave-yard! Oh, what a time! The Bible declares it: "They shall come forth, some to the resurrection of life, and some to the resurrection of damnation." Day of joy. Day of sorrow. Day of light. Day of darkness. Day of victory. Day of defeat. Day of resurrection. O God! prepare me for that day. Are we ready? There comes a voice from the dead steamer that overpowers all other voices as it says: "What thy hand findeth to do, do it with all thy might, for there is neither wisdom, nor device, nor knowledge in the grave whither we are all hastening."

## GRACE IN CRYSTALS.

"Salt is good."— *Luke* xiv., 34.

THE Bible is a dictionary of the finest similes. It employs, among living creatures, storks and eagles, and doves and unicorns, and sheep and cattle; among trees, sycamores and terebinths, and pomegranates, and almonds, and apples; among jewels, pearls and amethysts, and jacinths and chrysoprases. Christ uses no stale illustrations. The lilies that he plucks for his sermons are dewy fresh; the ravens in his discourses are not stuffed specimens of birds, but warm with life from wing-tip to wing-tip; the fish he points to are not dull about the gills, as though long captured, but a-squirm in the wet net just brought up on the beach of Tiberias. In my text, which is the peroration of one of his sermons, he picks up a crystal and holds it before his congregation as an illustration of divine grace in the heart, when he says, what we all know by experiment, "Salt is good."

I shall try to carry out the Saviour's idea in this text, and in the first place say to you that *grace is like salt in its beauty*. In Galicia there are mines of salt with excavations and under-ground passages reaching, I am told, two hundred and eighty miles. Far under-ground there are chapels and halls of reception, the columns, the altars, and the pulpits of salt. When the king and the princes come to visit these mines, the whole place is illumined, and the glory of crystal walls and crystal ceilings and crystal floors and crystal columns, under the glare of the torches and the lamps, needs words of crystal to describe it. But you need not go so far as that to find the beauty of salt. We live in a land which produces fourteen millions of bushels of it in a year, and you can take the morning rail train, and in a few hours get to the salt-mines and salt-springs; and you have this article morning, noon, and night, on your table. Salt has all the beauty of the snow-flake and water-foam, with durability added. It is beautiful to the naked eye, but under the glass you see the stars and the diamonds and the white tree-branches, and the splinters and the bridges of fire as the sun glints them. There is more architectural skill in one of these crystals of salt than human ingenuity has ever demonstrated in an Alhambra or St. Peter's. It would take all time, with an infringement upon eternity, for an angel of God to tell one-half the glories in a salt-crystal. So with the grace of God: it is perfectly beautiful. I have seen it smooth out wrinkles of care from the brow; I have seen it make an aged man feel almost young again; I have seen it lift the stooping shoulders, and put sparkle into the dull eye. Solomon discovered its anatomical qualities when he said, "It is marrow to the bones." It helps to digest the food, and to purify the blood, and to calm the pulses, and quiet the spleen; and instead of putting a man in a philosophical hospital to be experimented upon by prayer, it keeps him so well that he does not need to be prayed for as an invalid. I am speaking now of a *healthy* religion—not of that morbid religion that sits for three hours on a grave-stone, reading "Hervey's Meditations among the Tombs"—a religion that prospers best in a bad state of the liver! I speak of the religion that Christ preached. I suppose, when that religion has conquered the world, that disease will be banished; and that a man a hundred years of age will come in from business, and say, "I feel tired. I think it must be time for me to go," and without one physical pang, heaven will have him.

But the chief beauty of grace is in the soul. It takes that which was hard and cold and repulsive, and makes it all over again. It pours upon one's nature what David calls "the beauty of holiness." It extirpates every thing that is hateful and unclean. If jealousy and pride and lust and worldliness lurk about, they are chained, and have a very small sweep. Jesus throws upon the soul the fragrance of a summer garden as he comes in, saying, "I am the rose of Sharon;" and he submerges it with the glory of a spring morning as he says, "I am the light." Oh, how much that grace did for the three Johns! It took John Bunyan, the foul-mouthed, and made him John Bunyan, the immortal dreamer. It took John Newton, the infidel sailor, and in the midst of the hurricane made him cry out, "My mother's God, have mercy upon me!" It took John Summerfield from a life of sin, and by the hand of a Christian edge-tool maker led him into the pulpit that burns still with the light of that Christian eloquence which charmed thousands to the Jesus whom he once despised. Ah! you may search all the earth over for any thing so beautiful or beautifying as the grace of God. Go all through the deep mine passages of Wieliczka and amidst the under-ground kingdoms of salt in Hallstadt, and show me any thing so exquisite, so transcendentally beautiful as this grace of God fashioned and hung in eternal crystals.

Again, grace is like salt, in the fact that *it is a necessity of life*. Man and beast perish without salt. What are those paths across the Western prairies? Why, they were made there by deer and buffalo going to and coming away from the salt "licks." Chemists and physicians, all the world over, tell us that salt is a necessity of life. And so with the grace of God: you must have it or die. I know a great many people speak of it as a mere adornment, a sort of shoulder-strap adorning a soldier, or a light, frothing dessert, brought in after the greatest part of the banquet of life is over, or a medicine to be taken after calomel and mustard-plasters have failed to do their work; but ordinarily a mere superfluity, a string of bells around a horse's neck while he draws the load, and in no wise helping him to draw it. So far from that, I declare the grace of God to be the first and the last necessity. It is food we must take, or starve into an eternity of famine. It is clothing, without which we freeze to the mast of infinite terror. It is the plank, and the only plank, on which we can float shoreward. It is the ladder, and the only ladder, on which we can climb away from eternal burnings. And that young woman who sits before me and laughs must have it or die. It is a positive necessity for the soul. You can tell very easily what the effect would be if a person refused to take salt into the body. The energies would fail, the lungs would struggle with the air, slow fevers would crawl through the brain, the heart would flutter, and the life would be gone. That process of death is going on in many a one because they take not the salt of divine grace. The soul becomes weaker and weaker, and after a while the pulses of life will stop entirely. Stretch out that soul on the bier of eternal death! Coffin it in a groan! Strew on it wreaths of nightshade! Cover it with a pall of eternal blackness! Set no burning lamps at the head and at the feet, but rather the extinguished torches of the silly virgins whose lamps went out. Let the pall-bearers come in—Remorse and Despair and Anguish and Pain, and shoulder it, and take it away with solemn and awful tramp, remembering that they carry the corpse of a soul. "He that believeth and is baptized shall be saved, and he that believeth not shall be damned." Salt, a necessity for the life of the body—the grace of God a necessity for the life of the soul.

Again I remark, that grace is *like salt in abundance.* God has strewn salt in vast profusion all over the continents. Russia seems built on a salt-cellar. There is one region of that country that turns out ninety thousand tons in a year. England and Russia and Italy have inexhaustible resources in this respect. Norway and Sweden, white with snow above, white with salt beneath. Austria, yielding nine hundred thousand tons annually. Nearly all the nations rich in it—rock-salt, spring-salt, sea-salt. Christ, the Creator of the world, when he uttered our text, knew it would become more and more significant as the shafts were sunk, and the springs were bored, and the pumps were worked, and the crystals were gathered. So the grace of God is abundant. It is for all lands, for all ages, for all conditions. It seems to undergird every thing. Pardon for the worst sin, comfort for the sharpest suffering, brightest light for the thickest darkness. Around about the salt lakes of Saratov there are ten thousand men toiling day and night, and yet they never exhaust the saline treasures. And if the one thousand millions of our race should now cry out to God for his mercy, there would be enough for all; for those farthest gone in sin, for the murderer standing on the drop of the gallows, for Rosenzweig, and Stokes, and Foster. It is an ocean of mercy; and if Europe and Asia, Africa, North and South America, and all the islands of the sea, went down in it to-day, they would have room enough to wash and come up clean. Let no man in this house think that his case is too tough a one for God to act upon; though your sin may be deep and raging, let me tell you that God's grace is a bridge not built on earthly piers, but suspended, and spanning the awful chasm of your guilt, one end resting upon the rock of eternal promises, and the other on the foundations of heaven. Demetrius wore a robe so incrusted with jewels that no one after him ever dared to wear it; but our King, Jesus, takes off the robe of his righteousness, a robe blood-dyed and heaven-impearled, and reaches it out to the worst wretch in all the earth, and says, "Put that on! wear it now! wear it forever."

Again, the grace of God is *like salt in the way we come at it.* The salt on the surface is almost always impure —that which incrusts the Rocky Mountains and the South American pampas and in India; but the miners go down through the shafts and through the dark labyrinths, and along by galleries of rock, and, with torches and pickaxes, find their way under the very foundations of the earth, to where the salt lies that makes up the nation's wealth. To get to the best saline springs of the earth huge machinery goes down, boring depth below depth, depth below depth, until from under the very roots of the mountains, the saline water supplies the aqueduct. This water is brought to the surface, and is exposed in tanks to the sun for evaporation, or it is put in boilers mightily heated, and the water evaporates, and the salt gathers at the bottom of the tank—the work is completed, and the fortune is made. So with the grace of God. It is to be profoundly sought after. With all the concentred energies of body, mind, and soul we must dig for it. No man stumbles accidentally on it. We need to go down to the very lowest strata of earnestness and faith to find it. Superficial exploration will not turn it up. We must strive, and implore, and dig until we strike the spring foaming with living waters. Then the work of evaporation begins; and as when the saline waters are exposed to the sun, the vapors float away, leaving nothing but the pure white salt at the bottom of the tank, so, when the Christian's soul is exposed to the Sun of Righteousness, the vapors of pride and selfishness and worldliness float off, and there is chiefly left beneath pure white holiness of heart. Then, as in the case of the salt, the furnace is added. Blazing troubles, stirred by smutted stokers of darkness, quicken the evaporation of worldliness, and the crystallization of grace.

Have you not been in enough trouble to have that work go on? I was reading of Aristotle, who said there was a field of flowers in Sicily so sweet that once a hound, coming on the track of game, came to that field, and was bewildered by the perfumes, and so lost the track. Oh! that our souls might become like "a field which the Lord hath blessed," and exhale so much of the sweetness of Christian character that the hounds of temptation, coming on our track, might lose it, and go howling back with disappointment!

But, I remark again, that the grace of God is like the salt *in its preservative quality.* You know that salt absorbs the moisture of articles of food and infuses them with brine, which preserves them for a long while. Salt is the great antiputrefactive of the world. Experimenters, in preserving food, have tried sugar, and smoke, and airtight jars, and every thing else; but as long as the world stands Christ's words will be suggestive, and men will admit that, as a great preservative, "salt is good." But for the grace of God, the earth would have become a stale carcass long before this. That grace is the only preservative of laws, and constitutions, and literatures. Just as soon as a Government loses this salt of divine grace, it perishes. The philosophy of this day, so far as it is antagonistic to this religion, putrefies and stinks. The great want of our schools of learning and our institutions of science to-day is, not more Leyden jars, and galvanic batteries, and spectroscopes, and philosophical apparatus, but more of that grace that will teach our men of science that the God of the universe is the God of the Bible. How strange it is that in all their magnificent sweep of the telescope they have not seen the morning-star of Jesus, and that in all their experiments with light and heat they have not seen the light and felt the warmth of the Sun of Righteousness! We want more of the salt of God's grace in our homes, in our schools, in our colleges, in our social life, in our Christianity. And that which has it will live—that which has it not will die. I proclaim the tendency of every thing earthly to putrefaction and death—the religion of Christ the only preservative.

My subject is one of great congratulation to those who have within their souls this Gospel antiseptic. This salt will preserve them through the temptations and sorrows of life, and through the ages of eternity. I do not mean to say that you will have a smooth time because you are a Christian. On the contrary, if you do your whole duty, I will promise you a rough time. You march through an enemy's country, and they will try to double up both flanks, and to cut you off from your source of supplies. The war you wage will not be with toy arrows, but sword plunged to the hilt, and spurring on your steed over heaps of the slain. But I think that God omnipotent will see you through. I think he will. But why do I talk like an atheist, when I ought to say I *know* he will? "Kept by the power of God through faith unto complete salvation."

When Governor Geary, of Pennsylvania, died a few days ago, I lost a good friend. He impressed me mightily with the horrors of war. In the eight hours that it takes to come from Harrisburg to New York, he recited to me the scenes through which he had passed in the last war. He said that there came one battle upon which every thing seemed to pivot. Telegrams from Washington said that the life of the nation depended upon that struggle. He said to me: "I went into that battle, sir, with my son. His mother and I thought every thing of him. You know how a father will feel toward his son who is coming up manly, and brave, and good. Well, the battle opened and concentred, and it was awful! Horses and riders bent and twisted and piled up together: it was awful, sir! We quit firing, and took to the point of the bayonet. Well, sir, I didn't feel like myself that day.

I had prayed to God for strength for that particular battle, and I went into it feeling that I had in my right arm the strength of ten giants," and as the governor brought his arm down on the back of the seat, it fairly made the car tremble. "Well," he said, "the battle was desperate, but after a while we gained a little, and we marched on a little. I turned round to the troops and shouted, 'Come on, boys!' and I stepped across a dead soldier, and lo! it was my son. I saw at the first glance he was dead, and yet I did not dare to stop a minute, for the crisis had come in the battle; so I just got down on my knees, and I threw my arms around him, and I gave him one good kiss, and said, 'Good-bye, dear,' and sprang up and shouted, 'Come on, boys!'" So it is in the Christian conflict—it is a fierce fight. Eternal ages seem depending on the strife. Heaven is waiting for the bulletins to announce the tremendous issue. Hail of shot, gash of sabre, fall of battle-axe, groaning on every side. We can not stop for loss or bereavement, or any thing else. With one ardent embrace and one loving kiss, we utter our farewells, and then cry, "Come on, boys! There are other heights to be captured, there are other foes to be conquered, there are other crowns to be won."

Yet, as one of the Lord's surgeons, I must bind up two or three wounds. Just lift them now, whatever they be. I have been told there is nothing like salt to stop the bleeding of a wound, and so I take this salt of Christ's Gospel and put it on the lacerated soul. It smarts a little at first; but see! the bleeding stops, and lo! the flesh comes again as the flesh of a little child. "Salt *is* good!"

## GOSPEL ARCHERY.

"He was a mighty hunter before the Lord."—*Genesis* x., 9.

IN our day hunting is a sport; but in the lands and the times infested of wild beasts, it was a matter of life or death with the people. It was very different from going out on a sunshiny afternoon with a patent breech-loader, to shoot reed-birds on the flats, when Pollux and Achilles and Diomedes went out to clear the land of lions and tigers and bears. My text sets forth Nimrod as a hero, when it presents him with broad shoulders and shaggy apparel and sun-browned face, and arm bunched with muscle—"a mighty hunter before the Lord." I think he used the bow and the arrows with great success, practicing archery.

I have thought if it is such a grand thing and such a brave thing to clear wild beasts out of a country, if it is not a better and braver thing to hunt down and destroy those great evils of society that are stalking the land with fierce eye, and bloody paw, and sharp tusk, and quick spring. I have wondered if there is not such a thing as Gospel archery, by which those who have been flying from the truth may be captured for God and heaven. The Lord Jesus in his sermon used the art of angling for an illustration, when he said, "I will make you fishers of men." And so I think I have authority for using hunting as an illustration of Gospel truth; and I pray God that there may be many a man in this congregation who shall begin to study Gospel archery, of whom it may, after a while, be said, "He was a mighty hunter before the Lord."

How much awkward Christian work there is done in the world! How many good people there are who drive souls away from Christ instead of bringing them to him! All their fingers are thumbs—religious blunderers who upset more than they right. Their gun has a crooked barrel, and kicks as it goes off. They are like a clumsy comrade who goes along with skillful hunters; at the very moment he ought to be most quiet, he is crackling an alder, or falling over a log and frightening away the game. How few Christian people have ever learned the lesson of which I read at the beginning of this service, how that the Lord Jesus Christ at the well went from talking about a cup of water to the most practical religious truths, which won the woman's soul for God! Jesus in the wilderness was breaking bread to the people. I think it was very good bread; it was very light bread, and the yeast had done its work thoroughly. Christ, after he had broken the bread, said to the people, "Beware of the yeast, or of the leaven of the Pharisees." So natural a transition it was, and how easily they all understood him! But how few Christian people there are who understand how to fasten the truths of God and religion to the souls of men! Truman Osborne, one of the evangelists who went through this country some years ago, had a wonderful art in the right direction. He came to my father's house one day, and while we were all seated in the room, he said, "Mr. Talmage, are all your children Christians?" Father said, "Yes, all but De Witt." Then Truman Osborne looked down into the fire-place, and began to tell a story of a storm that came on the mountains, and all the sheep were in the fold; but there was one lamb outside that perished in the storm. Had he looked me in the eye I should have been angered when he told that story; but he looked into the fire-place, and it was so pathetically and beautifully done that I never found any peace until I was sure I was inside the fold, where the other sheep are.

The archers of olden-time studied their art. They were very precise in the matter. The old books gave especial directions as to how an archer should go, and as to what an archer should do. He must stand erect and firm, his left foot a little in advance of the right foot. With his left hand he must take hold of the bow in the middle, and then with the three fingers and the thumb of his right hand he should lay hold the arrow and affix it to the string—so precise was the direction given. But how clumsy we are about religious work! How little skill and care we exercise! How often our arrows miss the mark! Oh! that there were lay colleges established in all the towns and cities of our land, where men might learn the art of doing good—studying spiritual archery, and known as "mighty hunters before the Lord!"

In the first place, if you want to be effectual in doing good, you must be very *sure of your weapon*. There was something very fascinating about the archery of olden times. Perhaps you do not know what they could do with the bow and arrow. Why, the chief battles fought by the English Plantagenets were with the long-bow. They would take the arrow of polished wood, and feather it with the plume of a bird, and then it would fly from the bowstring of plaited silk. The bloody fields of Agincourt, and Solway Moss, and Neville's Cross heard the loud thrum of the archer's bowstring. Now, my Christian friends, we have a mightier weapon than that. It is the arrow of the Gospel; it is a sharp arrow; it is a straight arrow; it is feathered from the wing of the dove of God's Spirit; it flies from a bow made out of the wood of the cross. As far as I can estimate or calculate, it has brought down three hundred millions of souls. Paul knew how to bring the notch of that arrow on to the bowstring, and its whir was heard through the Corinthian theatres, and through the court-room, until the knees of Felix knocked together. It was that arrow that stuck in Luther's heart when he cried out, "Oh, my sins! Oh, my sins!" If it strike a man in the head, it kills his skepticism; if it strike him in the heel, it will turn his step; if it strike him in the heart, he throws up his hands, as did one of old when wounded in the battle, crying, "O Galilean! thou hast conquered!"

In the armory of the Earl of Pembroke, there are old corselets which show that the arrow of the English used to go through the breastplate, through the body of the warrior, and out through the backplate. What a symbol of that Gospel which is sharper than a two-edged sword, piercing to the dividing asunder of soul and body, and of the joints and marrow! Would to God we had more faith in that Gospel! The humblest man in this house, if he had enough faith in it, could bring a hundred souls to Jesus—perhaps five hundred. Just in proportion as this age seems to believe less and less in it, I believe more and more in it. What are men about that they will not accept their own deliverance? There is nothing proposed by men that can do any thing like this Gospel. The religion of Ralph Waldo Emerson is the philosophy of icicles; the religion of Theodore Parker was a sirocco of the desert, covering up the soul with dry sand; the religion of Rénan is the romance of believing nothing; the religion of Thomas Carlyle is only a condensed London fog; the religion of the Huxleys and the Spencers is merely a pedestal on which human philosophy sits shivering in the night of the soul, looking up to the stars, offering no help to the nations that crouch and groan at the base. Tell me where there is one man who has rejected that Gospel for another, who is thoroughly satisfied, and helped, and contented in his skepticism, and I will take the car to-morrow and ride five hundred miles to see him. The full power of the Gospel has not yet been touched. As a sportsman throws up his hand and catches the ball flying through the air, just so easily will this Gospel after a while catch this round world flying from its orbit, and bring it back to the heart of Christ. Give it full swing, and it will pardon every sin, heal every wound, cure every trouble, emancipate every slave, and ransom every nation. Ye Christian men and women who go out this afternoon to do Christian work, as you go into the Sunday-schools and the lay-preaching stations, and the penitentiaries, and the asylums, I want you to feel that you bear in your hand a weapon, compared with which the lightning has no speed, and avalanches have no heft, and the thunder-bolts of heaven have no power; it is the arrow of the omnipotent Gospel. Take careful aim! Pull the arrow clear back until the head strikes the bow! Then let it fly. And may the slain of the Lord be many!

Again, if you want to be skillful in spiritual archery, you must hunt *in unfrequented and secluded places.* Why does the hunter go three or four days in the Pennsylvania forests or over Raquette Lake into the wilds of the Adirondacks? It is the only way to do. The deer are shy, and one "bang" of the gun clears the forest. From the California stage you see, as you go over the plains, here and there, a coyote trotting along, almost within range of the gun—sometimes quite within range of it. No one cares for that; it is worthless. The good game is hidden and secluded. Every hunter knows that. So many of the souls that will be of most worth for Christ and of most value to the Church are secluded. They do not come in your way. You will have to go where they are. Yonder they are down in that cellar; yonder they are up in that garret—far away from the door of any church; the Gospel arrow has not been pointed at them. The tract distributer and the city missionary sometimes just catch a glimpse of them, as a hunter through the trees gets a momentary sight of a partridge or roebuck. The trouble is, we are waiting for the game to come to us. We are not good hunters. We are standing on Montague Street and Schermerhorn Street, expecting that the timid antelope will come up and eat out of our hand. We are expecting that the prairie-fowl will light on our church-steeple. It is not their habit. If the Church should wait ten millions of years for the world to come in and be saved, it will wait in vain. The world will not come. What the Church wants now is to lift its feet from damask ottomans, and put them in the stirrups. The Church wants not so much cushions as it wants saddle-bags and arrows. We have got to put aside the gown and the kid-gloves, and put on the hunting-shirt. We want a pulpit on wheels. We have been fishing so long in the brooks that run under the shadow of the Church that the fish know us, and they avoid the hook, and escape as soon as we come to the bank, while yonder is Upper Saranac and Big Tupper's Lake, where the first swing of the Gospel net would break it for the multitude of the fishes. There is outside work to be done. What is it that I see in the backwoods? It is a tent. The hunters have made a clearing, and camped out. What do they care if they have wet feet, or if they have nothing but a pine branch for a pillow, or for the north-east storm? If a moose in the darkness steps into the lake to drink, they hear it right away. If a loon cry in the midnight, they hear it. So, in the service of God, we have exposed work. We have got to camp out and rough it. We are putting all our care on the forty thousand people in Brooklyn who, they say, come to church. What are we doing for the three hundred and sixty thousand that do not come? Have they no souls? Are they sinless, that they need no pardon? Are there no dead in their houses, that they need no comfort? Are they cut off from God, to go into eternity—no wing to bear them, no light to cheer them, no welcome to greet them? I hear to-day, surging up from that lower depth of Brooklyn, a groan that comes through our Christian assemblages and through our beautiful churches; and it blots out all this scene from my eyes to-day, as by the mists of a great Niagara, for the dash and the plunge of these great torrents of life dropping down into the fathomless and thundering abysm of suffering and woe. I sometimes think that just as God blotted out the churches of Thyatira and Corinth and Laodicea because of their sloth and stolidity, he will blot out American and English Christianity, and raise on the ruins a stalwart, wide-awake missionary church that can take the full meaning of that command, "Go ye into all the world, and preach the gospel to every creature. He that believeth and is baptized shall be saved; but he that believeth not shall be damned"—a command, you see, punctuated with a throne of heaven and a dungeon of hell.

I remark, further, if you want to succeed in spiritual archery you must *have courage.* If the hunter stands with trembling hand or shoulder that flinches with fear, instead of his taking the catamount, the catamount takes him. What would become of the Greenlander if, when out hunting for the bear, he should stand shivering with terror on an iceberg? What would have become of Du Chaillu and Livingstone in the African thicket, with a faint heart and a weak knee? When a panther comes within twenty paces of you, and it has its eye on you, and it has squatted for the fearful spring, "Steady there!" Courage, oh, ye spiritual archers! There are great monsters of iniquity prowling all around about the community. Shall we not in the strength of God go forth and combat them? We not only need more heart, but more backbone. What is the Church of God that it should fear to look in the eye any transgression? There is the Bengal tiger of drunkenness that prowls around; and instead of attacking it, how many of us hide under the church-pew or the communion-table! There is so much invested in it we are afraid to assault it; millions of dollars in barrels, in vats, in spigots, in corkscrews, in gin-palaces with marble floors and Italian-top tables, and chased ice-coolers, and in the strychnine, and the logwood, and the tartaric acid, and the *nux vomica*, that go to make up our "pure" American drinks. I looked with wondering eyes on the "Heidelberg tun." It is the great liquor-vat of Germany, which is said to hold eight hundred hogsheads of wine, and only three times in a hundred years it has been filled. But, as I stood and looked at it, I said to myself, "That is nothing—eight hundred hogsheads. Why, our American vat holds five million two hundred thousand barrels of strong drinks, and we keep two hundred thousand men with nothing to do but to see that it is filled." Oh! to attack this great monster of Intemperance, and the kindred monsters of fraud and uncleanness, requires you to rally all your Christian courage. Through the press, through the pulpit, through the platform you must assault it. Would to God that all our American Christians would band together, not for crack-brained fanaticism, but for holy Christian reform! I think it was in 1793 that there went out from Lucknow, India, under the sovereign, the greatest hunting-party that was ever projected. There were ten thousand armed men in that hunting-party. There were camels, and horses, and elephants. On some princes rode, and royal ladies under exquisite housings, and five hundred coolies waited upon the train, and the desolate places of India were invaded by this excursion, and the rhinoceros, and deer, and elephant fell under the stroke of the sabre and bullet. After a while the party brought back trophies worth fifty thousand rupees, having left the wilderness of India ghastly with the slain bodies of wild beasts. Would to God that, instead of here and there a straggler going out to fight these great monsters of iniquity in our country, the millions of membership of our churches would band together and hew in twain these great crimes that make the land frightful with their roar, and are fattening upon the bodies and souls of immortal men! Who is ready for such a party as that? Who will be a mighty hunter for the Lord?

I remark, again, if you want to be successful in spiritual archery, you need not only to bring *down the game*, but bring it *in*. I think one of the most beautiful pictures of Thorwaldsen is his "Autumn." It represents a sportsman coming home, and standing under a grape-vine. He has a staff over his shoulder, and on the other end of that staff are hung a rabbit and a brace of birds. Every hunter brings home the game. No one would think of bringing down a reindeer or whipping up a stream for trout, and letting them lie in the woods. At even-tide the camp is adorned with the treasures of the forest—beak, and fin, and antler.

If you go out to hunt for immortal souls, not only bring them down under the arrow of the Gospel, but bring them into the Church of God, the grand home and encampment we have pitched this side the skies. Fetch them in; do not let them lie out in the open field. They need our prayers and sympathies and help. That is the meaning of the Church of God—*help*. Oh, ye hunters for the Lord! not only bring *down* the game, but bring it *in*.

If Mithridates liked hunting so well that for seven years he never went indoors, what enthusiasm ought we to have who are hunting for immortal souls! If

Domitian practiced archery until he could stand a boy down in the Roman amphitheatre with a hand out, the fingers apart like that, and then the king could shoot an arrow between the fingers without wounding them, to what drill and what practice ought not we to subject ourselves in order to become spiritual archers and "mighty hunters before the Lord!" But let me say you will never work any better than you pray. The old archers took the bow, put one end of it down beside the foot, elevated the other end, and it was the rule that the bow should be just the size of the archer; if it were just his size, then he would go into the battle with confidence. Let me say that your power to project good in the world will correspond exactly to your own spiritual stature. In other words, the first thing, in preparation for Christian work, is personal consecration.

"Oh for a closer walk with God,
A calm and heavenly frame,
A light to shine upon the road
That leads me to the Lamb."

I am sure that there are some here who at some time have been hit by the Gospel arrow. You felt the wound of that conviction, and you plunged into the world deeper; just as the stag, when the hounds are after it, plunges into Scroon Lake, expecting in that way to escape. Jesus Christ is on your track to-day, oh, impenitent man! not in wrath, but in mercy. Oh, ye chased and panting souls! here is the stream of God's mercy and salvation, where you may cool your thirst! Stop that chase of sin to-day. By the red fountain that leaped from the heart of my Lord, I bid you stop! There is mercy for you—mercy that pardons, mercy that heals, everlasting mercy.

Is there in all this house any one who can refuse the offer that comes from the heart of the dying Son of God? Why, do you know that there are, in the banished world, souls that, for that offer you get to-day, would fling the crown of the universe at your feet, if they possessed it? But they went out on the mountains, the storm took them, and they died.

There is in a forest in Germany a place they call the "deer-leap"—two crags, about eighteen yards apart, between them a fearful chasm. This is called the "deer-leap," because once a hunter was on the track of a deer; it came to one of these crags; there was no escape for it from the pursuit of the hunter, and in utter despair it gathered itself up, and in the death-agony attempted to jump across. Of course it fell, and was dashed on the rocks far beneath. Here is a path to heaven. It is plain; it is safe. Jesus marks it out for every man to walk in. But here is a man who says, "I won't walk in that path; I will take my own way." He comes on up until he confronts the chasm that divides his soul from heaven. Now his last hour has come, and he resolves that he will leap that chasm, from the heights of earth to the heights of heaven. Stand back now, and give him full swing, for no soul ever did that successfully. Let him try. Jump! jump! He misses the mark, and he goes down, depth below depth, "destroyed without remedy." Men! angels! devils! what shall we call that place of awful catastrophe? Let it be known forever as THE SINNER'S DEATH-LEAP.

## THE BEST WE HAVE.*

"And being in Bethany, in the house of Simon the leper, as he sat at meat, there came a woman having an alabaster box of ointment of spikenard very precious; and she brake the box, and poured it on his head. Verily I say unto you, Wheresoever this Gospel shall be preached throughout the whole world, this also that she hath done shall be spoken of for a memorial of her."—*Mark* xiv., 3, 9.

IN a village where I once lived, on a cold night there was a cry of "fire." House after house was consumed, but there was in the village a large, hospitable dwelling. As soon as people were burned out they came to this common centre. The good man of the house stood at the door, and said, "Come in," and the little children, as they were brought to the door, some of them wrapped in blankets and shawls very hastily, were taken up to bed, and as the old people that came in from their consumed dwellings were seated around the fire, the good man of the house told them that all would be well. This is a very cold day to be burned out of house and home, but we come into this hospitable home to-night, and gather around this great warm fire of Christian kindness and love. And it is good to be here. The Lord built the Tabernacle and the Lord let it burn down; blessed be the name of the Lord! We do not feel like sitting down in discouragement, although the place was very dear to us, our hearts often there

---

* Sermon preached at Plymouth Church on the evening of the day in which the Brooklyn Tabernacle was burned.

having been comforted; and many and many a time did Jesus appear, his face radiant as the sun. To-day, when the Christian sympathy came in from Plymouth Church and ten other churches of the city, all offering their houses of worship to us, I must say that it became very damp weather about the eyelashes.

If any body tells you that there is no kindness between churches—if any body tells you that there is no such thing as Christian brotherhood, tell him he lies! I find amidst the sorrows of the day one cause for extreme congratulation. I thank God that the fire took place when it did, and not an hour later. Had it come an hour later, when we were assembled for worship, many who are here to-night— (Mr. Talmage hesitated, and was visibly much affected. In a moment he continued.) I will not finish that.

I shall say to you what I would have said this morning if my pulpit had not been burned up, more especially addressing my own people, who, through the courtesy of this church, are here to-night.

A man pale and wasted with recent sickness is entertaining the doctor who cured him. Simon the host, Christ the guest. It is unpleasant to be interrupted at meals, and considerable indignation is aroused by the fact that a woman presses into the dining-hall with ointment made of spikes of nard, and pours this ointment on the head of Christ. It was an ointment so costly and so rare that the bestowment of it implied great admiration and affection. "Put her out!" cried the people; "what an outrageous interruption this is! why is this woman allowed to come in here?" Besides that, it is such a lack of economy. Here she takes a stone-jar made from the mountains near the city of Alabastron—a stone-jar filled with perfume so costly that it might have purchased bread for the poor, and pours it on the head of one who cares nothing for the fragrance. "Stop," said Jesus, "don't put her out!" He who had mingled the cup of all the flowers appreciated the breath of the nard, and he who had made the stone-jars in the factories of Alabastron knew the worth of that box. Jesus says: "The woman is right. She has done her best, and the perfume which fills this banqueting-house shall yet fill all the earth and all ages."

I notice in this subject, in the first place, a *very pleasant way of getting ourselves remembered.* Jesus says that this woman's action of kindness and love shall be a memorial of her. I can not understand the feelings of those who would like to be remembered far on in the future, but I think it is pleasant for us to think that our friends and associates will remember us when we are gone. To get worldly fame men tread on nettles, and work mightily and die wretchedly. Human aggrandizement gives no permanent satisfaction.

I had an aged friend who went into the White House when General Jackson was President of the United States, four days before he left the White House, and the President said to him, "I am bothered almost to death. People strive for this White House as though it were some grand thing to get here, but I tell you it is a perfect hell!" There was nothing in the elevation the world had given him that rendered him satisfaction, or could keep off the annoyances and vexations of life.

A man writes a book. He thinks it will circulate for

a long while. Before long it goes into the archives of the city library to be disturbed once a year, and that when the janitor cleans house! A man builds a splendid home, and thinks he will get fame from it. A few years pass along, and it goes down under the auctioneer's mallet at the executor's sale, and a stranger buys it.

The Pyramids were constructed for the honor of the men who ordered them built. Who built them? Do not know! For whom were they built? Do not know; their whole history is an obscuration and a mystery. There were men in Thebes and Tyre and Babylon who strove for great eminence, but they were forgotten; while the woman of the text, who lovingly accosted Jesus has *her* memorial in all the ages. Ah! men and women of God, I have found out the secret: that which we do for ourselves is forgotten; that which we do for Christ is immortal. They who are kind to the sick, they who instruct the ignorant, they who comfort the troubled, shall not be forgotten.

There have been more brilliant women than Florence Nightingale, but all the world sings her praise. There have been men of more brain than Missionary Carey; their names are forgotten, while his is famous on the records of the Christian Church. There may have been women with vases more costly than that which was brought into the house of Simon the leper; but their names have been forgotten, while I stand before you tonight reading the beautiful story of this Bethany worshiper. In the gallery of heaven are the portraits of Christ's faithful servants, and the monuments may crumble, and earth may burn, and the stars may fall, and time may perish; but God's faithful ones shall be talked of among the thrones, and from the earthly seed they sowed there shall be reaped a harvest of everlasting joy.

In contrast with the struggle for earthly aggrandizement, I put the life and the death of an aged Christian minister who lay down in the country parsonage the other day and died. A brilliant intellect, a large heart, and a consecrated life were the alabaster-box he brought to Jesus. For forty years he had toiled for the welfare of men, and then he laid down peacefully and died. We went out to put him away to his sleep. For hours the carriages came over the hills and through the valleys. The aged came, who had forty years ago entertained him at their own firesides. The young came, who had taken his benediction from the marriage altar. Ministers of all denominations of Christians came, with whom he had mingled in Christian counsel. We joined hands that day in new consecration to the cause for which he had lived and died, and there we put him away in the shadow of the old meeting-house, amidst the graves of his kindred, and whole generations in the door of whose sepulchre he had stood with consolation, and so on the morning of the resurrection, when he rises up, he will find his old friends all around him, and say: "I baptized you; I married you; I buried you; this is the day of which I often spoke; it is the resurrection!" When I came to talk of his departure, I did not have long to look for a text; this one immediately flashed upon my mind: "Let me die the death of the righteous—let my last end be like his."

I learn further from this subject that *Christ deserves the best of every thing.* That woman could have got a vase that would not have cost so much as those made of alabaster. She might have brought perfume that would have cost only fifty pence; this cost three hundred. As far as I can understand, her whole fortune was in it. She might have been more economical; but no—she gets the very best box, and puts in it the very best perfume, and pours it all out on the head of her Redeemer. My brothers and sisters in Christ, the trouble is that we bring to Christ too cheap a box. If we have one of alabaster and one of earthenware, we keep the first for ourselves, and we give the latter to Christ. We owe Jesus the best of our time, the best of our talents, the best of every thing. Is there an hour in the day when we are wider awake than any other, more capable of thought and feeling, let us bring that to Christ. We are apt to take a few moments in the morning when we are getting awake, or a few moments at night when we are getting asleep, to Jesus. If there be an hour in the day when we are most appreciative of God's goodness and Christ's pardon and heaven's joy, oh that is the alabaster-box to bring to Jesus. We owe Christ the very best years of our life. When the sight is the clearest, when the hearing is the acutest, when the arm is the strongest, when the nerves are the steadiest, when the imagination is the brightest, let us come to Jesus, and not wait until our joints are stiffened with rheumatism, and the glow is gone out of our temperament, and we arise in the morning as weary as when we laid down at night.

How often we bring the broken pitcher of exhausted faculties instead of the bright alabaster-box! Men come whole piles of broken ware thrown at his feet. We take the best of the lumber for our own structure, and give Christ the chips. We eat the ripe, luscious clusters, and give Christ the rinds and the peelings. The best thing we can do is to bring our infancy; the next best thing, our youth; the next best thing, our athletic manhood; but I tell you, the poorest thing we can do is to bring our emaciation and sickness. Would it not be sad if, after all the blessings we have had, we should bring to Christ a wasted skeleton and an empty skull? or a shattered box, when Jesus knows that for years we have had in our possession the vases of Alabastron?

The people of Circassia used, until sixty years of age, to worship on the outside of the temple. They let the younger people go in. These old men tarried outside, because they wanted to give themselves up to worldliness and vice. At sixty years of age they proposed to go in and worship. How many stand now on the outside of the temple of Christian sanctification and Christian work, expecting after a while to go in! I can think of but two aged men that the Bible speaks of as coming to God. Abraham, in the Old Testament, and Nicodemus, in the New. "Remember now thy Creator in the days of thy youth, while the evil days come not, nor the years draw nigh when thou shalt say, I have no pleasure in them." Oh that to-night I might twine all these youthful hearts into a wreath for my blessed Jesus!

But I remark further, that we owe to Christ the best of all our affections. If there is any body on earth you love better than Jesus, you wrong him. Who has ever been so loving and pure and generous? Which one of your friends offered to pay all your debts, and carry all your burdens, and suffer all your pains? Which one of them offered to go into the grave to make you richer? Tell me who he is, and where he lives, that I may go and worship him also. No, no, you know there has never been but one—Jesus—and that if he got his dues, we would bring to him all the gems of the mountains, and all the pearls of the sea, and all the flowers of the field, and all the fruits of the tropics, and all the crowns of dominion, and all the boxes of alabaster. If you have any brilliancy of wit, bring it; any clearness of judgment, any largeness of heart, any attractiveness of position, bring them. Away with the cheap bottles of stale perfume, when you may fill the banqueting-hall of Christ with exquisite aroma! Paul had made great speeches before, but he made his best speech for Christ. John had warmth of affection in other directions, but he had his greatest warmth of affection for Christ. Robert M'Cheyne was weary before, but he worked himself to death for Christ. Jesus deserves the best word we ever uttered, the gladdest song we ever sang, the lovingest letter we ever wrote, the healthiest day we ever lived, the strongest heart-throb we ever felt.

I will go further, and say we owe to Christ *all our kindred and friends.* Is there a child in your household especially bright and beautiful, take it right up to Jesus. Hold it in baptism before him; kneel beside it in prayer; take it right up to where Jesus is. Oh, do you not know, father and mother, that the best thing that could happen to that child would be to have Jesus put his hands on it? If some day Jesus should come to the household, and take one away to come back never, never, do not resist him; his heart is warmer, his arm stronger than yours. The cradle for a child is not so safe a place as the arms of Jesus. If Christ should come into your household where you have your very best treasures, and should select from all the caskets an alabaster-box, do not repulse him. It has seemed as if Jesus took the best; from many of your households the best one is gone. You knew that she was too good for this world; she was the gentlest in her ways, the deepest in her affections, and when at last the sickness came, you had no faith in medicines. You knew that Jesus was coming over the door-sill. You knew that the hour of parting had come, and when, through the rich grace of the Lord Jesus Christ, you surrendered that treasure, you said, "Lord Jesus, take it—it is the best we have— take it. Thou art worthy." The others in the household may have been of grosser mould; she was of alabaster.

The other day a man was taking me from the dépôt to a village. He was very rough and coarse, and very blasphemous; but after a while he mellowed down as he began to talk of his little son whom he had lost. "Oh, sir!" he said, "that boy was different from the rest of us. He never used any bad language; no, sir. I never heard him use a bad word in my life. He used to say his prayers, and we laughed at him; but he would keep on saying his prayers, and I often thought I can't keep that child; and I said to my wife, 'Mother, we can't keep that child.' But, sir, the day he was drowned, and they brought him in and laid him down on the carpet so white and so beautiful, my heart broke, sir. I knew we could not keep him." Yes, yes, that is Christ's way; he takes the alabaster-box.

Now, my friends, this woman made her offering to Christ. What offering have you to make to Jesus? She brought an alabaster-box, and she brought ointment. Some of you have been sick. In the hours of loneliness and suffering, you said, "Lord Jesus, let me get well this time, and I will be consecrated to thee." The medicines did their work; the doctor was successful; you are well; you are here to-night. What offering have you to make to the Lord Jesus who cured you? Some of you have been out to Greenwood, not as those who go to look at the monuments and criticise the epitaphs, but in the procession that came out of the gate with one less than when you went in. And yet you have been comforted. The grave-digger's spade seemed to turn up the flowers of *that* good land where God shall wipe away the tears from your eyes. For that Jesus who so comforted you and so pitied you, what offering have you to make? Some of you have passed without any special trouble. To-day at noon, when you gathered around the table, if you had called the familiar names, they would have all answered. Plenty at the table, plenty in the wardrobe. To that Jesus who has clothed and fed you all your life-long, to that Jesus who covered himself with the glooms of death that he might purchase your emancipation, what offering of the soul have you to make?

The woman of the text brought the perfumes of nard. You say, "The flowers of the field are all dead now, and we can not bring them." I know it. The flowers on the platform are only those that are plucked from the grim hand of Death; they are the children of the hothouse. The flowers of the field *are* all dead! We saw them blooming in the valleys and mountains; they ran up to the very lips of the cave; they garlanded the neck of the hills like a May-queen. They set their banquet of golden cups for the bee, and dripped in drops of honeysuckle for the humming-bird. They dashed their antlers against the white hand of the sick child, and came to the nostrils of the dying like spice gales from heaven. They shook in the agitation of the bride, and at the burial hour rang the silver chime of a resurrection. Beautiful flowers! Bright flowers! Sweet flowers! But they are all dead now. I saw their scattered petals on the foam of the wild brook, and I pulled aside the hedge and saw the place where their corpses lay. We can not bring the flowers. What shall we bring? Oh, from our hearts' affections to-night, let us bring the sweet-smelling savor of a Christian sacrifice! Let us bring it to Christ; and as we have no other vase in which to carry it, let this glorious Sabbath hour be the alabaster-box.

Rawlins White, an old martyr, was very decrepit, and for years he had been bowed almost double, and could hardly walk; but he was condemned to death, and on his way to the stake, we are told, the bonds of his body seemed to break, and he roused himself up as straight and exuberant as an athlete, and walked into the fire singing victory over the flames. Ah, it was the joy of dying for Jesus that straightened his body and roused his soul! If we suffer with him on earth, we shall be glorified with him in heaven. Choose his service; it is a blessed service. Let no man or woman go out of this house to-night unblessed. Jesus spreads out both arms of his mercy. He does not ask where you came from or what have been your wanderings; but he says, with a pathos and tenderness that ought to break you down, "Come unto me, all ye who are weary and heavy laden, and I will give you rest." Who will accept the offer of his mercy?

> "Shall Jesus bear the cross alone,
> And all the world go free?
> No, there's a cross for every one,
> And there's a cross for me."

## WASTED AROMA.

"Why was this waste?"—*Mark* xiv., 14.

LAST Sabbath night in Plymouth Church we saw a woman with a box of costly perfume pressing into the banqueting-hall where sat Christ the physician, and Simon the convalescent. The box in which she carried the perfume had been made in the city of Alabastron, from stone dug up from a hill near that city, and hence, you see, was very appropriately called an alabaster-box. According to an olden custom, she shook the box and poured the odor out on the head of the Jesus whom she very dearly loved. The guests were seized with a sudden fit of prudence, and pronounced the whole thing as uneconomical, crying out in the words of the text, "Why was this waste?" But Jesus applauded her, and said, "She hath done what she could," and proclaimed the fact that her behavior should be approvingly known through all the earth and through all the ages.

Now, before I come, this morning, to the main thought of my subject, I want you to see what a beautiful thing it is for a woman to approach Christ. This woman of Bethany might have done a great many pleasant things before; but this was the grandest, bravest, sweetest thing she ever did, and it is told as a memorial of her.

Woman's life is dull and monotonous in this country without Jesus. Men may go out into the world, as they do every day, and they see new sights and hear new sounds; but woman, for the most part, suffers and toils indoors. She needs a rest and inspiration she can not get from music and needle-work. She has affections deep and priceless, and will never be happy until she pours that alabaster-box on the head of Christ. She may try to satisfy her soul by drawing-room flatteries and elegancies of apparel, but will often feel great disquietude. She can not have peace here and a state of well-being hereafter, unless, like the woman of the text, she bursts into the room where Jesus sits, with all worshipful affection. Oh! that Mary would, this morning, sit down at the feet of Jesus, and Martha, and Rachel, and Rebecca, and the Israelitish waiting-maid, and grandmother Louise.

I see also that Christ asks no impossibilities. That woman brought an alabaster-box. What was it to Jesus? Why, he owns all the fragrance of earth and heaven; but he took it. He was satisfied with it. If it had been a wooden box, he would have been just as well satisfied, had it been the best one she could bring. I hear some one say, "If I only had this, that, or the other thing, I would do so much for God." In the last day it may be found that a cup of cold water given in the name of a disciple gets as rich a reward as the founding of a kingdom, and that the sewing-girl's needle may be as honorable in God's sight as a king's sceptre, and that the grandest eulogium that was ever uttered about any one was, "She hath done what she could."

There she sits at the head of the Sabbath-school class, and she says, "I wish I understood the Scriptures in Greek and Hebrew. I wish I had more faculty for instruction. I wish I could get the attention of my class.

I wish I could bring them all to Christ." Do not worry. Christ does not want you to know the Scriptures in Greek and Hebrew. Do as well as you can, and from the throne the proclamation will flame forth, "Crown that princess; she hath done what she could."

There is a man toiling for Christ. He does not get on much. He is discouraged when he hears Paul thunder, and Edward Payson pray. He says, "I wonder if I will ever join the song of heaven." He wonders if it would not look odd for him to stand amidst the apostles who preached, and the martyrs who flamed. Greater will be his wonder on the day when he shall find out that many who were first in the Church on earth are last in the Church of heaven, and when he sees the procession winding up among the thrones of the sorrowing ones, who never again shall weep, and the weary ones, who never again shall get tired, and the poor, who never again shall beg, and Christ, regardless of all antecedents, will put upon the head of his disciples a crown made from the gold of the eternal hills, set in with pearl from the celestial sea, inscribed with the words, "He hath done what he could."

But I also see in this subject *what wrong notions the world has of economy.* Just as soon as these people saw the ointment spilling on the head of Christ, they said, "Why this waste? Why, that ointment might have been sold and given to the poor!" The hypocrites! what did they care about the poor? I do not believe that one of them that made the complaint ever gave a farthing to the poor. I think Judas was most indignant, and he sold his Master for thirty pieces of silver. There is nothing that makes a stingy man so cross as to see generosity in others. If this woman of the text had brought in an old, worn-out box, with some stale perfume, and given that to Christ, they could have endured it; but to have her bring in a vessel on which had been expended the adroitness of skilled artisans, and containing perfume that had usually been reserved for palatial and queenly use, they could not stand it. And so it is often the case in communities and in churches, that those are the most unpopular men who give the most. Judas can not bear to see the alabaster-box broken at the feet of Christ.

Here is a man who gives a thousand dollars to the missionary cause. Men cry out, "What a waste! What's the use of sending New Testaments and missionaries, and spending your money in that way? Why don't you send plows, and corn-threshers, and locomotives, and telegraphs?" But is it a waste? Ask the nations that have been saved: Have not religious blessings always preceded financial blessings? Show me a community where the Gospel of Christ triumphs, and I will show you a community prospered in a worldly sense. Is it a waste to comfort the distressed, to instruct the ignorant, to balk immorality, to capture for God the innumerable hosts of men who erst with quick feet were tramping the way to hell? If a man buy railroad stock, it may decline; if a man invest in a bank, the cashier may abscond; if a man go into partnership, his associate may sink the store. Alas! for the man who has nothing better than "greenbacks" and Government securities! God ever and anon blows up the money-safe, and, with a hurricane of marine disaster, dismantles the merchantmen, and from the blackened heavens he hurls into the exchange the hissing thunder-bolts of his wrath.

People cry up this investment and cry down the other; but I tell you there is no safe investment save that which is made in the bank of which God holds the keys. The interest in that is always being paid, and there are eternal dividends. God will change that gold into crowns that shall never lose their lustre, and into sceptres that shall forever wave over a land where the poorest inhabitant is richer than all the wealth of earth tossed up into one glittering coin! So if I stand this morning before men who are now of small means, but who once were greatly prospered, and who in the days of their prosperity were benevolent, let me ask you to sit down and count up your investments. All the loaves of bread you ever gave to the hungry—they are yours yet; all the shoes you ever gave to the barefooted—they are yours yet; all the dollars you ever gave to churches, and schools, and colleges—they are yours yet. Bank-clerks sometimes make mistakes about deposits; but God keeps an unfailing record of all Christian deposits; and though on the great judgment there may be a "run" upon that bank, ten thousand times ten thousand men will get back all they ever gave to Christ—get all back, heaped up, pressed down, shaken together, and running over.

A young Christian woman starts to instruct the freedmen at the South, with a spelling-book in one hand and a Bible in the other. She goes aboard a steamer for Savannah. Through days, and months, and years she toils among the freedmen of the South, and one day there comes up a poisonous breath from the swamp, and a fever smites her low, and far away from home, watched tearfully by those whom she has come to save, she drops into an early grave. "Oh, what a waste! waste of beauty, waste of talent, waste of affection, waste of every thing," cries the world. "Why, she might have been the joy of her father's house; she might have been the pride of the drawing-room." But in the day when rewards are given for earnest Christian work, her inheritance will make insignificant all the treasures of Crœsus. Not wasted, her gentle words; not wasted, her home-sickness; not wasted, her heart-aches; not wasted, her tears of loneliness; not wasted, the pangs of her last hour; not wasted, the sweat on her dying pillow. The freedmen thought it was the breath of the magnolia in the thicket; the planter thought it was the sweetness of acacia coming up from the hedge. No, no; it was the fragrance of an alabaster-box poured on the head of Christ.

Our world will after a while burn up. So great have been its abominations and disorders, that one would think that when the flames touch it a horrible stench would roll into the skies: the coal-mines consuming, the impurities of great cities burning, you might think that a lost spirit from the pit would stagger back at the sickening odor. But no. I suppose on that day a cloud of incense will roll into the skies, all the wilderness of tropical flowers on fire, the mountains of frankincense, the white sheet of the water-lilies, the million tufts of heliotrope, the trellises of honeysuckle, the walls of "morning-glory." The earth shall be a burning censer held up before the throne of God, with all the sweet odors of the hemispheres. But on that day a sweeter gale shall waft into the skies. It will come up from ages past, from altars of devotion, and hovels of poverty, and beds of pain, and stakes of martyrdom, and from all the places where good men and women have suffered for God and died for the truth. It will be the fragrance of ten thousand boxes of alabaster, which, through the long reach of the ages, were poured on the head of Christ.

Last Sabbath morning, I think a great many persons, standing in the presence of our burning Tabernacle on Schermerhorn Street, said, "What a waste! Here all the toil expended gone in an hour." Indeed, those who have built churches know that there are a great many toils and anxieties and sacrifices connected with such an enterprise; the solicitation and collection of funds; the selection of a site for building; the choice of architects and plans and materials; the discussion of acoustics; the watching of building committees, themselves severely watched; the fatigue by day and the sleeplessness by night. It is a fact that, in many cases, after the church has been built, the congregation is exhausted, and the minister is kicked out. Oh, you people of the Brooklyn Tabernacle, what have you to show for all the toil, and prayer, and expenditure of the last two years? A heap of ashes, twisted walls, scorched pillars—an utter obliteration of all you have done. "Why was this waste?" Ah, my dear friends, there was not any waste. All the toil and money you put in that enterprise had a heavenly insurance, and it will be paid back to you in some shape. You may depend upon that. What money I gave toward it, I would rather have where it is—this morning—than have it in my pocket; having it in my pocket, I might lose it; but where it is, it is safe forever. I do not begrudge a nail, or a bolt, or a screw that went down in that great conflagration. Why, if it cost us nothing, do you think Christ would have wanted it?

Do not fling any of your useless, worn-out boxes at him! That was the great precious alabaster-box that the congregation poured on the head of Christ. When I say it was precious, I only say what is true. Our hearts had twined around that place very much. I can hear the old organ going yet, marshaling the hosts of God for the battle-shout of Christian song. I can see the audience rising yet to the "Old Hundred" doxology. I can see the pillars entwined with Christmas garlands, telling the people that Jesus is born, and every man has a chance for heaven. Oh! the place was all crowded with memories; days when Jesus rode through with dyed garments from Bozrah, smiting down our sins, and discomfiting our sorrows. On the last Sabbath-night I preached in that place, inviting men to the hope and joy of the Gospel, if I had known it was the last time, I would have kissed the old place good-bye. It seemed to me that when the roof went in, and we felt that all was gone, that the tears on the cheeks stopped and the sighs ceased, and as if there went through the street on that cold morning one great groan. But do not mourn the loss of that; Jesus is worthy of the most precious gift. Was it a waste? Are all the joys we felt there a waste? Are all the comforts that brooded over our souls in days of darkness, when trouble came to our souls and to our families, a waste? Were the hundreds and hundreds of souls who, in that building first found the peace of the Gospel, a waste? No, no, no; the building did its work, and it is gone! Let not the woman of Bethany begrudge the box, or begrudge the perfume. Let her rather go and get a better box, and put in it a sweeter odor, and come with another offering.

I have been bothered all the morning with a snatch of an old hymn which I can not quite catch. I wish some of you would hunt it up and tell it to me. I get only two or three lines of it:

> " Her dust and ruins that remain
> Are precious in our eyes;
> Those ruins shall be built again,
> And all that dust shall rise."

You remember that, Father Waterbury; find it for me sometime.

God means something by this disaster. If such a torch be lifted, it means to light us somewhere. I wish that fire had burned up all our sins. I wish that it might teach us what a poor foundation man builds on when he builds in this world, and that iron and brick and granite are wax when God breathes on them. We see that there is nothing of an earthly nature safe. Does not the telegraph flashing from all parts of the earth now bring baleful tidings? You are not safe on land or on sea. Witness the Portuguese bark driven, on night before last, on Peaked Head Bar, and the bark *Kadosh* on Aldernon Point. Ay, you are not safe on the other side of the sea. Witness the hurricane that last week swept over London; witness the floods that swept through Derbyshire. You are not safe on the rail train. The lightning express last week rolls over an embankment in Pennsylvania, and thirty lives are ground out. On last Tuesday night the floor gives way under a festival, and the mangled children are dragged out on the snow for fathers and mothers to look at. God, by fire, and earthquake, and storm, is crying to all the earth, saying: " Build higher;

build firmer; build on the rock." I am glad to hear that there were some of our people who, in the presence of that raving, thundering ruin last Sabbath morning, resolved to be the Lord's. They started for heaven. They say: "Is this the way things go on earth? Give me something better, something stronger, something that will last."

My friends, all these flames in Brooklyn and in Chicago and in Boston are only prefigurements of a great day of fire which you and I will see just as certainly as you sit there and I stand here. That day the fire will test us thoroughly. It will show whether our religion is a reality, or whether it is a false-face. When that fire comes over the fields, it will come swifter than an autumnal fire across the Illinois prairie. Before it, beasts will dash from the rocks in wild leap. Coming over the precipices, it will be a Niagara of fire. The continents of earth will wrap themselves in a winding-sheet of flame, and the mountains will cry to the plain, "Fire!" and the plain will cry to the sea, "Fire!" and the sea will cry to the sky, "Fire!" and heaven will answer back to earth, and the caverns will groan it, and the winds will shriek it, and the thunders will toll it, and the storms will wail it, and the nations will cry it, "Fire! fire!" And the day will burn on, and away will go all the churches you ever built, and away will go all your store-houses, and away will go all your cities. But what will become of those who have no Christ, no sins pardoned, no heaven secured? Oh, I wish that this morning, in our first service in this beautiful place, the hour might be signalized by a great stampede for heaven! I wish that you would all come in, fathers, mothers, brothers, sisters, husbands, wives, sons, daughters, friends, and neighbors. In the presence of the great sorrow that has come upon us, can you not do that? Do you believe that if this morning, with all the solemn surroundings of the past week, you reject the Gospel of Christ, you will ever feel? Do not some of you think that this is the last opportunity? Do you not feel that if you drive away the Spirit of God, he will never come back? Do you not think that God is speaking to me, and speaking to you all? Oh! that this house, set apart for secular song, might this morning hear sweeter music, namely, the angelic minstrelsy that sounds when sins are pardoned, and God is glorified, and Jesus sees the travail of his soul, and is satisfied. Strike all your harps, ye spirits blessed, the prodigal is come home! Clap your hands, all ye people, the lost is found!

## THINGS NOT BURNED UP.

"Comfort ye, comfort ye my people."—*Isaiah* xl., 1.

THESE words came to Isaiah after Jerusalem had been wasted with fire and famine and war; and I wish to-night, from these leaves of the tree of life, to compound a salve for a very sore burn.

Standing to-day in this brilliant Academy, by its trustees so kindly afforded us, our first feeling is one of gratitude to God and to them for so grand a refuge; but notwithstanding it is so much costlier a place than we are used to, we feel home-sick. The wanderer in a strange land, amidst palaces and temples and cathedrals, sits down and says to himself, "I would give the whole world for one hour under the thatched roof of my humble home." "Home, sweet home; there is no place like home." It was nothing but home-sickness that made the inspired writer say: "By the rivers of Babylon, there we sat down; yea, we wept when we remembered Zion. We hanged our harps upon the willows in the midst thereof. For there they that carried us away captive required of us a song; and they that wasted us required of us mirth, saying, Sing us one of the songs of Zion. How shall we sing the Lord's song in a strange land?"

The Brooklyn Tabernacle is gone! The bell that hung in its tower last Sabbath morning rang its own funeral knell. On that day we gathered from our homes with our families, to hear what Christ had of comfort and inspiration for his people. We expected to meet cheerful smiles and warm hand-shakings, and the triumphant song, and the large brotherhood that characterized that blessed place; but coming to the doors we found nothing but an excited populace and a blazing church. People who had given until they deeply felt it saw all the results of their benevolence going down into ashes, and on that cold morning the tears froze on the cheeks of God's people as they saw they were being burned out. Brooklyn Tabernacle is gone! The platform on which it was my joy to stand with messages of salvation; the pews in which you listened and prayed and wept and rejoiced; the altars around which you and your children were consecrated in baptism; the communion-table where we celebrated the Saviour's love—all that scene which to us was the shining gate of heaven is gone. I will not hide the loss. If I ever forget the glorious Sabbaths we spent there, and the sweet reunions, and the mighty demonstrations of God's Spirit among the people, may my right hand forget her cunning, and my soul be left desolate! But we have not come here to sound a dirge. "All things work together for good to them that love God." Sorrows are loathsome things, but they are necessary. They are leeches that suck out the hot inflammation from the soul. "Weeping may endure for a night, but joy cometh in the morning." I could cover up all this place with promises of hope and peace and comfort and deliverance. Hallelujah! for the Lord God omnipotent reigneth!

I am here to-night not to preach a formal sermon, but to tell you of *some things that last Sabbath were not burned up.*

First, the spirit of Christian brotherhood was not consumed. You never greeted the members of our church with such cordiality as this week on the street, in cars, and on the ferries. You stood on no cold formalities. The people who, during the last two years sat on the other side of the aisle, whose faces were familiar to you, but to whom you had never spoken, you greeted them this week with smiles and tears as you said, "Well, the old place is gone." You did not want to seem to cry, and so you swept the sleeve near the corner of the eye, and pretended it was the sharp wind that made your eyes weak. Ah! there was nothing the matter with your eyes; it was your soul bubbling over. I tell you that it is impossible to sit for two or three years around the same church fireside and not have sympathies in common. Somehow you feel that you would like those people on the other side of the aisle, about whom you know but little, prospered and pardoned and blessed and saved. You feel as if you are in the same boat, and you want to glide up the same harbor, and want to disembark at the same wharf. If you put gold and iron and lead and zinc in sufficient heat, they will melt into a conglomerate mass; and I really feel that last Sabbath's fire has fused us all, grosser and finer natures, into one. It seems as if we all had our hands on a wire connected with an electric battery; and when this church sorrow started, it thrilled through the whole circle, and we all felt the shock. The oldest man and the youngest child could join hands in this misfortune. Grandfather said, "I expected from those altars to be buried;" and one of the children last Sabbath cried, "I don't want the Tabernacle to burn, I have been there so many times." You may remember that over the organ we had the words, "One Lord, one faith, one baptism." That was our creed. Well, that is all burned down; but the sentiment is engraved with such durability in our souls that no earthly fire can scorch it, and the flames of the Judgment-day will have no power to burn it.

Another thing that did not burn up is *the cross of Christ.* That is used to the fire. On the dark day when Jesus died, the lightning struck it from above, and the flames of hell dashed up against it from beneath. That tearful, painful, tender, blessed cross still stands. On it we hang all our hopes; beneath it we put down all our sins; in the light of it we expect to make the rest of our pilgrimage. Within sight of such a sacrifice, who can feel he has it hard? In the sight of such a symbol, who can be discouraged, however great the darkness that may come down upon him? Jesus lives! The loving, patient, sympathizing, mighty Jesus! It shall not be told on earth, or in hell, or in heaven, that three Hebrew children had the Son of God beside them in the fire, and that a whole church was forsaken by the Lord, when they went through a furnace one hundred and fifty feet front by one hundred deep. O Lord Jesus! shall we take out of thy hand the flowers and the fruits, and the brightness and the joys, and then turn away because thou dost give us one cup of bitterness to drink? Oh no, Jesus! we will drink it dry. But how it is changed! Blessed Jesus, what hast thou put into the cup to sweeten it? Why, it has become the wine of heaven, and our souls grow strong. I come to-night, and place both of my feet deep down into the blackened ashes of our consumed church, and I cry out with an exhilaration that I never felt since the day of my soul's emancipation, "Victory! victory! through our Lord Jesus Christ!"

> "Your harps, ye trembling saints,
> Down from the willows take;
> Loud to the praise of love divine
> Bid every string awake."

I remark, again, that the *catholicity of the Christian churches has not been burned up*. We are in the Academy to-day not because we have no other place to go. Last Sabbath morning at nine o'clock we had but one church; now we have twenty-six, all at our disposal. Their pastors and their trustees say, "You may take our main audience-rooms, you may take our lecture-rooms, you may take our church parlors, you may baptize in our baptisteries, and sit on our anxious-seats." Oh! if there be any larger-hearted ministers or larger-hearted churches anywhere than in Brooklyn, tell me where they are, that I may go and see them before I die. The millennium has come. People keep wondering when it is coming. It *has* come. The lion and the lamb lie down together, and the tiger eats straw like an ox. I should like to have seen two of the old-time bigots, with their swords, fighting through that great fire on Schermerhorn Street last Sabbath. I am sure the swords would have melted, and they who wielded them would have learned war no more. I can never say a word against any other denomination of Christians. I thank God I never have been tempted to do it. I can not be a sectarian. I have been told I ought to be, and I have tried to be, but I have not enough material in me to make such a structure. Every time I get the thing most done, there comes a fire, or something else, and all is gone. The angels of God shake out on this Christmas air, "Glory to God in the highest, and on earth peace, good will toward men." I do not think the day is far distant when all the different branches of the Presbyterian Church will be one, and all the different branches of the Methodist Church will be one, and all the different branches of the Episcopal Church will be one. I do not know but I see on the horizon the first gleam of the morning which shall unite all evangelical denominations in one organization; churches distinguished from each other, not by varieties of creeds, but difference of locality, as it was in the time of the apostles. It was then the Church of Thyatira, and the Church of Thessalonica, and the Church of Antioch, and the Church of Laodicea. So I do not know but that in the future history, and not far off either, it may be simply a distinction of locality, and not of creed, as the Church of New York, the Church of Brooklyn, the Church of Boston, the Church of Charleston, the Church of Madras, the Church of Constantinople.

My dear brethren, we can not afford to be severely divided. Standing in front of the great foes of our common Christianity, we want to put on the whole armor of God, and march down in solid column, shoulder to shoulder! one commander! one banner! one triumph!

> "The trumpet gives a martial strain
> O Israel! gird thee for the fight:
> Arise, the combat to maintain,
> Arise, and put thy foes to flight."

I have to announce also, among the things not burned

up is *heaven*. Fires may sweep through other cities—we heard the tolling of the bell as we came in to-night; but I am glad to know that the New Jerusalem is fireproof. There will be no engines rushing through those streets; there will be no temples consumed in that city. Coming to the doors of that Church, we will find them open, resonant with songs, and not cries of fire. Oh, my dear brother and sister! if this short lane of life comes up so soon to that blessed place, what is the use of our worrying? I have felt a good many times this last week like Father Taylor, the sailor-preacher. He got in a long sentence while he was preaching one day, and lost himself, and could not find his way out of the sentence. He stopped, and said, "Brethren, I have lost the nominative of this sentence, and things are generally mixed up, but I am bound for the kingdom anyhow." And during this last week, when I saw the rushing to and fro and the excitement, I said to myself, "I do not know just where we shall start again, but I am bound for the kingdom anyhow." I do not want to go just yet. I want to be pastor of this people until I am about eighty-nine years of age, but I have sometimes thought that there are such glories ahead that I might be persuaded to go a little earlier—for instance, at eighty-two or eighty-three; but I really think that if we could have an appreciation of what God has in reserve for us, we would want to go to-night, stepping right out of the Academy of Music into the glories of the skies. Ah! that is a good land. Why, they tell me that in that land they never have a heartache. They tell me that a man might walk five hundred years in that land and never see a tear or hear a sigh. They tell me that our friends who have left us and gone

there, their *feet* are radiant as the sun, and that they take
hold of the hand of Jesus familiarly, and that they open
that hand and see in the palm of it a healed wound that
must have been very cruel before it was healed. And
they tell me that there is no winter there, and that they
never get hungry or cold, and that the sewing-girl never
wades through the December snow-bank to her daily
toil, and that the clock never strikes twelve for the night,
but only twelve for the day.

See that light in the window. I wonder who set it
there. "Oh!" you say, "my father that went into glory
must have set that light in the window." No; guess
again. "My mother, who died fifteen years ago in Jesus I think must have set that light there." No; guess
again. You say, "My darling little child, that last summer I put away for the resurrection, I think she must
have set that light there in the window." No; guess
again. *Jesus* set it there; and he will keep it burning
until the day we put our finger on the latch of the door
and go in to be at home forever. Oh! when my sight
gets black in death, put on my eyelids that sweet ointment. When in the last weariness I can not take another step, just help me put my foot on that door-sill. When
my ear catches no more the voices of wife and child, let
me go right in, to have my deafness cured by the stroke
of the harpers whose fingers fly over the strings with the
anthems of the free. Heaven never burns down! The
fires of the last day, that are already kindled in the heart
of the earth, but are hidden because God keeps down the
hatches—those internal fires will after a while break
through the crust, and the plains, and the mountains, and
the seas will be consumed, and the flames will fling their

long arms into the skies; but all the terrors of a burning world will do no more harm to that heavenly temple than the fires of the setting sun which kindle up the window-glass of the house on yonder hill-top. Oh, blessed land! But I do not want to go there until I see the Brooklyn Tabernacle rebuilt. You say, "Will it be?" You might as well ask me if the sun will rise to-morrow morning, or if the next spring will put garlands on its head. You and I may not do it—you and I may not live to see it; but the Church of God does not stand on two legs nor on a thousand legs. I am here to tell you that among the things not burned up is *our determination, in the strength and help of God, to go forward.*

You say, "Where are you going to get the means?" I do not know. The building of the Tabernacle within two years, and then an enlargement, at great expense, within that same time, and the establishment and the maintenance of the Lay College, have taken most of our funds. Did I say just now that I did not know where the funds are to come from? I take that back. I do! I do! From the hearts of the Christian people, and the lovers of the cause of morality all over this land. I am sure they will help us, and we shall go on, and the new structure shall rise. How did the Israelites get through the Red Sea? I suppose somebody may have come and said, "There is no need of trying; you will get your feet wet; you will spoil your clothes; you will drown yourselves. Whoever heard of getting through such a sea as that?" How did they get through it? Did they go back? No. Did they go to the right? No. Did they go to the left? No. They went *forward* in the strength of the Lord Almighty; and that is the way *we* mean to get through the Red Sea. Do you tell me that God is going to let the effort for the establishment of a free Christian church in Brooklyn fail? Why, on the dedication-day of our Tabernacle, I was not more confident, and was not so happy as I am now. That building did its work. We wanted to support a free Christian church; we did it, and got along pleasantly and successfully, and demonstrated the fact. The building is gone. The ninety-five souls received at the first communion in that building more than paid us for all the expenditure. We only put up the Tabernacle for *two years*. Do you know that? Here sits a member of the Board of Trustees right under me, and he remembers that when we built we said, "We shall put it up for two years; it will be a temporary residence; and at the close of that time we will know how large a building we want, and what style of building we want." But having put it up, we liked it so well, we concluded to stay there permanently. But God decided otherwise; and I take it as one of the providential indications of that fearful disaster that we are to build a larger church, and ask all the people to come in and be saved. You know how we were crowded, and pushed, and jammed in that building; and last summer some of us talked about an enlargement, but we found it impossible without changing the whole structure of the building. The difficulty now is gone; and if the people North, South, East, and West will help us, we shall build on a larger scale, and the hundreds and thousands who have wanted to be with us, but could not, shall have room for themselves and families, where they may come and be comforted in their sorrows, and, by the grace of the Lord Jesus, find out the way to heaven. Do you tell me that the human voice can not reach more people than we used to have there? It is a mistake. I have been wearing myself out for the last two years in trying to keep my voice in. Give me room where I can preach the glories of Christ and the grandeurs of heaven.

The old iron-clad has gone down with a shot amidships. We will build next time of brick. The building shall be amphitheatrical in shape; it shall be very large; it shall be very plain. Whether the material will be any better than the one used in the old structure, I can not say, for there are four things that God has demonstrated within a short time are not fire-proof. One is corrugated iron: witness the Brooklyn Tabernacle. Another is brick: witness the fire last week in Centre Street, New York. Another is Joliet stone: witness Chicago. Another is Quincy granite: witness Boston. When God rises up to burn any thing, a stone wall is shavings. Hear that, oh you men who are building on nothing but earthly foundations! The people will rise up, and all our friends, North, South, East, and West, who have been giving us their sympathies, will translate their sympathies and their "God bless yous" into "greenbacks," and next winter the people will cry out, "The glory of the second temple is greater than the first."

There was a king of olden time who prided himself on doing that which his people thought impossible; and it ought to be the joy of the Christian Church to accomplish that which the world thinks can not be done.

But I want you to know that it will require more prayer than we have ever offered, and more hard work

than we have ever put forth. Mere skirmishing around
the mercy-seat will not do. We have to take the
kingdom of heaven by violence. We have to march
on, breaking down all bridges behind us, making retreat
impossible. Throw away your knapsack if it impedes
your march. Keep your sword-arm free. Strike for
Christ and his kingdom while you may. No people ever
had a better mission than you are sent on. Prove yourselves worthy. If I am not fit to be your leader, set me
aside. The brightest goal on earth that I can think of is
a country parsonage amidst the mountains. But I am
not afraid to lead you. I have a few hundred dollars;
they are at your disposal. I have good physical health;
it is yours as long as it lasts. I have enthusiasm of soul;
I will not keep it back from your service. I have some
faith in God, and I shall direct it toward the rebuilding
of our new spiritual house. Come on, then! I will lead
you. Come on, ye aged men, not yet passed over Jordan! Give us one more lift before you go into the promised land. You men in mid-life, harness all your business faculties to this enterprise. Young man, put the
fire of your soul in this work. Let women consecrate
their persuasiveness and persistence to this cause, and
they will be preparing benedictions for their dying hour
and everlasting rewards; and if Satan really did burn
that Tabernacle down, as some people say he did, he
will find it the poorest job he ever undertook.

Good-bye, old Tabernacle! your career short but blessed; your ashes precious in our sight. In the last day,
may we be able to meet the songs there sung, and the
prayers there offered, and the sermons there preached.
Good-bye, old place, where some of us first felt the Gos-

pel peace, and others heard the last message ere they fled away into the skies! Good-bye, Brooklyn Tabernacle of 1870! But welcome our new church (I see it as plainly as though it were already built)! Your walls firmer; your gates wider; your songs more triumphant; your ingatherings more glorious. Rise out of the ashes, and greet our waiting vision! Burst on our souls, oh day of our church's resurrection! By your altars, may we be prepared for the hour when the fire shall try every man's work of what sort it is. Welcome, Brooklyn Tabernacle of 1873!

## WICKEDNESS IN HIGH PLACES.

"Their right hand is full of bribes."—*Psalm* xxvi., 10.
"Woe to thee, O land, when thy king is a child, and thy princes eat in the morning."—*Ecclesiastes* x., 16.

THOSE two passages are descriptive of wickedness in high places. The morals of a nation hardly ever rise higher than the virtue of the rulers. Henry VIII. makes impurity national and popular. William Wilberforce in the Parliament is perpetual elevation to an empire. Sin, epauleted and bestarred, comes to respect and canonization; vice, elevated, is recommended. Malarias rise from the marsh, float upward and away; but moral distempers descend from the mountain to the plain. The "Five Points" and Coal Street disgust men with the bestiality of sin; but dissolute French court and corrupt Congressional delegation put a premium upon crime. The most of the vices of the world are kingly exiles that had a throne once, but, driven out, they have come down in tattered robes to be entertained by the humble and the insignificant.

I do not believe that there is any nation on earth which has more noble-minded and pure-hearted men in places of authority than this nation. There is not a meeting of Legislature or Congress or Cabinet but has in it the best specimens of Christian character—men whose hands would consume a bribe; whose cheek has never been flushed with intoxication; whose lips have never been smitten of blasphemy, or stung of a lie; men whose speeches against the wrong and in behalf of the right make us think of the fiery words of the Scotch Covenanters, and of the daring challenge of Martin Luther, and of the red lightning of Micah and Habakkuk. I do not believe that our legislative and political councils are any more corrupt than they were in olden time. I will not believe it so long as I read in history of Aaron Burr, stuffed with corruption until he could hold no more—body, mind, and soul soaked in abomination, the debaucher of the debauched, yet a member of the State Legislature, afterward Attorney-general, afterward United States Senator, and, last of all, Vice-president of the Union. You can not make me believe that political dishonesty is peculiar to our day when I find out that the governor of this very State, almost fifty years ago, disbanded the Legislature because it was too corrupt to sit in council; and when, in the State of Massachusetts, there was a man in the gubernatorial chair so offensive that when he made his proclamation for Thanksgiving-day, ending with his own signature as governor, and the stereotyped phrase, "God save the Commonwealth," a minister of Christ, while reading the Governor's proclamation for Thanksgiving, put this emphasis after reading the proclamation, saying, "Marcus Morton, Governor of Massachusetts? *God save the Commonwealth!*"

There has been a tendency to contrast the past with the present, to the advantage of the former; and I suppose that sixty years from now political writers will make angels out of us, although the material now seems so very unpromising. But the crimes in high places in olden times are no apology for the crimes in high places in modern times; and I shall this morning, in the fear of God, and with reference to my last account, unroll before you the scroll of public wickedness.

If there was ever a time when the minister of the Gospel and the philanthropist should speak out, this is the time. King David must feel the rebuke of Nathan; Felix must be made to tremble; sin must be denounced; God must be honored; the nation must be saved. We may hold back the truth on these subjects, and walk with muffled feet lest we wake up some big sinner. But what will we answer in the day when men who have stood in the high places of the earth, warring against God, shall fall like lightning from heaven? or, as John Milton has it:

> "Hurled headlong flaming from the ethereal sky,
> With hideous ruin and combustion, down
> To bottomless perdition."

I stand this morning in the presence of men who hold in their hands the suffrages of the nation, and by whose vote, and by whose printing-press, and by whose social influence, and by whose prayer, the future character of this country is to be decided.

In unrolling, then, this scroll of wickedness in high places, the first thing that I mark especially is *incompetency for office.* If a man seek for a place and win it when he is incompetent, he is committing a crime against God and a crime against man. It is not a sin for me to be ignorant of medical science; but if, without medical attainment, I set myself up among professional men, and trifle, in my ignorance, with the lives of those whose confidence I have won, then my charlatanism becomes highhanded knavery. The ignorance that in the one case was innocence, in the other case becomes a crime. It is not a sin for me to be ignorant of machinery; but if I attempt to engineer a steamer across the Atlantic, amidst darkness and hurricane, holding the lives of hundreds of people in my grasp, then the blood of all the shipwrecked is on my garment. But what shall we say of men who attempt to engineer our State and national affairs over the rough waters, without the first element of qualification?—men not knowing enough to vote "aye" or "no," until they have looked for the wink of others of their party? So we have had Legislative and Congressional committees to make tariffs and homestead bills, and arrange about the fisheries, and think out the best way of collecting indemnities—men whose incompetency has been the laughing-stock of the country. In this country, to-day, qualification for office is not the question, but "How much has the man done for the party?" And so we had a Congressional committee that made one tariff for flaxseed-oil and another for linseed-oil—not knowing, in their stupidity, that flaxseed and linseed oil are the same thing. No depth or length or breadth of disqualification in this country hinders a man from holding office. The polished civilian of acknowledged integrity, profoundly acquainted with the spirit of our institutions, is run over by the great stampede of men who rush out from their bloated and unthinking ignorance to take the positions of trust in this country. So we have had, in some parts of the country, school-commissioners nominated in a grog-shop, hurraed for by the rabble, hardly able to read their own commissions when they were handed to them; judges of courts in important cases giving the charge with so much inaccuracy of phraseology that the thief in the prisoner's-box was more amused at the stupidity of the bench than alarmed at his own prospective punishment. We arraign, to-day, incapacity for office as one of the crimes to be seen in our national and State councils.

I unroll the scroll a little farther, and find *intemperance* and the co-ordinate crimes. I admit there has been some improvement in this thing. The grog-shop that used to flourish in the basement of the Capitol, where senators once went to get inspiration for their speeches, has been abolished. There is a temperance society in Congress. But the plague is not yet stayed. I knew a man who, only a few years ago, was an example of integrity, and honored everywhere. Last winter I went to Washington. I had not seen him for years, and I thought I would send my card into the House of Representatives, and call him out. The card went in by the sergeant-at-arms, and my old friend that I had not seen in ten years came out staggering drunk. In this country, the temptations to intemperance in public life are so great that more of our men in office die of *delirium tremens*, and the kindred diseases that come from intemperance and an impure life, than from all the other causes combined. There is one weapon that slays more senators and congressmen and legislators and common councilmen than any other, and that is the bottle. How few of the men who were in prominent political offices twenty-five or thirty years ago, when they died, came to honorable graves! The family physician, to relieve the family and keep them from national disgrace, said it was gout, or it was epilepsy, or it was obstruction of the liver, or it was exhaustion from patriotic services! But God knew it was whisky. It was the same habit that smote the great man down that smote the dark villain in the alley. The one you wrapped up in a coarse cloth, and threw into a rough coffin, and carried out in a box-wagon, and put down in a pauper's grave, without prayer or benediction; the other gathered the pomp of the city, and the name was on the silver plate, and lordly men walked uncovered beside the hearse with tossing plumes, on the way to a grave soon to be adorned with a marble pillar of four sides, which shall be covered with the story of the man who died of *exhaustion from patriotic services!* The difference between the two was this: the one put an end to his existence with logwood-rum at two cents a glass, and the other perished in a beverage at three dollars a bottle. I write both of their epitaphs: on a shingle over the pauper's grave I write it with a lead-pencil; on the white shaft over a senator's tomb I cut it with a chisel—"*Slain by strong drink!*"

It is a simple fact that dissipated habits have not, in this country, been a hinderance to a man's getting office: if he be sober sometimes; if the governor can get straight enough to write his message; if the judge's tongue is not positively thick when he delivers the charge; if the vice-president is not drunk when he is sworn in—that will do. So we have had world-renowned secretaries of state carried out drunk from their office, and senators of the United States arrested at midnight in houses of shame for uproarious behavior; judges and jurors and lawyers by night, while the trial is going on by day, gambling and singing the song of the drunkard. Oh, it is a sad thing to have a hand tremulous with intoxication holding the scales of justice, when the lives of men and the destinies of a nation are in the balance; to have a chariotcer with unskillful hands on the reins while the swift destinies of governments are harnessed, on a road where governments have been dashed to pieces and empires have gone down in darkness and woe!

What was it that drove back your armies in the last war so often? Were your sons and fathers cowards and poltroons? No! It was because so often drunkenness sat in the saddle. What are those graves on the heights of Fredericksburg, as you pass down to Richmond? Was it the sword or the bottle that slew them? The bottle! for that day drunkenness rode in some of the stirrups, leading forth your sons and fathers to death. Dissipation in all the high circles as well as the low. A trial in the courts ever and anon reveals the fact that Impurity walks in robes, and dances under the palatial chandelier, and drowses on the damask upholstery. Sin is tolerable, if it is only rich. Stand back and let the libertine go by, for he rides in a three-thousand-dollar turn-out. The Congressional galleries are thrilled by the appeals of men who on the following night fulfill what Solomon said, "He goeth after her straightway, as an ox to the slaughter and as a fool to the correction of stocks, until a dart strike through his liver." Meanwhile, political parties are silent, lest they lose votes; and newspapers are quiet, lest they lose subscribers; and ministers of the Gospel are still, lest some affluent pew-holder should be disgusted. But God's indignation gathers like the fiery flashes around the edges of a blackening cloud just before the swoop of a tornado. His voice sounds through this country to-day, in the words of the text: "Woe unto thee, O land, when thy king is a child, and thy princes drink in the morning." Oh, the land groans to be delivered! It sweats great drops of blood! It is crucified—not between two thieves, but between a thousand, while the nations ride past, wagging their heads and crying, "Aha! aha!"

I unroll the scroll of wickedness in high places still farther, and I see the crime of *bribery*. It was that which corrupted Lord Bacon in his magnificent position—it was that which led Chief-justice Thorpe to the gallows. You know as well as I that in the past few years it has been almost impossible to get a law passed by State or National Legislature unless there was some financial consideration. When a bill has appeared at the door, the question among your representatives has been, "How much money is in this?" Reformers and philanthropists, with some scheme for the elevation of the nation, approach the door of the Legislature, or the door of Congress, and are laughed at because their hands are empty. Political bribes, offered in the shape of preferment for office: "If you vote so and so, you shall have so and so." "If you will vote for my bill giving a monopoly to my moneyed institution, then I will vote for your bill giving a monopoly to your moneyed institution." "Here is a bill with which we shall have a great deal of trouble, but it must go through. Crowd the lobbies with railroad men, and manufacturers, and contractors. Make an entertainment for the members, and when they are good and drunk, have them promise to vote that way. Put a thousand dollars or five thousand dollars in the hand of this man, who will be prudent in the distribution of it. Put two thousand dollars in the hand of this man, who will see that 'it does good.' Be very cautious how you approach men. Now we want only four more votes, and this matter will be all right. Give a thousand dollars to that very intelligent member from Westchester. Give five hundred dollars to that stupid member from Ulster. Now we have but two more votes to regulate. Give three hundred dollars to this man, and he will be sick and stay at home, and then give three hundred to this man, and he will go to the bedside of his great-aunt languishing in her last sickness!" The day for the passage of the bill has come. The speaker thumps his gavel on the desk and says, "Senators, are you ready for the question? All in favor of this bill that will vote one or two hundred thousand dollars, or a million dollars, into the hands of unprincipled speculators, will say, Aye." Aye! aye! aye! aye! "All opposed, No." "The ayes have it." The money is wasted, the public treasure is gone, business is embarrassed, and our National and State Legislatures become the sewers into which the filth and the vomit of this nation empty themselves. If you think that I exaggerate the matter, go to any of these places just before a bill is to be passed, and learn that I have not more than half represented the truth in the case, and that this crime of bribery is smiting the whole country, depleting your wealth, oh, you men of affluence! grinding harder your faces, oh, you children of the poor!

The Democratic party filled its cup of iniquity before it went out of power at the beginning of the war. The Republican party came along, and as it had more opportunity, by reason of the contracts, filled its cup of iniquity in shorter time; and there they are, two carcasses lying side by side—the Republican party and the Democratic party—putrefied until they have no more power to rot!

The bribery during the war is cursing us yet, and I fear will curse us for a century. You know how it was then. "If you give me the contract above all others who apply for it, I'll give you ten per cent. of the profits. If you will only pass these worn-out cavalry horses and certify that they are fit for service, I'll give you five thousand dollars bonus." "Bonus" was the word. So it went down to your sons and fathers in the army—rice that was worm-eaten, crackers that were mouldy, garments that were shoddy, meat that was rank, horses that stumbled in the charge, tents that sifted the rain into the faces of the exhausted. But it was all right, for they got the *bonus!*

The argument in behalf of the stability of republics is stronger in my mind now than it ever was. If our Government had not been thoroughly established, all this bribery and theft and outrage would have swamped it forever. The amount of money that has been spent in this country in railroads that ought never to have been constructed, in canals that ought never to have been dug, in loans that ought never to have been allowed, in farcical schemes that ought never to have been countenanced, would have swamped any three monarchies.

We sit to-day, this whole nation, under the shadow of Congressional dishonor. The white marble of our beautiful Capitol has become the vast mausoleum of the slain. Both political parties implicated. The stables of Augeas, uncleaned after three thousand oxen had stood there for thirty years, was a small job for Hercules, compared with what the Poland Committee found of national dirt in the Congressional halls. On that Union Pacific Railroad many of your representatives took a through ticket to hell. They paid their fare in eighty per cent. dividends.

They sold out political influence, honor, Christian principle, and immortal soul. But be careful, my friends, lest you smite the innocent with the guilty. I think the nation is on the track of some men who have not been proven guilty. We take men to be innocent until they are found villainous. I can not believe that men, after thirty years of integrity, amidst temptations where they might have made millions of dollars, would now sell heaven for a few hundred. A solid column of defamers reaching from Brooklyn to Washington, with uplifted hand in solemn oath, could not make me believe that some of the men arraigned are iniquitous. But, my friends, we must admit that this nation sits to-day in the shadow of national dishonor and Congressional disgrace. The crimes found in public places are only the index of political abandonment. The blotches on the surface only show the disease within. I do not believe the men inculpated in public places to-day are any worse than thousands of the political hucksters who in your legislatures and your congresses have been bought up by moneyed institutions. Some of the finest houses ever built on Fifth Avenue, and Beacon Street, and Rittenhouse Square, have been built out of money paid for votes by railroad companies in New York, New Jersey, Pennsylvania, and Massachusetts. I was glad when the explosion came. Public men will see that they must beware, since there are thunders on the track, and God has said that he "will wound the hairy scalp of him who goeth on still in his trespasses." You throw up your hands and say, "Why, we can't help it." Can you not? If I thought there was nothing for you and me to do, I would not preach this sermon. There are four things for you to do.

First, stand off from all political office unless your own principles are thoroughly settled. Do not go into the blaze of temptation unless you are fire-proof. Common council, water-board, legislative hall, and congressional assemblage have been the damnation of a great many respectable people. But if you go into political life without your principles thoroughly settled, before you get through with it you will drink, and you will swear, and you will lie, and you will take bribes. "Ah!" you say, "that is not complimentary." Well, I always was clumsy at compliments.

The second thing to do is to take the counsel of Paul, and pray for your rulers; pray for all in authority. Do you know that Shadrach and Abed-nego did not need the Son of God beside them in the fire so much as your rulers do? We pray every Sunday for the President of the United States, because that is in the liturgy. But have we been entirely cleared of all responsibility for the national corruption, from the fact that we have not prayed as we should for our representatives? When I take up the paper and see this awful defalcation in character, I feel just as I did when I saw the account of the wreck of the *Northfleet* a few nights ago in English waters—the *Northfleet* run down by a strong steamer; for those men were crashed into by temptations, with fiery furnace and thundering wheel-bucket; and there was no life-boat. Pray for your rulers!

In the next place, be faithful at the ballot-box. Do not stand on your dignity and refuse to vote because the rabble go. Put on your old clothes, and elbow your way through the unwashed, and the wretched, and the abandoned, and go to the polls. Cast your own vote.

Make up your mind in a Christian way as to who are the men best for office; then vote for the man who loves God and hates rum, and believes in having the Bible read every day as long as the world stands in all our common schools. Refuse to vote, or vote the wrong way, and you sin against the graves of the men who died for the Government, and you sin against your children, who may live to feel the curse of your negligence or your political dishonesty.

But I have a better prescription than all. It is the fourth thing I have to say in the way of counsel, and that is, *Evangelize the people.* Gospelize this country, and you will have pure representatives and pure men everywhere. I have no faith in the conversion of an old politician. I never knew one to be converted. I suppose the grace of God can do it, but seldom tries it. I should be no more surprised to see the Pope of Rome and the cardinals come in and sit down on the "anxious-seat" in a Methodist meeting-house than I would to see a long row of politicians converted. What work we have to do we are to do with the great masses of the people who cast the votes, and with our children who are coming up to be the sovereigns. That woman who this afternoon, in the Sabbath-school class, teaches six boys how to be Christians, does more for our political future than all the fine essays that were ever written about the Constitution, or the arraignment of the American Senate for holding stock of the Crédit Mobilier. I want you to understand there is work for you and me to do. Change men's hearts, and their lives will be right. There were good men this last week in Cooper Institute, New York, trying to have the Christian religion recognized in the Constitution of the United States. But, my friends, you get the people converted by the grace of God, and I do not care about the mere technicality of a Constitutional recognition. What we want in this country is just four revivals—revivals that come like those in the days of Nettleton and Jonathan Edwards and George Whitefield. We want four revivals all at once: one starting from the North, rolling South; one starting from the South, rolling North; one starting from the East, rolling West; one starting from the West, rolling East. And then I want to stand on the spot where the four seas meet, that I may shout, "Hallelujah! for the Lord God omnipotent reigneth. Hallelujah! for the kingdoms of this world are becoming the kingdoms of our Lord Jesus Christ." But remember, that if there be forty millions of people in this country, upon you personally rests a forty-millionth of the responsibility. The least thing you can do for the country is to contribute toward it a heart changed by the grace of God, and a life all pure. Remember that it is not as nations we are at last to be judged, but as individuals, each man answering for himself in that day when monarchies and republics alike shall perish, and the earth itself shall become a heap of ashes, scattered in the blast of the nostrils of the Lord God Almighty!

## THE FOURTH ANNIVERSARY.

"He thanked God, and took courage."—*Acts* xxviii., 15.

PAUL had just come ashore at Puteoli, and was soon to go across the country to Rome, to meet, perhaps, a great many trials and perplexities. The Christians at Rome hear that Paul has landed at Puteoli and is on the way, so they go out to escort him to the city. When he saw them, his heart revived, or, as my text says, "He thanked God, and took courage." That is descriptive of my own feelings this morning. You may not be aware that this is the anniversary of my settlement as the pastor of this church. Fifty-two times the shuttle has flown, in each flight weaving a week, with a golden border of Sabbath. Three hundred and sixty-four times the clock has struck twelve for the noon and twelve for the night. In that time, how many marriage garlands have been twisted, how many graves dug, how many sorrows suffered, how many fortunes won, how many souls lost, how many immortals saved!

Four years ago, this month, I came to you with chastened spirit, for only the Sabbath before I had delivered my valedictory sermon in Philadelphia, and the sharp laceration of soul which I felt that Sabbath-night as, standing at the foot of the pulpit, I bade farewell to long-tried friends, many of them my own children in the Gospel, can be appreciated only by those who have gone through the same process. Coming here, I found strangers in both boards of the church, and a building almost empty. Still my heart failed not, for I was sure that God had called me to the work, and, however weak a man may feel in himself, he is strong while leaning against the throne of the Lord Almighty. Instead of standing among strangers to-day, I look off upon familiar faces, and upon those with whom I have been taking sweet counsel, and those whom I know are remembering me, day by day, in their prayers. So I shall address them this morning as one large, Christian family. I have thought that in this, my anniversary sermon, it might be well if I should tell you what, by the help of God, I have been trying to do in this congregation.

In the first place, I remark, I have been trying *to win your confidence and love*, not by sycophancy or by the consultation of your prejudices, but by preaching a straightforward Gospel, regardless as to where it hit. A minister living amidst people who do not believe in him can not be useful. When a congregation wish that their pastor would be called to some other position, he really has a call to go. When they have the idea that he is influenced by selfish and worldly motives, his usefulness is done, and he as really has a call to go as he had a call to come. There are churches being depleted and blasted by a ministry not adapted to them. A minister has no more right to kill a church than a church has a right to kill a minister. I know a man who professes to be a minister of Christ, who is in his third settlement. The two previous churches that he served have come to extinction as the result of that ministry, and there is not much prospect that the third will long survive; while, on the other hand, there are ministers of Christ who have for thirty and forty years stood in the same places, and the tie of affection and confidence between pastor and people has all the time strengthened.

A good many years ago, a lad, fifteen years of age, heard, in England, John Flavel preach from the text: "If any man love not our Lord Jesus Christ, let him be Anathema Maranatha." The lad grew up, came to this country, and lived to be one hundred years of age, not having found Christ. One day he stood in the field, and the memory of that sermon of John Flavel crossed his mind, and the thought of how that minister of Christ, at the close of the service, said: "How can I pronounce the benediction, when there may be some here who love not the Lord Jesus Christ, and are Anathema Maranatha." The remembrance of that minister brought the old man to Christ at one hundred years of age, and eighty-five years after he had heard that Gospel sermon. Oh! it is a grand thing to preach earnestly, faithfully, and successfully this glorious Gospel. Now let me be frank, and say to you, my dear people, that I have tried to win your confidence and your deep sympathy in my Christian work. If you have seen in me many shortcomings, be aware of the fact that I have had a deeper realization of them than you possibly could have had, and I am here to say that you have given me more than I deserve, and that your kindness through the last four years has made my ministry in this place an undisturbed satisfaction.

I remark again, I have tried, in my ministry during the past year and the past four years, to create amidst this people *Christian sociality.* There are churches that are arctic seas, iceberg grinding against iceberg. The attendants upon them come as men come into the ferry-boat, sitting down beside each other—no nod of recognition, no hand-grasping of fellowship, no throb of brotherly and sisterly affection. They come in, they sit down, they go out. From Saturday to Monday morning they are ferried over by Christian ordinances, and that is all there is of it. Now, my dear brother, if you are cold and hard and selfish, then the higher the wall you build around your soul, the better. You would do well to be exclusive; but if there is in you any thing kind, any thing lovely, any thing noble, any thing useful, let it shine out. Suppose a vessel were driven on the rocks, and while fifty people were struggling in the surf, one man gets safely to the beach, and runs up to the fisherman's hut and sits down and warms himself, regardless of those who are still struggling in the water—what a cruel thing that would be! How much better, like the survivors of the *Atlantic* shipwreck, toiling with both hands until the left hand gave out, and until the right hand gave out, and then with their teeth seizing the clothing of the suffering ones and pulling them ashore! And what do you suppose God thinks of us if, having escaped from the floods of sin and darkness and death, we are culturing an unchristian selfishness, while there are hundreds and thousands all around about us still struggling in the wave? I say, let us have a kindly sympathy and helpfulness toward those who are all around us. Every church was intended by God to be a large family circle—of fathers and mothers, and brothers and sisters. What kind of a family circle would that be where the brothers did not recognize each other, and the parents were characterized by frigidity and heartlessness? Sons and daughters of God, have you no higher appreciation of the larger Christian brotherhood in which you are gathered in churches? Who is that that used to sit before you in the Tabernacle? Do not know. Who is that that used to sit at your right hand and at your left hand? Do not know. You ought to have known. It is a sin not to be acquainted with those who sit by us in the house of God year after year. Do not stand upon the formalities of society. In the name of Christ, I declare to you the privilege of giving the right hand of fellowship to every one who comes to the same church. We have tried to culture this Christian sociality in the sociable; much has already been accomplished, and when our new church shall be built, we will put our hand more earnestly to the work. The church sociable ought to be the most cheerful of all places. Let there be in it a time to laugh. Do not with long faces overshadow the young people. You go to church and to the prayer-meeting to worship; then worship, and have nothing but worship. You go to the sociable; then have nothing but sociality. Yet there are church reunions so entirely formal that the liveliest thing in all the evening is the long-metre doxology. Be cheerful, be kind, be sympathetic with all with whom you are associated. If fish go in schools, and if sheep go in flocks, and if flowers go in tribes, and if stars swing in galaxies, then let all those who worship in the same church move together in loving and shining bands. "Behold, how good and how pleasant it is for brethren to dwell together in unity!"

Again, I have tried in this church to preach an every-day religion. The vast majority of my congregation are in business life. It would have been absurd for me to talk about abstract trials when I saw by the paper that gold was going down, and men were losing their fortunes. We must bring a Gospel comfort just suited to the condition of the people to whom we preach. Here is a physician who comes into a sick-room where there is a case of diphtheria. Does he apply to it medicines for cholera, or yellow fever, or marasmus? Oh no, it is a specific for diphtheria. And if we want to make the Gospel successful in the hearts of men in the way of comfort, we must bring that particular phase of it which is thoroughly adapted to the case. So I have from time to time tried to bring you a Gospel that would be appropriate in Wall Street, and in Broadway, and in Schermerhorn Street, and in Montague Street.

It is a simple fact that there are but few men who take the comforts of religion into their business. You get sick, or a member of your family dies; you say, "Send for the minister!" But suppose you are in a business corner; suppose the sheriff is after you; suppose your best friend betrays you; suppose there are three or four men in the front office with duns for debts that you can not meet; suppose that you can no more sleep at night than if you were on the top of a mast in a Mediterranean hurricane; suppose with flushed cheek you walk the floor nights, your head aching as though it would split open—why, then, do you not send for religious consolation? No, you do not. You send for some poor, miserable skinflint, and ask him if he will lend you a thousand dollars at two per cent. a month, and he will not do it! You go to a friend you helped in time of trouble, and want to get his name on your note, and he will not give it, and in utter despair, and wild with trouble, you say, "If it were not for my wife and children, I would jump off the dock." I remember a man who, in 1857, helped a dozen people through the financial straits. He loaned a thousand dollars here, and five thousand there, and ten thousand there, and took his friends to the bank, and allowed them to go on his credit, and helped them through. Five years after *his* trial came. Where were those old friends? Gone; or, if they came into his store, it was only to say, "God bless you!" forgetful of the fact that one ounce of pure financial help at that time would have been worth fifty tons of "God bless yous." Instead of going at such a time to worldly resources, why did you not go to God? Why did you not lock the door of your private office, and get down on your knees, and say, "Oh Lord! thou seest my business trouble. There is that note at the bank. I have no money to meet it. There is my rent, it has become due: what shall I do about it? There are my unsalable goods at the warehouse. Lord Jesus, help me out of this trouble." God would have done it as certainly as he sits upon the throne and offers help to men who want it. You did not go for it, and you did not get it. If you had made your religion do that, it would have been worth something. Your religion, instead of being a robe to wrap around you and keep you warm in the chill blasts of trial, has been merely a string of beads around your neck, very beautiful to look at, and that is all. In the last panic in New York, amidst all the excitement, there was a man found in Wall Street, in his back office, with a loaded pistol lying on the table where he was writing a farewell letter to his family. What did that man most need? Was it the counsel of the brokers? The help of the note-shavers? No! He wanted the comfort and the peace of Christ's religion. I have seen a man in a business strait go through, sustained by the grace of God. By disaster, in one night his fortune all went. When I saw him before, he was worth hundreds of thousands of dollars; now he was not worth a farthing. Yet he was counting up his heavenly treasures. If God had knocked out the bottom of his earthly fortunes, that bottom was found to be the top of the chest in which are the jewels of heaven! And if his riches took wings and flew away, in their flight they met the ravens of God coming down to hungry Elijah! That man to-day, on a salary of twelve hundred dollars as a clerk in the same store over which he had presided with great dignity, is happier than Henry VIII. was on the day when Anne Boleyn came to the palace—than Napoleon III., at the time of his coronation—than any man who trusts in the wealth or honor of this world for his chief satisfaction. I expect the day will come when I can set the consolations of that Gospel on your counting-room desk; under its light the bank protests, and the letters of angry creditors, reading like the full title-deed to the thrones and principalities of heaven. That is what I call an every-day religion.

Again, I have tried in these four years in which I have been your pastor, *to dispel the conventionalities of the Church.* There is a tendency among Christian people to walk in religious things on ecclesiastical stilts, instead of coming down upon a plain, common-sense level. How few people talk religion; they whine about it! What charm is there for a wide-awake, warm-hearted, enthusiastic man amidst the cold formalities of the Church of God? He sees through them; he sees they are a sham. Friday morning, you go into a merchant's store and buy a bill of hosiery. How his face lights up! How cheerful he is! How fascinating he is while he is selling the bill of goods! You go away, saying, "That is one of the most agreeable men I ever met in my life." That very Friday evening you go into the prayer-meeting where that same Christian merchant worships, and you find him getting up and recommending the religion of Jesus Christ with a funereal countenance and a doleful phraseology, enough to make an undertaker burst into tears. How few people there are who talk cheerfully about the religion of Jesus! In other words, that man of whom I spoke had more exhilaration when he was selling a bill of goods than in recommending the religion which makes all heaven ring with the anthems of the free. Now, ought that so to be? How many are driven from the doors of the churches by the simple reason that they do not want such a repulsive religion. They are afraid to shake hands with a Christian man, lest they shall be religiously assaulted. I remember very well how it was when I was a boy. I laid one hour and a half under the raspberry-bushes in the garden, to escape from the minister and the elder who came to my father's house on a family visit; and my father came out on the back steps, and cried, "De Witt, where are you?" De Witt made no answer! Ought our religion to repel or attract? My little child, four years old, said to her mother: "Ma, ma, I saw in a book a picture of a man and a picture of God, and the man looked awfully frightened because he saw

God. Now," she says, "if I had been there and God had come in, I would not have been frightened; I would have just gone right up and put my arms around his neck and kissed him." Well, I thought that was pretty good theology. In other words, religion ought to invite our caresses, instead of driving the world howling away, as though it were something disagreeable, repulsive, and to be hated.

Again, I have, in these four years in which I have ministered to you, tried *to preach a Gospel of comfort to the bereaved.* This is the most delicate work to which the preacher is ever called. If you do not know how to treat a wound, you had better not touch it. How many people come to the wounds of the soul with a spiritual quackery, and they irritate and poison the wounds instead of cure. It may require no great skill to take a sloop across the North River, but it does to engineer a steamship across the Atlantic; and there may be no great skill required to heal a little sorrow of the soul, but to take one through the storms and tossing seas of tribulation and trial does require some tact, and ingenuity, and especial grace. I do not suppose that in the four years in which I have ministered to you a single family has escaped bereavement—if not in your immediate circle, then in a near circle. Oh! how many households have been broken up by bereavement since I came among you. From most other sorrows you can run away. You can go home, but how if a part of the home itself is gone? Then it is not so easy. Then every thing reminds you of your loss. Suppose you should sit down at a piano, put a piece of music on the rack, then put your foot on the pedal and your fingers on the keys—the music would start off magnificently. But suppose you struck one key and the chord did not respond, because it was broken. Why, that ruins the entire accompaniment. Well, sometimes in life you have been going on in great joy and hilarity, when suddenly you have thought of a voice, just one voice, that has been hushed, of one heart that is still, and the silent key spoiled all the music.

Oh, if we could all die together! If we could keep the lambs and the sheep of our family flock all together until some bright spring day, the birds a-chant, and the water a-glitter, and then we together could hear the voice of the good Shepherd, and we could all go through the flood, hand in hand! If we only knew when we were to die, and we could gather our family and say, "Now Jesus calls us, and we must away;" and then we could put our little ones in the bed and straighten out their limbs, and say, "Sleep, now, the last sleep," and then we could go to our own couches and lie down, and say, "Master, we are all ready. The children have gone, and we are ready." But it is not that way. It is one by one—one by one. It may be in mid-winter, and the snow comes down twenty inches deep above our fresh grave; or it may be in the dark, damp, chill March midnight; or it may be in a hotel, our arm too weak to pull the bell for help; or it may be so suddenly we can not say good-bye. Oh, death is bitter—a racking, tremendous curse! The apple that our first parents plucked from the forbidden tree had in it two black seeds, one called Sin, the other called Death. But I bless God that I have been able during these four years to preach to you resurrection hope. A gale from heaven has blown off the "white-caps" of the billow of sorrow, and the feet of Christ have trampled the waves to a level, until over the glittering floor of the hushed waters have marched all the consolations of God, troop by troop.

> "Oh, weep no more,
> Your comfort slain;
> The Lord is risen,
> He lives again."

So now I take the harp of Gospel comfort, and play three tunes: "Weeping may endure for a night, but joy cometh in the morning"—that is one; "All things work together for good to those who love God"—that is two; "And the Lamb which is in the midst of the throne shall lead them to living fountains of water, and God shall wipe away all tears from their eyes"—and that is the third.

Above all, during the past year I have tried to present to you *Christ the only Saviour from sin, and death, and hell.* I have tried to show you that unless a man be born again he can not get into heaven. If there be any truth about God or Christ, or death or judgment, or heaven or hell, that I have not presented, I wish you would let me know what it is, that now I may declare it. I have tried to show you that religion was an indispensable thing, not a mere adornment, but something that you must have or die. I know that truth is not always considered popular at this day; but somehow people have continued to come and hear it. I feel it is a vital truth of Christianity: "Believe in Christ and be saved—refuse him and die." Christ has been so lovely to me that I want all the world to love him, and I have, with all the types and figures of God's word that I could find, presented this Jesus to you, and I am glad to know that many of you have accepted the offer. The angels of God have not stopped singing "Harvest Home." There are scores and scores of souls who during this past year have entered the Church on earth prepared, as I trust, for the Church in heaven.

Now the year is done. If you have neglected any duty, or if I have neglected any duty, it is neglected forever. Each year has its work; if we do not do the work during that year, we never do it. The year has been to me one of great happiness—the happiest year of my ministry, and the happiest year in my life. The great calamity that put our Tabernacle in ashes has, under the good hand of God, been the best blessing that could possibly have come to us. I think we all feel that. It has consolidated us as nothing could have done, and it has gathered the sympathy and the good feeling of Christians of all denominations in this country, and from the other side of the seas. And it has shown me that in this church there is a great band of Christian men and women who will stop at no self-denial, and who will be afraid of no hard work that is to be endured for Christ. The success of the recent effort made in another room in this building is significant of that, and the masons have already begun the foundations of a grand, glorious, free Christian church. While the best men and the best newspapers in this land are in sympathy with us, you know very well that there are some who are not in sympathy with the work done by this church. They do not understand it, and never will. In proportion as you are faithful will you be abused; in other words, the faster a ship goes, the more angrily will the waters boil. So there are some secular and religious newspapers of this day that are full of spite and full of venom. You say you do not understand it. There is no mystery to me about it. It is natural. It is the history of the Church of God all the world over in all ages. I feel that our church is on the right track, and I defy all earth and hell; for if God be for us, who can be against us? If God spared not his Son, but gave him up for us, shall he not with him also freely give us all things? I am persuaded that neither height, nor depth, nor length, nor breadth shall separate us from the love of God, which is in Christ Jesus our Lord. Our church will go up, and Christ will appear in it, and he will save thousands and thousands of souls. I see it coming, and I am in exultation at the prospect.

We enter now upon another year. It will be an eventful year. You and I may not live to see its close, for God can spare you and me, and ten thousand better persons than we are, and still carry on his work; but his Church will be prospered. Having risen up as you have to the work of giving the Gospel to the masses of Brooklyn, nothing can put you to confusion. We need no pillar of cloud by day to lead us, for God's angels are sworn to defend us; and success in the future is as certain as though on that wall I saw coming out in letters of fire, while I speak, "Lo, I am with you alway, even unto the end of the world." I will live to see the completion of the work undertaken. I know if God calls me before that time, he will let me come out on the battlements of heaven, and look off on the establishment of that work for which my soul longed. Roll on, sweet days of the world's emancipation! when the mountains and the hills shall break forth into singing, and all the trees of the wood shall clap their hands; and instead of the thorn shall come up the fir-tree, and instead of the brier shall come up the myrtle-tree; and it shall be to the Lord for a name for an everlasting sign that shall not be cut off.

## MIGRATION HEAVENWARD.

"The stork in the heaven knoweth her appointed time; and the turtle and the crane and the swallow observe the time of their coming; but my people know not the judgment of the Lord."—*Jeremiah* viii., 7.

WHEN God would set fast a beautiful thought, he plants it in a tree. When he would put it afloat, he fashions it into a fish. When he would have it glide the air, he moulds it into a bird. My text speaks of four birds of beautiful instinct—the stork, of such strong affection that it is allowed familiarly to come, in Holland and Germany, and build its nest over the door-way; the sweet-dispositioned turtle-dove, mingling in color white, and black, and brown, and ashen, and chestnut; the crane, with voice like the clang of a trumpet; the swallow, swift as a dart shot out of the bow of heaven, falling, mounting, skimming, sailing—four birds started by the prophet twenty-five centuries ago, yet flying on through the ages, with rousing truth under glossy wing and in the clutch of stout claw. I suppose it may have been this very season of the year—autumn—and the prophet out-of-doors, thinking of the impenitence of the people of his day, hears a great cry overhead.

Now, you know it is no easy thing for one with ordinary delicacy of eye-sight to look into the deep blue of the noonday heaven; but the prophet looks up, and there are flocks of storks, and turtle-doves, and cranes, and swallows, drawn out in long lines for flight southward. As is their habit, the cranes had arranged themselves into two lines making an angle, a wedge splitting the air with wild velocity, the old crane, with commanding call bidding them onward; while the towns, and the cities, and the continents slid under them. The prophet, almost blinded from looking into the dazzling heavens, stoops down and begins to think how much superior the birds are in sagacity about their safety than men about theirs; and he puts his hand upon the pen, and begins to write: "The stork in the heaven knoweth her appointed times; and the turtle and the crane and the swallow observe the time of their coming; but my people know not the judgment of the Lord."

If you were in the field to-day, in the clump of trees at the corner of the field, you would see a convention of birds, noisy as the American Congress the last night before adjournment, or as the English Parliament when some unfortunate member proposes more economy in the Queen's household—a convention of birds all talking at once, moving and passing resolutions on the subject of migration; some proposing to go to-morrow, some moving that they go to-day, some moving that they go to Brazil, some to Florida, some to the table-lands of Mexico, but all unanimous in the fact that they must go soon, for they have marching orders from the Lord, written on the first white sheet of the frost, and in the pictorial of the changing leaves. There is not a belted kingfisher, or a chaffinch, or a fire-crested wren, or a plover, or a red-legged partridge but expects to spend the winter at the South, for the apartments have already been ordered for them in South America, or in Africa; and after thousands of miles of flight, they will stop in the very tree where they spent last January. Farewell, bright plumage! Until spring weather, away! Fly on, great band of heavenly musicians! Strew the continents with music, and whether from Northern fields, or Carolinian swamps, or Brazilian groves men see your wings, or hear your voice, may they bethink themselves of the solemn words of the text: "The stork in the heaven knoweth her appointed times; and the turtle and the crane and the swallow observe the time of their coming; but my people know not the judgment of the Lord."

I propose, so far as God may help me, this morning, carrying out the idea of the text, to show that the birds of the air have more sagacity than men. And I begin by particularizing and saying that *they mingle music with their work.* The most serious undertaking of a bird's life is this annual travel from the Hudson to the Amazon, from the Thames to the Nile. Naturalists tell us that they arrive there thin, and weary, and plumage ruffled, and yet they go singing all the way; the ground, the lower line of the music, the sky, the upper line of the music, themselves, the notes scattered up and down between. I suppose their song gives elasticity to their wing, and helps on with the journey, dwindling a thousand miles into four hundred. Would God that we were as wise as they in mingling Christian song with our every-day work! I believe there is such a thing as taking the pitch of Christian devotion in the morning, and keeping it all the day. I think we might take some of the dullest, heaviest, most disagreeable work of our life, and set it to the tune of "Antioch" or "Mount Pisgah."

It is a good sign when you hear a workman whistle. It is a better sign when you hear him hum a roundelay.

It is a still better sign when you hear him sing the words of Isaac Watts or Charles Wesley. A violin chorded and strung, if something accidentally strike it, makes music, and I suppose there is such a thing as having our hearts so attuned by divine grace, that even the rough collisions of life will make a heavenly vibration. I do not believe that the power of Christian song has yet been fully tried. I believe that if you could roll the "Old Hundred" doxology through Wall Street, it would put an end to the panic! I believe that the discords, and the sorrows, and the sins of the world are to be swept out by heaven-born hallelujahs. Some one asked Haydn, the celebrated musician, why he always composed such cheerful music. "Why," he said, "I can't do otherwise. When I think of God, my soul is so full of joy that the notes leap and dance from my pen." I wish we might all exult melodiously before the Lord. With God for our Father, and Christ for our Saviour, and heaven for our home, and angels for future companions, and eternity for a lifetime, we should strike all the notes of joy. Going through the wilderness of this world, let us remember that we are on the way to the summery clime of heaven, and from the migratory populations flying through this autumnal air learn always to keep singing.

> "Children of the heavenly King,
> As ye journey, sweetly sing;
> Sing your Saviour's worthy praise,
> Glorious in his works and ways.
>
> "Ye are traveling home to God,
> In the way your fathers trod;
> They are happy now, and we
> Soon their happiness shall see."

The Church of God never will be a triumphant church until it becomes a singing church.

I go further, and remark that the birds of the air are wiser than we, in the fact that, in their migration, *they fly very high*. During the summer, when they are in the fields, they often come within reach of the gun; but when they start for the annual flight southward, they take their places mid-heaven, and go straight as a mark. The longest rifle that was ever brought to shoulder can not reach them. Would to God that we were as wise as the stork and crane in our flight heavenward! We fly so low that we are within easy range of the world, the flesh, and the devil. We are brought down by temptations that ought not to come within a mile of reaching us. Oh for some of the faith of George Müller of England, and Alfred Cookman, once of the Church militant, now of the Church triumphant! So poor is the type of piety in the Church of God now, that men actually caricature the idea that there is any such thing as a higher life. Moles never did believe in eagles. But, my brethren, because we have not reached these heights ourselves, shall we deride the fact that there are any such heights? A man was once talking to Brunel, the famous engineer, about the length of the railroad from London to Bristol. The engineer said, "It is not very great. We shall have, after a while, a steamer running from England to New York." They laughed him to scorn; but we have gone so far now that we have ceased to laugh at any thing as impossible for human achievement. Then, I ask, is any thing impossible for the Lord? I do not believe that God exhausted all his grace in Paul, and Latimer, and Edward Payson. I believe there are higher points of

Christian attainment to be reached in the future ages of the Christian world. You tell me that Paul went up to the tiptop of the Alps of Christian attainment. Then I tell you that the stork and crane have found above the Alps plenty of room for free flying. We go out and we conquer our temptations by the grace of God, and lie down. On the morrow, those temptations rally themselves and attack us, and by the grace of God we defeat them again; but, staying all the time in the old encampment, we have the same old battles to fight over. Why not whip out our temptations, and then forward march, making one raid through the enemy's country, stopping not until we break ranks after the last victory. Do, my brethren, let us have some novelty of combat, at any rate, by changing, by going on, by making advancement, trading off our stale prayers about sins we ought to have quit long ago, going on toward a higher state of Christian character, and routing out sins that we have never thought of yet. The fact is, if the Church of God—if we, as individuals, made rapid advancement in the Christian life, these stereotyped prayers we have been making for ten or fifteen years would be as inappropriate to us as the shoes, and the hats, and the coats we wore ten or fifteen years ago. Oh for a higher flight in the Christian life, the stork and the crane in their migration teaching us the lesson!

> "Dear Lord, and shall we ever live,
> At this poor dying rate—
> Our love so faint, so cold to thee,
> And thine to us so great?"

Again, I remark that the birds of the air are wiser than we, because they *know when to start*. If you should go out now and shout, "Stop, storks and cranes, don't be in a hurry!" they would say, "No, we can not stop; last night we heard the roaring in the woods bidding us away, and the shrill flute of the north wind has sounded the retreat. We must go. We must go." So they gather themselves into companies, and turning not aside for storm or mountain top or shock of musketry, over land and sea, straight as an arrow to the mark they go. And if you come out this morning with a sack of corn and throw it in the fields and try to get them to stop, they are so far up they would hardly see it. They are on their way south. You could not stop them. Oh that we were as wise about the best time to start for God and heaven! We say, "Wait until it is a little later in the season of mercy. Wait until some of these green leaves of hope are all dried up and have been scattered. Wait until next year." After a while we start, and it is too late, and we perish in the way when God's wrath is kindled but a little. There are, you know, exceptional cases where birds have started too late, and in the morning you have found them dead on the snow. And there are those who have perished half-way between the world and Christ. They waited until the last sickness, when the mind was gone, or they were on the express train going at forty miles an hour, and they came to the bridge and the "draw was up" and they went down. How long to repent and pray? Two seconds! Two seconds! To do the work of a lifetime and to prepare for the vast eternity in two seconds! I was reading of an entertainment given in a king's court, and there were musicians there, with elaborate pieces of music. After a while Mozart came and began to play, and he had a blank piece of paper before him, and the king familiarly looked over his shoulder and said, "What are you playing? I see no music before you." And Mozart put his hand on his brow, as much as to say, "I am improvising." It was very well for him, but oh, my friends, we can not extemporize heaven. If we do not get prepared in this world, we will never take part in the orchestral harmonies of the saved. If we go out of this world unpardoned, we secure for our souls a blasted residence. Oh that we were as wise as the crane and the stork, flying away, flying away from the tempest!

Some of you have felt the pinching frost of sin. You feel it to-day. You are not happy. I look into your faces, and I know you are not happy. There are voices within your soul that will not be silenced, telling you that you are sinners, and that without the pardon of God you are undone forever. What are you going to do, my friends, with the accumulated trangressions of this lifetime? Will you stand still and let the avalanche tumble over you? Oh that you would go away into the warm heart of God's mercy. The Southern grove, redolent with magnolia and cactus, never waited for Northern flocks as God has waited for you, saying, "I have loved thee with an everlasting love. Come unto me, all ye who are weary and heavy laden, and I will give you rest."

Another frost is bidding you away—it is the frost of sorrow. Where do you live now? "Oh," you say, "I have moved." Why did you move? You say, "I don't want as large a house now as formerly." Why do you not want as large a house? You say, "My family is not so large." Where have they gone to? Eternity! Your mind goes back through that last sickness and through the almost supernatural effort to keep life, and through those prayers that seemed unavailing, and through that kiss which received no response because the lips were lifeless, and I hear the bells tolling and I hear the hearts breaking—while I speak, I hear them break. A heart! Another heart! Alone! alone! alone! This world, which in your girlhood and boyhood was sunshine, is cold now, and oh! weary dove, you fly around this world as though you would like to stay, when the wind and the frost and the blackening clouds would bid you away into the heart of an all-comforting God. Oh, I have noticed again and again what a botch this world makes of it when it tries to comfort a soul in trouble! It says, "Don't cry!" How can we help crying when the heart's treasures are scattered, and father is gone, and mother is gone, and companions are gone, and the child is gone, and every thing seems gone? It is no comfort to tell a man not to cry. The world comes up and says, "Oh, it is only the body of your loved one that you have put in the ground!" But there is no comfort in that. That body is precious. Shall we never put our hand in that hand again, and shall we never see that sweet face again? Away with your heartlessness, oh world! But come, Jesus! and tell us that when the tears fall they fall into God's bottle; that the dear bodies of our loved ones shall rise radiant in the resurrection; and all the breakings down here shall be liftings up there, and "they shall hunger no more, neither thirst any more, neither shall the sun light on them nor any heat, for the Lamb which is in the midst of the throne shall lead them to living fountains of water, and God shall wipe all tears from their eyes."

You may have noticed that when the chaffinch or the stork or the crane starts on its migration, it calls all those of its kind to come too. The tree-tops are full of chirp and whistle and carol and the long roll-call. The bird does not start off alone. It gathers all of its kind. Oh that you might be as wise in this migration to heaven, and that you might gather all your families and your friends with you! I would that Hannah might take Samuel by the hand, and Abraham might take Isaac, and Hagar might take Ishmael. I ask you if those who sat at your breakfast-table this morning will sit with you in heaven? I ask you what influences you are trying to bring upon them, what example you are setting them? Are you calling them to go with you? Ay, ay, have you started yourself? I say it in all love. I could not stand here in any other spirit and say this. I ask you what the prospects are that you will be united families in heaven? I have heard of whole families saved, and so have you. I suppose there is such a thing also as a whole family lost. Father lost, mother lost, sons and daughters lost, the estate of wretchedness going down from generation to generation, the tide of blackness deepening and swiftening into wilder rapids and mightier plunges of despair. Impenitent father, impenitent mother! if you reject Christ, and your children come up to years of discretion, and through your influence reject him and are lost, it will be your fault. Oh, if there should come through the darkness of the lost world words from their own lips, saying, "Father, you never invited me to Christ; mother, your example led me away from Jesus, and I am lost; you got me here; you can not get me out!"

Start for heaven yourself, and take your children with you. Come thou and all thy house into the ark. Tell your little ones that there are realms of balm and sweetness for all those who fly in the right direction. Heaven beckons from above; hell gapes from beneath; and this is the only safe hour. Oh, make the best of it. Swifter than eagle's stroke, put out for heaven. Like the crane or the stork, stop not night nor day until you find the right place for stopping. Seated to-day in Christian service, will you be seated in the same glorious service when the heavens have passed away with a great noise, and the elements have melted with fervent heat, and the redeemed are gathered around the throne of Jesus? Oh, is it impossible that the separating line goes through any family in my beloved flock? Is the father on one side and the mother on the other side of the line that divides the two eternities? If you are saved, take your friends with you. Invite all your children to go along. Together on earth, may you be together in heaven!

It is strange how out of the same bell you may get such different sounds—glad and sad—just as the janitor rings it fast or slow. So when Independence-day comes he rings the bell merrily, and every stroke seems to say "Independence," "liberty;" and then, when the long procession winds into the church-yard, that very same bell tolls for the dead. So it is with this Gospel bell. I lay hold the rope to-day, and offer you pardon, peace, and heaven. How gladly the bell rings out! Free! Free! But there is another story to be told. Those who reject God and wander away from him, go into perpetual sorrow; and so I lay hold the rope of the bell and give it slow, sad, solemn pull, and it rings out, through the darkness of the destroyed spirit, Woe! Woe!

> "To-day the Saviour calls,
> Ye wanderers come.
> Oh, ye benighted souls,
> Why longer roam?
>
> The Spirit calls to-day,
> Yield to his power.
> Oh, grieve Him not away,
> 'Tis mercy's hour."

## THE LAVER OF LOOKING-GLASSES.

"And he made the laver of brass, and the foot of it of brass, of the looking-glasses of the women assembling."—*Exodus* xxxviii., 8.

WE often hear about the Gospel in John, and the Gospel in Luke, and the Gospel in Matthew; but there is just as surely a Gospel of Moses, and a Gospel of Jeremiah, and a Gospel of David. In other words, Christ is as certainly to be found in the Old Testament as in the New.

When the Israelites were marching through the wilderness, they carried their church with them. They called it the tabernacle. It was a pitched tent; very costly, very beautiful. The frame-work was made of forty-eight boards of acacia-wood set in sockets of silver. The curtains of the place were purple, and scarlet, and blue, and fine linen, and were hung with most artistic loops. The candlestick of that tabernacle had shaft, and branch, and bowl of solid gold, and the figures of cherubim that stood there had wings of gold; and there were lamps of gold, and snuffers of gold, and tongs of gold, and rings of gold; so that skepticism has sometimes asked, Where did all that precious material come from? It is not my place to furnish the precious stones, it is only to tell that they were there.

I wish now more especially to speak of the laver that was built in the midst of that ancient tabernacle. It was a great basin from which the priests washed their hands and feet. The water came down from the basin in spouts and passed away after the cleansing. This laver or basin was made out of the looking-glasses of the women who had frequented the tabernacle, and who had made these their contribution to the furniture. These looking-glasses were not made of glass, but they were brazen. The brass was of a very superior quality, and polished until it reflected easily the features of those who looked into it. So that this laver of looking-glasses spoken of in my text did double work: it not only furnished the water in which the priests washed themselves, but it also, on its shining, polished surface, pointed out the spots of pollution on the face which needed ablution. Now, my Christian friends, as every thing in that ancient tabernacle was suggestive of religious truth, and for the most part positively symbolical of truth, I shall take that laver of looking-glasses spoken of in the text as all-suggestive of the Gospel, which first shows us our sins as in a mirror, and then washes them away by divine ablution.

> "Oh happy day, happy day,
> When Jesus washed my sins away!"

I have to say that this is the only looking-glass in which a man can see himself as he is. There are some mirrors that flatter the features, and make you look better than you are. Then there are other mirrors that distort your features, and make you look worse than you are; but I want to tell you that this looking-glass of the Gospel shows a man just as he is. When the priests entered the ancient tabernacle, one glance at the burnished side of this laver showed them their need of cleansing;

so this Gospel shows the soul its need of divine washing. "All have sinned, and come short of the glory of God." That is one showing. "All we, like sheep, have gone astray." That is another showing. "From the crown of the head to the sole of the foot there is no health in us." That is another showing. The world calls these, defects, imperfections, or eccentricities, or erratic behavior, or "wild oats," or "high living;" but the Gospel calls them sin, transgression, filth—the abominable thing that God hates. It was just one glance at that mirror that made Paul cry out, "Oh wretched man that I am, who shall deliver me from the body of this death?" and that made David cry out, "Purge me with hyssop, and I shall be clean;" and that made Martin Luther cry out, "Oh my sins, my sins!" I am not talking about bad habits. You and I do not need any Bible to tell us that bad habits are wrong, that blasphemy and evil-speaking are wrong. But I am talking of a sinful nature, the source of all bad thoughts, as well as of all bad actions. The Apostle Paul calls their roll in the first chapter of Romans. They are a regiment of death encamping around every heart, holding it in a tyranny from which nothing but the grace of God can deliver it.

Here, for instance, is ingratitude. Who has not been guilty of that sin? If a man hand us a glass of water, we say, "Thank you;" but for the ten thousand mercies that we are every day receiving from the hand of God, how little expression of gratitude—for thirst slaked, for hunger fed, for shelter, and sunshine, and sound sleep, and clothes to wear—how little thanks! I suppose there are men fifty years of age who have never yet been down on their knees in thanksgiving to God for his goodness. Besides that ingratitude of our hearts, there is pride (who has not felt it?)—pride that will not submit to God, that wants its own way—a nature that prefers wrong sometimes instead of right—that prefers to wallow instead of to rise up. I do not care what you call that; I am not going to quarrel with any theologian, or any man who makes any pretensions to theology. I do not care whether you call it "total depravity," or something else; I simply make the announcement of God's word, affirmed and confirmed by the experience of hundreds of people in this house: the imagination of the heart of man is evil from youth. "There is none that doeth good; no, not one." We have a bad nature. We were born with it. We got it from our parents; they got it from their parents. Our thoughts are wrong, our action is wrong; our whole life is obnoxious to God before conversion; and after conversion, not one good thing in us but that which the grace of God has planted and fostered. "Well," you say, "I can't believe that to be so." Ah! my dear brother, that is because you have never looked into this laver of looking-glasses.

If you could catch a glimpse of your natural heart before God, you would cry out in amazement and alarm. The very first thing this Gospel does is to cut down our pride and self-sufficiency. If a man does not feel his lost and ruined condition before God, he does not want any Gospel. I think the reason that there are so few conversions in this day is because the tendency of the preaching is to make men believe that they are pretty good anyhow—quite clever, only wanting a little fitting up—a few touches of divine grace, and then you will be all right; instead of proclaiming the broad, deep truth that

Payson, and Baxter, and Whitefield thundered to a race trembling on the verge of infinite and eternal disaster. "Now," says some one, "can this really be true? Have we all gone astray? Is there no good in us?" In Hampton Court I saw a room where the four walls were covered with looking-glasses; and it made no difference which way you looked, you saw yourself. And so it is in this Gospel of Christ. If you once step within its full precincts, you will find your whole character reflected; every feature of moral deformity, every spot of moral taint. If I understand the Word of God, its first announcement is that we are lost. I care not, my brother, how magnificently you may have been born, or what may have been your heritage or ancestry, you are lost by reason of sin. "But," you say, "what is the use of all this—of showing a man's faults when he can't get rid of them?" None! "What was the use of that burnished surface to this laver of looking-glasses spoken of in the text, if it only showed the spots on the countenance and the need of washing, and there was nothing to wash with?" Glory be to God, I find that this laver of looking-glasses was filled with fresh water every morning, and the priest no sooner looked on its burnished side and saw his need of cleansing, than he washed and was clean—glorious type of the Gospel of my Lord Jesus, that first shows a man his sin, and then washes it all away!"

I want you to notice that this laver in which the priest washed—the laver of looking-glasses—was filled with *fresh water every morning.* The servants of the tabernacle brought the water in buckets and poured it into this laver. So it is with the Gospel of Jesus Christ; it has a fresh salvation every day. It is not a stagnant pool filled with accumulated corruptions. It is living water, which is brought from the eternal rock to wash away the sins of yesterday—of one moment ago. "Oh," says some one, "I was a Christian twenty years ago!" That does not mean any thing to me. What are you now? We are not talking, my brother, about pardon ten years ago, but about pardon now—a fresh salvation. Suppose a time of war should come, and I could show the Government that I had been loyal to it twelve years ago, would that excuse me from taking an oath of allegiance now? Suppose you ask me about my physical health, and I should say I was well fifteen years ago—that does not say how I am now. The Gospel of Jesus Christ comes and demands present allegiance, present fealty, present moral health; and yet how many Christians there are seeking to live entirely in past experience, who seem to have no experience of present mercy and pardon! When I was on the sea, and there came up a great storm, and officers and crew and passengers all thought we must go down, I began to think of my life insurance, and whether, if I were taken away, my family would be cared for; and then I thought, Is the premium paid up? and I said Yes. Then I felt comfortable. Yet there are men who in religious matters are looking back to past insurance. They have let it run out, and they have nothing for the present, no hope nor pardon—falling back on the old insurance policy of ten, twenty, thirty years ago. If I want to find out how a friend feels toward me, do I go to the drawer and find some old yellow letters written to me ten or twelve years ago? No; I go to the letter that was stamped the day before yesterday in the post-office, and I find how he feels toward me. It is not in regard to old communications we had with Jesus Christ, it is communications we have now. Are we not in sympathy with him this morning, and is he not in sympathy with us? Do not spend so much of your time in hunting in the wardrobe for the old, worn-out shoes of Christian profession. Come this morning and take the glittering robe of Christ's righteousness from the Saviour's hand. You say you were plunged in the fountain of the Saviour's mercy a quarter of a century ago. That is nothing to me; I tell you to wash now in this laver of looking-glasses and have your soul made clean.

I notice also, in regard to this laver of looking-glasses spoken of in the text, that the priests always washed *both hands and feet*. The water came down in spouts, so that, without leaving any filth in the basin, the priests washed both hands and feet. So the Gospel of Jesus Christ must touch the very extremities of our moral nature. A man can not fence off a small part of his soul, and say, "Now this is to be a garden in which I will have all the fruits and flowers of Christian character, while outside it shall be the devil's commons." No, no; it will be all garden or none. I sometimes hear people say, "He is a very good man except in politics." Then he is not a good man. A religion that will not take a man through an autumn election will not be worth any thing to him in June, July, and August. They say he is a useful sort of a man, but he overreaches in a bargain. I deny the statement. If he is a Christian anywhere, he will be in his business. It is very easy to be good in the prayer-meeting, with surroundings kindly and blessed, but not so easy to be a Christian behind the counter, when by one skillful twitch of the goods you can hide a flaw in the silk so that the customer can not see it. It is very easy to be a Christian with a psalm-book in your hand and a Bible in your lap, but not so easy when you can go into a shop, and falsely tell the merchant you can get those goods at a cheaper rate in another store, so that he will sell them to you cheaper than he can afford to sell them. The fact is, the religion of Christ is all-pervasive. If you rent a house, you expect full possession of it. You say, "Where are the keys of those rooms? If I pay for this whole house, I want possession of those rooms." And the grace of God when it comes to a soul takes full possession of a man, or goes away and takes no possession. It will ransack every room in the heart, every room in the life, from cellar to attic, touching the very extremities of his nature. The priests washed hands and feet.

I remark, further, that this laver of looking-glasses spoken of in the text was a very large laver. I always thought, from the fact that so many washed there, and also from the fact that Solomon afterward, when he copied that laver in the Temple, built it on a very large scale, that it was large; and so suggestive of the Gospel of Jesus Christ and salvation by him—vast in its provisions. The whole world may come and wash in this laver and be clean.

When the last war had passed, the Government of the United States made proclamation of pardon to the common soldiery in the Confederate army, but not to the chief soldiers. The Gospel of Christ does not act in that way. It says pardon for all, but especially for the chief of sinners. I do not now think of a single passage that says a small sinner may be saved, but I do think of passages that say a great sinner may be saved. If there be sins only faintly hued, just a little tinged, so faintly colored that you can hardly see them, there is no special pardon promised in the Bible for those sins; but if they be glaring, red like crimson, then they shall be as snow. Now, my brother, I do not state this to put a premium upon great iniquity. I merely say this to encourage that man in this house who feels he is so far gone from God that there is no mercy for him. I want to tell him there is a good chance. Why, Paul was a murderer; he assisted at the execution of Stephen; and yet Paul was saved. The dying thief did every thing bad. The dying thief was saved. Richard Baxter swore dreadfully; but the grace of God met him, and Richard Baxter was saved. It is a vast laver. Go and tell every body to come and wash in it. Let them come up from the penitentiaries and wash away their crimes. Let them come up from the alms-houses and wash away their poverty. Let them come up from their graves and wash away their death. If there be any one so worn out in sin that he can not get up to the laver, you will take hold of his head and put your arms around him, and I will take hold of his feet, and we will plunge him in this glorious Bethesda, the vast laver of God's mercy and salvation. In Solomon's Temple there were ten lavers, and one molten sea—this great reservoir in the midst of the temple filled with water—these lavers and this molten sea adorned with figures of palm-branch, and oxen, and lions, and cherubim. This fountain of God's mercy is a vaster molten sea than that. It is adorned not with palm-branches, but with the wood of the cross; not with cherubim, but with the wings of the Holy

Ghost; and around its great rim all the race may come and wash in the molten sea. I was reading the other day of Alexander the Great, who, when he was very thirsty and standing at the head of his army, had brought to him a cup of water. He looked off upon his host and said, "I can not drink this, my men are all thirsty;" and he dashed it to the ground. Blessed be God! there is enough water for all the host—enough for captains and host. "Whosoever will may come and take of the water of life freely"—a laver broad as the earth, high as the heavens, and deep as hell.

But I notice also, in regard to this laver of looking-glasses spoken of in the text, that the washing in it was *imperative, and not optional.* When the priests come into the tabernacle (you will find this in the thirtieth chapter of Exodus), God tells them that they must wash in that laver or die. The priest might have said, "Can't I wash elsewhere? I washed in the laver at home, and now you want me to wash here." God says, "No matter whether or not you have washed before. Wash in this laver or die." "But," says the priest, "there is water just as clean as this—why won't that do?" "Wash here," says God, "or die." So it is with the Gospel of Christ—it is imperative. There is only this alternative: keep our sins and perish, or wash them away and live. But says some one, "Why could not God have made more ways to heaven than one?" I do not know but he could have made half a dozen. I know he made but one. You say, "Why not have a long line of boats running from here to heaven?" I can not say, but I simply know that there is only one boat. You say, "Are there not trees as luxuriant as that on Calvary?—more luxuriant, for that had neither buds nor blossoms; it was stripped and barked!" Yes, yes, there have been taller trees than that and more luxuriant; but the only path to heaven is under that one tree. Instead of quarreling because there are not more ways, let us be thankful to God there is one—one name given unto men whereby we can be saved—one laver in which all the world may wash. So you see what a radiant Gospel this is I preach. I do not know how a man can stand stolidly and present it, for it is such an exhilarant Gospel. It is not a mere whim or caprice; it is life or death; it is heaven or hell. You come before your child, and you have a present in your hand. You put your hands behind your back and say, "Which hand will you take? In one hand there is a treasure, in the other there is not." The child blindly chooses. But God our Father does not do that way with us. He spreads out both hands, and says, "Now this shall be very plain. In that hand are pardon, and peace, and life, and the treasures of heaven; in *that* hand are punishment, and sorrow, and woe. Choose, choose for yourselves!" "He that believeth and is baptized shall be saved, but he that believeth not shall be damned."

Oh, my dear friends, I wish I could this morning coax you to accept this Gospel. If you could just take one look in this laver of looking-glasses spoken of in the text, you would begin now spiritual ablution. You will not feel insulted, will you, when I tell you that you are a lost soul without pardon? Christ offers all the generosity of his nature to you this morning. The love of Christ—I dare not, toward the close of my sermon, begin to tell about it. The love of Christ! Do not talk to me about a mountain; it is higher than that. Do not talk to me about a sea; it is deeper than that.

An artist in his dreams saw such a splendid dream of the transfiguration of Christ that he awoke and seized his pencil, and said, "Let me paint this and die." Oh, I have seen the glories of Christ! I have beheld something of the beauty of that great sacrifice on Calvary, and I have sometimes felt I would be willing to give any thing if I might just sketch before you the wonders of that sacrifice. I would like to do it while I live, and I would like to do it when I die. "Let me paint this and die!" He comes along, weary and worn, his face wet with tears, his brow crimson with blood, and he lies down on Calvary for you. No, I mistake. Nothing was as comfortable as that. A stone on Calvary would have made a soft pillow for the dying head of Christ. Nothing so comfortable as that. He does not lie down to die; he stands up to die; his spiked hands outspread as if to embrace a world. Oh, what a hard end for these feet that had traveled all over Judea on ministries of mercy! What a hard end for those hands that had wiped away tears and bound up broken hearts! Very hard, oh dying Lamb of God! and yet there are those here this morning who do not love thee. They say, "What is that all to me? What if He does weep, and groan, and die, I don't want Him." Lord Jesus Christ, they will not help thee down from the cross! The soldiers will come, and they will tear thee down from the cross, and put their arms around thee and lower thee into the tomb; but *they* will not help. They see nothing to move them. Oh dying Christ! turn on them thine eyes of affection now, and see if they will not change their minds!

> "I saw One hanging on a tree,
>   In agony and blood,
> Who fixed his languid eyes on me,
>   As near his cross I stood.
>
> "Oh, never till my latest breath
>   Will I forget that look!
> He seemed to charge me with his death,
>   Though not a word he spoke."

And that is all for you! Oh, can you not love him? Come around this laver, old and young. It is so burnished, you can see your sins; and so deep, you can wash them all away. Oh mourner, here bathe your bruised soul; and, sick one, here cool your hot temples in this laver. Peace! Do not cry any more, dear soul! Pardon for all thy sins, comfort for all thy afflictions. The black cloud that hung thundering over Sinai has floated above Calvary, and burst into the shower of a Saviour's tears.

I saw in Kensington Garden, London, a picture of Waterloo a good while after the battle had passed, and the grass had grown all over the field. There was a dismounted cannon, and a lamb had come up from the pasture and lay sleeping in the mouth of that cannon. So the artist had represented it—a most suggestive thing. Then I thought how the war between God and the soul had ended; and instead of the announcement, "The wages of sin is death," there came the words, "My peace I give unto thee;" and amidst the batteries of the law that had once quaked with the fiery hail of death, I beheld the Lamb of God which taketh away the sin of the world.

> "I went to Jesus as I was,
>   Weary, and worn, and sad:
> I found in him a resting-place,
>   And he has made me glad."

## CRUMBS UNDER THE TABLE.

"But he answered and said, It is not meet to take the children's bread, and to cast it to dogs. And she said, Truth, Lord: yet the dogs eat of the crumbs which fall from their masters' table. Then Jesus answered and said unto her, O woman, great is thy faith: be it unto thee even as thou wilt. And her daughter was made whole from that very hour.— *Matthew* xv., 26–28.

IT was a Sabbath afternoon in the Belleville parsonage. I had been trying for two years to preach, but to me the Christian life had been nothing but a struggle. I sat down at the table, took up my Bible, and asked for divine illumination, and it poured like sunlight upon my soul through the story of the Syrophenician woman.

This woman was a mother, and she had an afflicted daughter. The child had a virulent, exasperating, convulsive disease, called the possession of the devil. The mother was just like other mothers; she had no peace as long as her child was sick. She was a Gentile, and the Jews had such a perfect contempt for the Gentiles that they called them dogs. Nevertheless, she comes to Christ, and asks his help in her family troubles. Christ makes no answer. The people are afraid there is going to be a "scene" there, and they try to get the woman out of Christ's presence; but he forbids her expulsion. Then she falls down and repeats her request. Christ, to rally her earnestness, and to make his mercy finally more conspicuous, addresses her, saying, "It is not meet to take the children's bread"—that is, the salvation appointed for the Jews—"and cast it to dogs"—the Gentiles. Christ did not mean to characterize that woman as a dog. That would have been most unlike him, who from the cross said, "Behold thy mother." His whole life so gentle and so loving, he could not have given it out as his opinion that that was what she ought to be called; but he was only employing the ordinary parlance of the Jews in regard to the Gentiles. Yet that mother was not to be put off, pleading as she was for the life of her daughter; she was not to be rebuffed, she was not to be discouraged. She says, "Yea, Lord, I acknowledge I am a Gentile dog, but I remember that even the dogs have some privileges, and when the door is open they slink in and they crawl under the table, and when the bread or the meat sifts through the cracks of the table, or falls off the edge of it, they pick it up, and the master of the house is not angry with them. I don't ask for a big loaf; I don't ask even for a big slice; I only ask for that which drops down through the chinks of the table—the dogs' portion. It is the crumbs I am after." Christ felt the wit and the earnestness and the stratagem and the faith of that woman. He turns upon her, and says, "You have conquered me; your daughter is well now. Go home, mother; but before you get there she will come down, skipping out to meet you."

There I see the mother going. She feels twenty years younger—getting on in life, but she goes with a half-run. Amidst an outburst of hysterical laughter and tears they meet. The mother breaks down every time she tries to tell it; the daughter with cheeks as rosy as before she fell in the first fit; the doctors of the village prophesying that the cure will not last, because it was not according to their prescription. But I read in the oldest medical journal of the world, "The daughter was made whole from that very hour."

In the first place, I learn from my subject that *sin treats us like a dog*—not as dogs are now treated. Landseer, in his pictures, makes princes of all the canine family. You sometimes find the kennel lined and cushioned. The St. Bernard dogs are admired all the world over. There is one of them with a collar on his neck inscribed with the names of twenty-five persons whose lives he saved from the snow. The sagacity and faithfulness and kindness of the dog have conquered the respect of the world. He dashes from the ship's deck to save the life of the man overboard. He rushes into the wild surf and brings ashore the exhausted bather. With his warm tongue he licks into life the freezing wayfarer. From the Liffy Bridge a child fell into the water. A dog stood on the bridge and saw it fall, and leaped after the child as it came to the surface, and seizing it gently but firmly, brought it ashore. A gentleman stood on the bridge, looking down at it, and said, "How very sagacious that dog is—how very kind and faithful!" But he was thrilled through when he saw it was his own child that had been saved. There is no way in which you can so deeply offend a hunter as by maltreating his hounds. The finest picture in the room of Dr. John Brown, of Edinburgh, the celebrated author, is a picture of "Rab," the dog immortal. Walter Scott sang his praise. The mastiff, lying, toothless, and blind, and lame, on the door-mat, is the pet of the whole household.

But it was not so in the time of Christ, nor is it so in the East to-day. That whole land is filled with mean curs; they are foul and vermin-covered and snarly, and the most significant thing that a Jew could say about a Gentile, in the way of depicting hatred, was to call him a dog. It seems as if the sagacity of the dog were not discovered in those days. Job gives him a kick in his thirtieth chapter. Abishai said, in regard to David, "Shall this dead dog curse the king?" Goliath said to David, "Am I a dog, that thou comest out against me with stones?" Hazael, wishing to depict his hatred for some kind of sin, said, "Is thy servant a dog, that he should do this great thing?" Paul, writing to the Philippians, tried to set forth the danger of consorting with certain persons, and said, "Beware of dogs." John, in Revelation, describing the fact that the abandoned and the dissolute and the sinful shall finally be thrust out of heaven, says, "Without are dogs." This I say to show you what intense hatred the Jew of olden time had against the Gentile. You must all admit that it must have been a positively sinful hatred, and so through my subject, the first lesson I learn is that sin treats us like a dog. It may flatter you for a while; it may caress you for a while; but no Eastern traveler ever more mercilessly beat a whelp in the streets of Beirut or Damascus than sin will beat you and me if it gets a chance. "The way of the transgressor is hard."

Sin is a scarification of the soul. Sin comes to the young man. It says, "Take a game of cards—it won't hurt you. Besides that, it is the way men make their fortune." It is only a small stake. See how easy it is. The young man plays and wins a horse and carriage and a house—wins a fortune! "See how easy it is," says sin; "it don't cost you any thing! Look at those young men who stick to their salaries, away down at the foot of the ladder, while you are in great prosperity." The young man is encouraged. He goes on, and plays larger and larger; the tide turns against him; he loses the horse, loses the carriage, loses the house, loses the fortune. Crack! goes the sheriff's mallet on the last household valuable. Down lower and lower the man falls, until he pitches pennies for a drink, or clutches for devils that trample him in wild delirium. "The way of the transgressor is hard."

Sin comes to a young man and says, "Take this glass —it won't hurt you. It has a very fine flavor. Take a glass in the morning; it will be an appetizer. Take a glass at noon; it will aid digestion. Take a glass at night; it will make you sleep well." You are in a glow, while others are chilly. How bright it makes the eye— how elastic it makes the step! One day you meet him, and you say, "What are you doing here at noon? I thought you were at business." "Oh, I lost my place." "Lost your place?" God have mercy upon the young man when, through misdemeanor, he loses his place! Every temptation in hell takes after him. Hoppled and handcuffed, at thirty years of age, by evil habit! Save that young man; he is on the express train that stops not until it tumbles over the embankment of perdition. "The way of the transgressor is hard."

Sin comes to a young man, and says, "Take a dollar out of your employer's drawer; he won't miss it; you can put it back after a while. Take another! take another! Don't you see how easy it is? Hundreds of dollars added to your salary in a year!" One day the police knock at the door, and say, "I want you."

"What!" "I want you." Discovery has come; disgrace, imprisonment, loss of the soul. "The way of the transgressor is hard."

But you need not look through the wicket of the prison to learn this, and to find the frozen feet, and the bruised brow, and to hear the coughing lungs, resulting from crime. Every man has found out in his own experience that "The way of the transgressor is hard." Sin demeans us, sin is cruel, sin is desperate—it lacerates, it mauls the soul, it chains you like a dog, it drives you out like a dog, it throws refuse to you like a dog, it whips you with innumerable stripes like a dog. There is a legend abroad, of some one of whom it was foretold that she would die of a serpent's bite. The father, to keep her away from that, built a castle far out in the sea. He said no serpent could crawl there; but one day a boat came under the castle, and the daughter saw grapes in it, and, letting down a rope, she got the grapes, and was eating them, when she found a serpent entwined in the clusters. It stung her, and she died. Sin may seem luscious and ripe, and to have all the wealth of the vineyard, but at the last "it biteth like a serpent, and stingeth like an adder." Oh, have nothing to do with its approaches. It promises you a robe; it will cover you with rags. It offers you a chalice of luxurious beverage; it will fill you with wormwood. It promises you a throne; it will drive you into a kennel.

Again, my subject shows you *Jesus with his back turned.* That woman came to him and said, "Lord, spare the life of my child; it will not cost you any thing." Jesus turns his back. He throws positive discouragement upon her petition. Jesus stood with his *face* to blind Bartimeus, and the foaming demoniac, and the limping paralytic, and the sea when he hushed it, and the grave when he broke it; but now he turns his back. I asked an artist, a day or two ago, if he ever saw a representation of Jesus Christ with his back turned. He said, no. And it is a fact that you may go through all the picture-galleries of London and Dresden and Rome and Florence and Naples, and you will find Christ with full-face and profile, but never with his back turned. Yet here, in this passage, he turned away from the woman. And so, some of you have come at times and found Jesus with his face away from you. Here is somebody who is striving to be a Christian. He has cried to God for mercy, and he has been in as much anxiety about his soul as that Syrophenician woman was about her daughter. He has come to Christ and said, "Lord, look this way." No answer. He said, "Lord Jesus Christ, look this way. I come with a soul sin-sick. Look this way." What did Christ say? "You are a sinner, you are a vile sinner, you are a condemned sinner, you are a dying sinner. Do you expect all the glories of heaven to be given to one as wayward as you have been?" But do not be discouraged, oh seeking soul! put down the pack of thy sins at Jesus's feet anyhow. If his face is turned away from thee, then put down thy pack of sins at his heel. Then, if perchance he step backward, he will fall over it into thine outstretched arms, oh waiting sinner! Jesus will turn his face at the right time. Remember that mercy postponed is mercy augmented. If the waters of thy soul come to flood-tide, they will break away the dam. If the arrowhead be drawn clear back to the bow, it is only that it may be projected farther. If Christ turn his back to thee, it is only that the dawn on his face may be more effulgent. Oh, what are a few days or hours of darkness and struggle compared with the eternal illumination! What were the five minutes in which this Syrophenician woman stood in bitterness behind Jesus, compared with the eighteen hundred years in which she has rejoiced before him? Courage, oh sorrowing soul! "Weeping may endure for a night, but joy cometh in the morning." Many a man has put his hand over his shoulder to find the cross, and lo! it was gone; but in bringing his hand back again, he has struck the crown on his head, radiant with pardon and glory. I see horses dashing down the street. They draw a chariot. Who is in it? A man with a bandage over his mouth, and his head wrapped in folds. Who is it? Naaman, the leper. He drives up in front of the place where the prophet lives. The charioteer cries, "Whoa! Whoa!" They stop there. They wait for the prophet to come out. He does not come. He merely sends word, "Go wash in the Jordan, and thou shalt be healed." And so we come for Christ's mercy. That mercy may not have appeared as we expected, but let us be willing to take it at any time and in any way it shall come. Blessed are all they who put their trust in him.

Again, I see in my subject *Jesus conquered by a human soul.* That woman said, "Take this disease away from my daughter." Christ responded to her, "It is not meet to take the children's bread, and cast it to dogs." Then she roused her soul into an acuteness of expression seldom equaled by poet or painter, or orator or satirist, when she said, "Yea, Lord, but even the dogs eat of the crumbs that fall from their master's table." Then he turned, and flung pardon and healing and help into her soul with the words, "O woman! great is thy faith; be it unto thee even as thou wilt. And her daughter was made whole from that very hour." I have talked to you sometimes of Jesus, the conqueror. Listen now about Jesus, the conquered. You have seen him on the white horse of victory, all heaven following him on white horses, in his right hand the drawn sword of universal dominion; the moon under his feet, the stars his tiara; the sun only the rocket shot up in the signal-service of his great host; burning worlds only the bonfires of his victory. But now see him surrender—faith, humility, and prayer triumphant.

There are some things which are impossible for Christ: he can not break his oath; he can not despise the humble; he can not resist the cry of faith. Heaven sheathes its sword. It seems as if the prayer of the Syrophenician woman has conquered Omnipotence. The cavalry troop that John saw coming down the hills of heaven fall back. Behold the victories of prayer! History tells us of Queen Caroline, who, in 1820, tried to get into Westminster Abbey, at the coronation of George IV., her offended husband. With six shining bays, and in a carriage of state, she rode up to the door. She tried this door; no admittance. She tried another door; they demanded tickets. She came to another door, and said, "Surely you will not keep out your queen;" but they said, "We have no orders for your admittance." So she mounted her carriage and rode away in derision. Let me say that the attempt to get into the temple of Christ's mercy will be fruitless if we come with pride and come in pomp. We can not ride through the gates in state—

we can not come with plumes or pretension. Richly-robed Queen Caroline failed at Westminster Abbey with George IV.; but the Syrophenician woman of the text, at the door of Christ's mercy, succeeded with the Lord of earth and heaven. She wanted only the crumbs—she is invited to sit up as a banqueter. Bitter Valley Forge comes before victorious Yorktown. The kingdom of heaven is large enough when you get into it, but the gate is so low that you can not come in save on your knees. O man! O woman out of Christ! push your way this day into that kingdom. With earnest, importunate, confident, persistent prayer conquer all the obstacles in your way. I suppose that the people who were standing around about the woman and around about Christ said, "Don't bother Jesus with that matter. You can't make any impression on him. He has no medicine. If the doctors of the village can't cure your daughter, Christ can't do it; besides that, you can see, from his looks, that he don't care any thing for you." The woman knew better. With prayer she seized Christ, and with omnipotent cure Christ seized the invalid, and "she was made whole from that very hour." Oh, bring the diseases of your body, bring the diseases of your soul, to Christ! If his face be turned away from you, keep on until he shall turn his face to you. Persevere, implore, beseech, agonize, and conquer.

Why, my friends, you talk as though there were a greater amount of perseverance to be used in the matter of becoming a Christian than in any thing else. Let me say, you have five hundred times in your life exerted more perseverance and put forth more determination than would have made you a Christian. You put it out in worldly directions. If you had taken a thousandth part of your worldly earnestness, and with it gone toward Christ, you would have found him. How men seek for the wealth of this world! Is any man utterly discouraged if he does not make a fortune this year? Does he not keep on trying and trying? Who here, especially among the young, has given up the idea of getting at least a competency? Not one. And yet how treasures do fall out by the way! I was reading, a day or two ago, of the fact that in 1861 there were in this country failures in business amounting to two hundred millions of dollars, and that in 1857 there were failures in this country amounting to two hundred and ninety-seven millions of dollars. Yet who stopped seeking after money? Let me tell you that if you had sought with one-half of the earnestness after Christ and eternal treasures which characterized your search for earthly perishables, you would long ago have had the joy and peace of the Gospel. So it is with the honors of the world. How men push out their energies in that direction, and toil and drudge, and yet how little they are worth after they are gotten! How mightily it was illustrated in the history of William the Conqueror. The world bowed down before him, and yet, when he came to die, the rabble rushed into the room and stole the pictures, and actually stole the last shred of clothing off the corpse of William the Conqueror. And then, when they came to bury him in the chancel of the church, a man stood up with a strong protest that actually staggered back the pall-bearers and procession, and inquired why such a miserable carcass as that should be let down into the church chancel? All the world honoring him a little while before—now all the glory departed! But the failure of the world's honors have not discouraged you; you have pushed on after them. When I see that one-half of that energy put out in the direction of the Lord Jesus Christ would have brought you into the peace and the life of the Gospel, I do not ask you to exert any more energy in the divine direction than you do in the worldly direction, but just as much. Strive to enter into the straight gate. Take the kingdom of heaven by violence. Come up to Christ as this Syrophenician woman did, and refuse to be put off, and pray, and pray, and pray again, until he shall turn his face of benediction and mercy upon you.

Are you sitting here this morning unmoved while your last opportunity of salvation is going away from you? Spring is coming. Do you see the ice going out of the river? You see the snow melting. Soon the voice of the turtle will be heard in the land. Are there any signs that the winter is breaking up in your soul? Is the only sound there that of the bittern, and the owl of the night, and the petrel crying through the everlasting storm? When I think of the perils that hang around those who have not secured the pardon of the Gospel, I feel that I must leave the platform and take you by the shoulder, and cry out in your ear, as the angel did to Lot, "Escape for thy life; look not behind thee, neither stay thou in all the plain; escape to the mountain, lest thou be consumed." I know that the critics sometimes say I am too importunate in pleading with men about their souls; but how can I observe formalities and oratorical proprieties when I see sitting before me thousands within a short time of hell or heaven?

Will you be like the Syrophenician woman upon

whom Christ turned his back? Oh, he will not turn it for five minutes. But from those who finally reject him Christ will turn away; and no entreaty, no cry for mercy, no groaning will win his favor. The harvest will be past, and the summer ended, and the day of grace gone forever! Can that be all true, or is this a fable? Am I merely imagining it? Will there be no great ordeal when you and I, my brethren, must stand naked and hear our doom—Christ saying to some on that day, "Come, ye blessed"—that invitation chiming like the very bells of heaven? Will there be a cry, "Depart, ye cursed?" Coming from the study of the Bible this morning into your presence, I feel overwhelmed by these truths, and I cry out, If the Lord be God, follow him. Make up your mind whether the Bible is right or not. If it is wrong, quit these assemblages; they do not amount to any thing. If the Bible is wrong, stop praying; it does not amount to any thing. But if it is all truth, if I am an immortal man, and yet a dying man, if this body must soon perish, and then my soul rise up into the presence of Almighty God, and stand before him in judgment, oh let me appreciate it, and let me act upon it! By the crushed heart of the Son of God, by the flaming throne of heaven, by the raging furnaces of hell, fly for thy life! "Let the wicked forsake his way." I do not ask what sins you have committed. I do not come with a partial Gospel. I do not say, "This man may receive the Gospel, and for that man there will be no mercy." I tell you Christ's arm of mercy is stretched out far enough to take in all this audience, saying, "Whosoever will, let him take the water of life freely." Did you ever have a better offer than that? — pardon for all your sins, comfort for all your trouble, shelter in all your temptations, peace when you die, and joy forever. And all "without money and without price." May that Almighty Spirit, without which the heart stays hard, and all Christian entreaty is unavailing—may that Spirit this morning set before you the stupendous issue of this hour. Oh, eternity! where shall I spend it? Where will you spend it? Oh, eternity! Joys that will never fade! sorrows that never end!—which shall be mine? Which shall be yours?

## ORDERED BACK TO THE GUARD-ROOM.

"Felix trembled, and answered, Go thy way for this time; when I have a convenient season, I will call for thee."—*Acts* xxiv., 25.

A CITY of marble was Cesarea—wharves of marble, houses of marble, temples of marble. This being the ordinary architecture of the place, you may imagine something of the splendor of Governor Felix's residence. In a room of that palace, floor tesselated, windows curtained, ceiling fretted, the whole scene affluent with Tyrian purple, and statues, and pictures, and carvings, sat a very dark-complexioned man by the name of Felix, and beside him a woman of extraordinary beauty, whom he had stolen by breaking up another domestic circle. She was only eighteen years of age, a princess by birth, and unwittingly waiting for her doom—that of being buried alive in the ashes and scoria of Mount Vesuvius, which in sudden eruption, one day, put an end to her abominations. Well, one afternoon, Drusilla, seated in the palace, weary with the magnificent stupidities of the place, says to Felix: "You have a very distinguished prisoner, I believe, by the name of Paul. Do you know he is one of my countrymen? I should very much like to see him, and I should very much like to hear him speak, for I have heard so much about his eloquence. Besides that, the other day, when he was being tried in another room of this palace, and the windows were open, I heard the applause that greeted the speech of Lawyer

Tertullus, as he denounced Paul. Now, I very much wish I could hear Paul speak. Won't you let me hear him speak?" "Yes," said Felix, "I will. I will order him up now from the guard-room." Clank, clank, comes a chain up the marble stairway, and there is a shuffle at the door, and in comes Paul, a little old man, prematurely old through exposure—only sixty years of age, but looking as though he were eighty. He bows very courteously before the Governor and the beautiful woman by his side. They say: "Paul, we have heard a great deal about your speaking; give us now a specimen of your eloquence." Oh! if there ever was a chance for a man to show off, Paul had a chance there. He might have harangued them about Grecian art, about the wonderful water-works he had seen at Corinth, about the Acropolis by moonlight, about prison life in Philippi, about "what I saw in Thessalonica," about the old mythologies; but "No!" Paul said to himself: "I am now on the way to martyrdom, and this man and woman will soon be dead, and this is my only opportunity to talk to them about the things of eternity." And just there and then, there broke in upon the scene a peal of thunder. It was the voice of a judgment-day speaking through the words of the decrepit apostle. As that grand old missionary proceeded with his remarks, the stoop begins to go out of his shoulders, and he rises up, and his countenance is illumined with the glories of a future life, and his shackles rattle and grind as he lifts his fettered arm, and with it hurls upon his abashed auditors the bolts of God's indignation. Felix grew very white about the lips. His heart beat unevenly. He put his hand to his brow, as though to stop the quickness and violence of his thoughts.

He drew his robe tighter about him, as under a sudden chill. His eyes glare and his knees shake, and, as he clutches the side of his chair in a very paroxysm of terror, he orders the sheriff to take Paul back to the guard-room. "Felix trembled, and said, Go thy way for this time; when I have a convenient season, I will call for thee." A young man came one night to our services, with pencil in hand, to caricature the whole scene, and make mirth of those who should express any anxiety about their souls; but I met him at the door, his face very white, tears running down his cheek, as he said, "Do you think there is any chance for me?" Felix trembled, and so may God grant it may be here to-night!

I propose to give you two or three reasons why I think Felix sent Paul back to the guard-room, and adjourned this whole subject of religion. The first reason was, he *did not want to give up his sins.* He looked around; there was Drusilla. He knew that when he became a Christian, he must send her back to Azizus, her lawful husband, and he said to himself, "I will risk the destruction of my immortal soul, sooner than I will do that." How many there are now who can not get to be Christians, because they will not abandon their sins! In vain all their prayers and all their church-going. You can not keep these darling sins and win heaven; and to-night some of you will have to decide between the wine-cup, and unlawful amusements, and lascivious gratifications on the one hand, and eternal salvation on the other. Delilah sheared the locks of Samson; Salome danced Herod into the pit; Drusilla blocked up the way to heaven for Felix; and unless some of you repent, you shall likewise perish. Yet when I present the subject to-night, I fear that some of you will say, "Not quite yet. Don't be so precipitate in your demands. I have a few tickets yet that I have to use. I have a few engagements that I must keep. I want to stay a little longer in the whirl of conviviality—a few more guffaws of unclean laughter, a few more steps on the road to death, and then, sir, I will listen to what you say. 'Go thy way for this time; when I have a convenient season, I will call for thee.'" Do you know that your boat is on the edge of the maelstrom, and that the foam on the wave is the frothing lip of the destroyed; and that the gleam in the water is the glaring eyeballs of the banished; and that the roar of the wave is the groan of the damned? Oh, I know that it is a great deal easier, when you are in a boat, to pull ahead the same way you are going; but if to-night you see that you are within a few yards of the vortex, and that this may be your last hour —aye, your last moment, you had better turn around in the boat, you had better clutch with both hands the handles of the oars, as with a death grip, and, putting the blades down into the black waters, pull for your eternal life, crying, "Lord, save me, I perish!" Can you not offer such a prayer to-night, oh man! long wandering away from your God? Who is that I see running up and down in the prison-house of the lost, now trying to break through this gate, and failing, turning around and rushing to the other gate, and beating against it, and in despair crying, "Let me get out?" Who is it? Some soul to-night that will not give up his indulgences; some soul to-night that is bound hand and foot by the powers of darkness; some soul here that has a darling sin that he will not sacrifice, and who says to me, when

I present the great themes of God and eternity to his soul, "Not yet; go thy way for this time; when I have a convenient season, I will call for thee."

Another reason why Felix sent Paul back to the guard-room and adjourned this subject was, *he was so very busy.* In ordinary times he found the affairs of state absorbing, but those were extraordinary times. The whole land was ripe for insurrection. The Sicarii, a band of assassins, were already prowling around the palace, and I suppose he thought, "I can't attend to religion while I am so pressed by affairs of state." It was business, among other things, that ruined his soul, and I suppose there are three thousand people in this house to-night who are not children of God because they have so much business. It is business in the store—losses, gains, unfaithful employés. It is business in your law office —subpœnas, writs you have to write out, papers you have to file, arguments you have to make. It is your medical profession, with its broken nights, and the exhausting anxieties of life hanging upon your treatment. It is your real estate office, your business with landlords and tenants, and the failure of men to meet their obligations with you. Ay, with some of those who are here, it is the annoyance of the kitchen, and the sitting-room, and the parlor—the wearing economy of trying to meet large expenses with a small income. Ten thousand voices of "business, business, business," drown the voice of the Eternal Spirit, silencing the voice of the advancing judgment-day, overcoming the voice of an agonizing eternity; and they can not hear, they can not listen. They say, "Go thy way for this time." Some of you look upon your goods, you look upon your profession, you look upon your memorandum-books, and you see the demands that are made this very week upon your time and your patience and your money; and while I am entreating you about your soul and the danger of procrastination, you say, "Go thy way for this time; when I have a convenient season, I will call for thee." Oh Felix, why be bothered about the affairs of this world so much more than about the affairs of glory or perdition? Do you not know that when death comes you will have to stop business, though it be in the most exacting period of it—between the payment of the money and the taking of the receipt. The moment he comes you will have to go. Death waits for no man, however high, however low. Will you put your office, will you put your shop in comparison with the affairs of an eternal world? affairs that involve thrones, palaces, dominions eternal. Will you put two hundred acres of ground against immensity? Will you put forty or fifty years of your life against millions of ages? Oh Felix, you might better postpone every thing else! for do you not know that the upholstering of Tyrian purple in your palace will fade, and the marble blocks of Cesarea will crumble, and the breakwater at the beach, made of great blocks of stone sixty feet long, must give way before the perpetual wash of the sea; but the redemption that Paul offers you will be forever? and yet, and yet, and yet you wave him back to the guard-room, saying, "Go thy way for this time; when I have a convenient season, I will call for thee."

Again, Felix adjourned this subject of religion and put off Paul's argument, because he *could not give up the honors of the world.* He was afraid somehow he would be compromised himself in this matter. Remarks he made afterward showed him to be intensely ambitious. Oh how he hugged the favor of men!

I never saw the honors of this world in their hollowness and hypocrisy so much as I have seen them within the last few days, as I have been looking over the life and death of that wonderful man just departed, Charles Sumner. Now that he is dead, the whole nation takes off the hat. As he goes out toward the place of burial, even Independence Hall, in Philadelphia, asks that his remains may stop there on their way to Boston. The flags are at half-mast, and the minute-guns on Boston Common throb, now that his heart has ceased to beat. Was it always so? While he lived, how censured of legislative resolutions, how caricatured of the pictorials; how charged with every motive mean and ridiculous; how all the urns of scorn and hatred and billingsgate emptied upon his head; how, when struck down in Senate chamber, there were hundreds of thousands of people who said, "Good for him, served him right!" how, summer before last, he had to put the ocean between him and his maligners, that he might have a little peace, and how, when he went off sick, they said he was broken-hearted because he could not get to be President or Secretary of State. Oh Commonwealth of Massachusetts! who is that man that sleeps to-night in your public hall, covered with garlands and wrapped in the stars and stripes? Is that the man who, only a few months ago, you denounced as the foe of republican and democratic institutions? Is that the same man? You were either wrong then or you are wrong now—a thing most certain, oh Commonwealth of Massachusetts! Ye American people, ye can not, by one week of funeral eulogium and newspaper leaders, which the dead senator can neither read nor hear, atone for twenty-five years of maltreatment and caricature. When I see a man like that, pursued by all the hounds of the political kennel so long as he lives, and then buried under great piles of garlands, and amidst the lamentations of a whole nation, I say to myself, What an unutterably hypocritical thing is all human applause and all human favor! You took twenty-five years in trying to pull down his fame, and now you will take twenty-five years in trying to build his monument. You were either wrong then, or you are wrong now. My friends, was there ever a better commentary on the hollowness of all earthly favor? If there are young men in this house who are postponing religion in order that they may have the favors of this world, let me persuade them of their complete folly. If you are looking forward to gubernatorial, senatorial, or presidential chair, let me show you your great mistake. Can it be that now in the presence of these great national solemnities there is any young man saying, "Let me have some political office, let me have some of these high positions of trust and power, and then I will attend to religion; but not now. 'Go thy way for this time; when I have a convenient season, I will call for thee!'"

And now my subject takes a deeper tone, and it shows what a dangerous thing is this deferring of religion. When Paul's chain rattled down the marble stairs of Felix, that was Felix's last chance for heaven. Judging from his character afterward, he was reprobate and abandoned.

It is eighteen centuries now since Felix lost his soul;

it is lost yet. I suppose that Drusilla went to the same place. One day in Southern Italy there was a trembling of the earth, and the air got black with smoke intershot with liquid rocks, and Vesuvius rained upon her and upon her son a horrible tempest of ashes and fire. They did not reject religion; they only put it off. They did not understand that that day, that that hour when Paul stood before them, was the pivotal hour upon which every thing was poised, and that it tipped the wrong way. Their convenient season came when Paul and his guardsman entered the palace: it went away when Paul and his guardsman left. Have you never seen men waiting for a convenient season? There is such a great fascination about it, that though you may have come in here to-night, and may sit or stand with great respect to the truth of Christ, yet somehow there is in your soul the thought, "Not quite yet. It is not time for me to become a Christian." I say to a boy, "Seek Christ." He says, "No; wait until I get to be a young man." I say to the young man, "Seek Christ." He says, "Wait until I come to mid-life." I meet the same person in mid-life, and I say, "Seek Christ." He says, "Wait until I get old." I meet the same person in old age, and say to him, "Seek Christ." He says, "Wait until I am on my dying bed." I am called to his dying couch. His last moments have come. I bend over the couch and listen for his last words. I have partially to guess what they are by the motion of his lips, he is so feeble; but rallying himself, he whispers, until I can hear him say, "I—am—waiting —for—a more—convenient—season"—and he is gone!

I can tell you when your convenient season will come. I can tell you the year—it will be 1874. I can tell you the month—it will be the month of March. I can tell you what kind of a day it will be—it will be the Sabbath-day. I can tell you what hour it will be—it will be between eight and ten o'clock. In other words, it is *now*—a word of three letters; but each one an anthem, or a jubilee, or a coronation, or a dungeon, or a groan. Do you ask me how I know this is your convenient season? I know it because you are here, and because the Holy Spirit is here, and because the elect sons and daughters of God in this church are praying for your redemption, and because the women of the church, last Thursday afternoon, especially implored the blessing of God upon the morning and evening services of to-day. I know it because this matter was up on Friday evening at the prayer-meeting, and this morning in the prayer-meeting, and in the preceding prayer-meeting this evening. We prayed that God would come by his Holy Spirit and save your souls, and so I know this is your convenient season. I know it also from the fact that two great national funeral bells, one from the East and the other from the West, are tolling through all the valleys, and over all the mountains of the land—tolling, tolling, "Put not your trust in princes, neither in the son of man in whom there is no help; their breath goeth forth, in that very day their thoughts perish." Ay, I know it is your convenient season because some of you, like Felix, tremble as all your past life comes upon you with its sin, and all the future life comes upon you with its terror. This night air is aglare with torches to show you up or to show you down. It is rustling with wings to lift you into light, or smite you into despair, and there is a rushing to and fro, and a shouting, and a wailing, and a leaping, and a falling, and a beating against the door of your soul as with a great thunder of emphasis, telling you, "Now, now is the best time, as it may be the only time."

My friends, be quick. You have no time to waste. Be quick, the days of your life are going. Be quick, the hour of your death is coming. Be quick, the time of grace has almost closed with some of you; perhaps it may be closed with some of you to-night. Be quick, lest some paralysis seize upon you as upon our venerable ex-President, just carried out, or you have no more time than the illustrious senator who fell this week—only time to say as he did, putting his hand upon his heart, "*Oh!* oh!" and you be gone!

May God Almighty forbid that any of you, my brethren or sisters, act the part of Felix and Drusilla, and put away this great subject. If you are going to be saved ever, why not begin to-night? Throw down your sins and take the Lord's pardon. Christ has been tramping after you many a day.

An Indian and a white man became Christians. The Indian, almost as soon as he heard the Gospel, believed and was saved; but the white man struggled on in darkness for a long while before he found light. After their peace in Christ, the white man said to the Indian, "Why was it that I was kept so long in the darkness, and you immediately found peace?" The Indian replied, "I will tell you. A prince comes along, and he offers you a coat. You look at your coat, and you say, 'My coat is good enough,' and you refuse his offer; but the prince comes along and he offers me the coat, and I look at my old blanket and I throw that away, and take his offer.

You, sir," continued the Indian, "are clinging to your own righteousness, you think you are good enough, and you keep your own righteousness; but I have nothing, nothing, and so when Jesus offers me pardon and peace, I simply take it." My hearer, why not now throw away the worn-out blanket of your sin and take the robe of a Saviour's righteousness—a robe so white, so fair, so lustrous, that no fuller on earth can whiten it? Oh, Shepherd, to-night bring home the lost sheep! Oh, Father, to-night give a welcoming kiss to the wan prodigal! Oh, friend of Lazarus, to-night break down the door of the sepulchre, and say to all these dead souls as by irresistible fiat, "*Live!* LIVE!"

## FREE CHURCHES ADVOCATED.

"The rich and poor meet together: the Lord is the maker of them all."—*Proverbs* xxii., 2.

NO one class in a community is independent of the other classes. That is not a healthful condition of society in which men stand aloof from each other. That is a better state when people, moving in different circles, at some time come upon a common platform. What is true in the world is true in the Church: "the rich and the poor *ought* to meet together: the Lord is the maker of them all." I do not think that the Church of Christ has kept pace with the enterprise of the world. Some years ago, it took a long time to make a nail. The blacksmith would take the bar of iron, thrust it into the hot coals, move the bellows, bring the iron out on the anvil, smite it, cleave it, round it, fashion it into nails. It was a long and tedious process; but now the iron is put into a machine, and in a moment hundreds of nails are showered upon the floor of the manufactory. Once it required some time to thresh wheat from the straw. The farmer would take the sheaf of wheat, tear off the straw that bound it, scatter it on the floor of the barn, and then the slow flail would pound the wheat out of the straw; now the horses start, and the machine rumbles, and a sheaf of wheat is threshed instantly.

In olden times that was considered a wonderful printing-press which could make two hundred and fifty impressions in an hour; now, by our modern steam printing-press, thousands and tens of thousands are made in the same length of time.  The Post-office was formerly a slow affair.  Once in two weeks the mail would go from London to Edinburgh, and at about the same distance of time go from New York to Boston; but now, half a dozen times a day, you must look out or you will be run over by the wagons that come down Nassau Street with whole tons of United States mails, seven hundred millions of letters and papers having passed through the public post-offices of this country in one year.

So there has been an advance in jurisprudence.  In 1846 the constitution of our State was changed, improvements were made in the criminal code, in the civil code—law that would do very well in 1777, not doing at all in 1873.  Now, I ask if the Church of God has kept pace with worldly enterprise? with the post-office? with modern railroad transportation? with the arts? with the sciences? with optics? with geology? with astronomy? "Oh," you say, "there is no new principle in religion to be developed."  Well, I respond, there is no new principle in science to be developed.  They are only the old principles that have come to light and demonstration.  There was just as much electricity in the clouds before Benjamin Franklin played kite with the thunder-storms as there has been since.  The law of gravitation did not wait for Newton to come.  There was just as much power in steam before Fulton discovered it as since.  The carboniferous and jurassic strata of the earth did not wait to take their position until Hugh Miller planted his crow-bar.  So, in matters of religion, if a man comes, and says, "I have now discovered an entirely new principle in religion;" I say, "I have no faith in what you are going to say. I have but one standard, and that is the Bible." But if he says, "I have an old Bible principle that I wish to evolve and demonstrate," then, with all the possible attention of my soul, I say, "Hear! hear!"

I propose to-night to argue on behalf of a Free Church. There are a great many who do not quite understand the plans and policies of such a church. In the first place, I believe in such a church because it seems to me to be *the Scriptural idea*. The apostle James says: "If there come into your assembly a man with a gold ring, in goodly apparel, and there come in also a poor man in vile raiment; and ye have respect to him that weareth the gay clothing, and say unto him, Sit thou here in a good place; and say to the poor, Stand thou there, or sit here under my footstool: are ye not then partial in yourselves, and are become judges of evil thoughts?" In other words, the apostle James draws a picture. It is a meeting of Christian people; the usher stands at the door; two people come to the door and ask for seats. The usher looks at the one man, examines him from head to foot, sees that his garments are dictated by the recent fashion, and says, "Come here, sir, I'll give you an excellent seat;" takes him far up in front, gives him a seat, and says, "I hope you will be very comfortable." Then the usher goes back, sees the other man, scrutinizes him very thoroughly, and says, "Poor coat, worn shoes, old hat. I think you will find a very good place to stand in that corner." Now, the lightnings of that passage strike such an usher; in other words, you have no right to arrange a man's position in the house of God according to his financial qualifications. Do you suppose that the seats in the tabernacle of olden time, the temple, and the synagogue, were ever rented by worshipers? Oh no; you tell me those were miraculous times. You say in our times churches are such expensive institutions. We want all this costly machinery. Let me tell you no church of the day costs half so much as did the old temple, and yet that temple in olden times was supported by voluntary contributions. When the farmer brought his harvest in, he said, "These sheaves are for the Lord." When the flocks were drawn up, he said, "These lambs are for God." When the birds were caught, he said, "These pigeons, and these doves, are for sacrifice." The temple, the tabernacle, all supported by voluntary contributions. But you say men were more generous in those times. No, no; the world has been advancing all the time; there has never been so much generosity on earth as now.

Do you suppose it would have been possible for the Christian and Sanitary commissions that we had during the last war to have prospered in those ancient times? No, they could not have been supported two thousand, one thousand, or five hundred years ago. They are projected in this Christian age. Now, I say, if in those dark times, and in that wicked city of Jerusalem, the temple could be supported by voluntary contributions, can we not in this Christian age, and in the full blaze of the Gospel light, and when the doctrine of Christian beneficence is so much inculcated, support a plain church? The fact is, that the modes of constructing church finances have chilled the voluntary principle, and dammed back the charities of the world; when, if we had gone back to the old Bible plan in all our churches, there would have been larger benevolence and a more extensive support of the institutions of religion. So that I come back now with more emphasis than ever, to say, "If there come into your assembly a man with a gold ring and goodly apparel, and there come in also a poor man with vile raiment, and ye have respect to him that weareth the gay clothing, and say unto him, Sit thou here in a good place, and say to the poor, Stand thou there, or sit here under my footstool, are ye not then partial in yourselves, and are become judges of evil thoughts?" Oh, how different it would be in all our churches if, instead of having them supported by a few men, we could have the great masses of the people bring their mites into the Lord's treasury.

I argue, farther, in behalf of a Free Church, because I think it is the only practical common-sense mode for city evangelization. The Church has tried scores of ways. We have gone out with tracts, and with our Bibles and religious books, among the people in the destitute parts of the city. Some have refused to take them. Some have burned them up. Some have read them and tried to reform; but as long as we leave them down amidst the evil influences by which they are surrounded, and do not bring them into some Christian church—if you reform them fifty times, fifty times they will be unreformed. In other words, here is a man down by the marshes with chills and fever. The physician comes and gives him quinine, and stops the chills; but just as long as that man continues to live down by the swamps, he will be subjected to the same ailment. Bring him out on the hill-top, where the atmosphere is clear, if you want him to be permanently restored. Now, I say of those people who live in the slums of city destitution, as long as you leave them there they will fall into their old sins; but if you bring them into the healthy atmosphere of a Christian church, then you may hope for their permanent reformation. If you can say to them, "There is a free church, there is a free Bible, there is a free cross, and yonder is a free heaven," they will accept the invitation and come with you.

Mark this, my friends, that when you save the cities, you save the world. When Pekin comes to Christ, all China will come. When Paris surrenders to God, all France will surrender. When London prays, England will pray with her. When New York bows at the feet of Christ, the United States will bow with her. Save the cities, and you save the world.

I knew this city of Brooklyn eighteen years ago. Since then there have been great efforts made for the evangelization of the city, and yet you know as well as I that there is more sin in the city to-day, more Sabbath-breaking, and a vaster population who come not under any kind of religious influence. Where is Brooklyn to-day? In the churches? No! Where is New York to-day? In the churches? No! No! No! It is the exception when people go to church. A vast majority of the masses are traveling on down toward death, unassisted because uninvited. Now, if a surgeon goes into a hospital, and there are three hundred patients, and he cures twenty of them and the other two hundred and eighty die, I call that unsuccessful treatment. If the Church of God has saved some, when I compare the few that have been redeemed with the vast multitude that have perished, I say it has been a comparative failure;

and if the old plan of conducting the Church of Christ has failed, let us start the ship on another tack and try another plan. In other words, come back to the Gospel theory, and throw wide open the doors of our church and tell the people to come in, without regard to their past history or their present financial or moral condition.

Again, I argue in behalf of a Free Church, because there are *three or four classes of people that will especially be touched by it.* Among them will be men who were once very influential in the churches, but who lost their property, and consequently can not meet the pew-rents. I am not speaking of imaginary cases. I have seen scores of that kind of cases in the city of Brooklyn. In 1837, or in 1857, or 1867, they lost their property. They used to sit near the pulpit. The next year they went farther back in the church. The next year farther back, and farther back as their finances entirely failed them, until at last they sat back by the door; and when the treasurer went down the aisle, he tapped the man's shoulder and said, "If you don't pay up, you will have to vacate this seat." What became of that man? He went out from the house of God. What becomes of the great multitude who once were influential in the Church of God, who, having lost their property, can not meet the pew-rents in the churches? They have gone—some to infidelity—some into lives of dissipation—God only knows where they have gone! Will men of any self-respect go to church under such a state of circumstances? I tell you, nay. If it were my case, I would stay at home and gather my children about me, and read to them of Christ and a free heaven, out of which a man is never pitched because he can not pay his pew-rent! At the very time a man most needs the consolation of religion—when his earthly fortunes have failed—at the very time that he needs most to be told about treasures that never fail, in banks that never break—the Church of God turns its back upon that man, and the work of breaking down that the Wall Street gamblers began, the Church of God finishes. It seems as if Christ, in the infinity of his foreknowledge, could not think of a Church pretending to love him that would unanimously bar out the destitute. He said, "The poor ye have always with you." He made it not merely as a statement, but as a prophecy and a promise; and yet it does really *seem* as if, in this respect, the Lord God had been thwarted.

There is another class of persons to whom a Free Church will appeal, and that is *the middle classes*. And let me say they are the suffering ones in religious things. The wealthy may purchase religious advantages anywhere; the positively beggared may feel so humiliated, they will be willing to go into a mission chapel: but the middle classes have not money enough to buy positions in the wealthy churches, and they are too proud to go among the beggared. So they stay at home. When I say the middle classes, I mean those whose income just about meets their outgo; and you will immediately see that is the condition of nine hundred and ninety-nine out of every thousand in this city and in every city. The fact is, God does not trust us with money—I mean the majority of us. Your son is at school. You do not give him a large amount of money at the start. You say to the teacher, "Send in the bills." When the bills come in, you pay for the tuition, you pay for clothing, you pay for traveling expenses. Now God treats us very much in that way. He clothes us, pays our traveling expenses, shelters us, but never trusts us with a large amount of money. Hence the middle classes are in the majority—those men in a community are in the majority who, when they have met the butcher's bill, and the grocer's bill, and the gas bill, and the clothing bill, and paid their house-rent, have nothing left. The wife says to her husband, "My dear, I think we ought to go to church somewhere. Why don't we take a pew in Dr. Well-to-do's church?" "Oh," he says, "we can't afford it. I have more now to pay than I can pay. We can't go there. We've got to deny ourselves a little longer. We'll get a little religion perhaps at home. We'll occasionally read the Bible, and once in a while go to a funeral, and that won't cost us any thing; and we will pick up a little religion here and there; and after a while we may have good luck, and we will then rent a pew, and go to heaven respectably." Many a husband and wife have consulted with each other upon matters of church economy, and before taking a pew, the husband said to the wife, "Now, you know that our income only meets our outgo. What are you willing to deny yourself? Will you have this old carpet another year? Will you wear that set of furs another winter? Will you consent to have no more dresses this season?" "No," she says. "Then," he says, "we can't afford religion, and we can't afford the church." And so they stay at home. My friends, open the doors of a free church, where men may meet together without invidious comparisons, and they will pour in like the tides of the sea. We have been barring out this class of men from the house of God, and barring them out from the very gate of heaven.

The fact is, that the Church has become a sort of spiritual insurance company; and the man comes to get a policy, and you take him into a private room and sound the lungs, and listen to the beating of the heart, and then practically—not literally, but practically—you ask him if he is sound on the dollar question, and if he has been afflicted with any thing like bankruptcy, and if there has been any thing like financial sickness in the family; and if it is all right, you charge him a great premium, and tell him to be very careful and pay it promptly, for if the policy should run out, that very night he might die, and so lose all the advantages of all the pew-rent he had ever paid; and where his soul would go to would be very uncertain.

There is another class of people to whom a Free Church will appeal, and that is the *rich*. I am yet to find an intelligent and rich Christian man who does not believe in such an institution. He may doubt the financial success of it; but I am yet to find one such who does not believe in the principle of it. In other words, our moneyed men do not like to see the principles of Wall Street applied to the Church of God. When I say a rich man, I mean a man who has riches—not a man who has gained a little money and who is very anxious lest he can not sufficiently display it—but I mean a man who has a fortune, who masters it, and who has not allowed his fortune to master him. When you shall throw open the churches of the living God as free churches, then I want to tell you that the gold, and the silver, and the myrrh, and the frankincense will come down to the feet of Jesus. I am not merely theorizing. We demonstrated it in the old Tabernacle. There were the poor there. Then we had the middle classes—men who toiled; some with hand, and some with brain—for brain-work is poorly paid in this country. We had many of that class, and they had a hard struggle. Then we had more rich men than we ever had in the old city church—more than we ever expected—men who said, "I will pay for the Gospel not only for myself and my family, but *there* is a man in that pew who can not afford to pay any thing; I will pay for him. *There* is another man; I will pay for him. And instead of sending my money to foreign lands, where I have no doubt it does good, I will preach the Gospel to all those in the same church who can not afford to purchase religious advantages." So it was practically demonstrated; and we shall, God willing, on a larger scale demonstrate it in the new Tabernacle. And if you shall be afraid to come to such a place lest you be socially contaminated, I hope you will stay away, lest you contaminate us!

I am in favor of a Free Church, further, because *all the Providential indications*, so far as we are concerned, are in that direction. It has been the all-absorbing principle in my soul ever since I entered the ministry. It was the thing that brought me to this city. I had a comfortable home in Philadelphia, but this was a Gospel principle I thought I would like to see tried. I came here, and it so happened that all the people who gathered around me were of the same opinion, and so we have been unanimous. We were unanimous in the style of the new church, and about the architecture of the second. We were unanimous about having it free. When we were burned down we were unanimous about reconstruction, and the principle we developed in the old church we will try to develop in the new. Where the old Tabernacle stopped when it burned down, the new Tabernacle will begin when it rises up.

Again, I am in favor of the Free Church, because it appeals to *men of the world, as no other kind of church does.* A prominent minister of New York said to me a week or two ago, "There are no people who come into our churches here in New York but Christian people. Somehow, we do not get hold of the world." I said, "The majority of those who come into my religious services are of the world, and I think it must be that the free Christian principle is attracting them. In other words, men of the world can not understand the limitations and the exclusiveness of the house of God. They say, 'If you are brothers and sisters, why do not the rich and poor meet together? the Lord is the Maker of them all.'" "Oh," you say, "those men of the world do not do their duty." I know they do not do their duty; but if this world is to be brought to Christ—if Bibles are to be printed, if churches are to be built, if Christian institutions are to be supported—I ask you are not the dollars of the man of the world worth as much as the dollars of the man of the church? Besides that, we expect these men of the world *en masse* to march after a while into the kingdom of Christ. Having seen the frank, sympathetic men of the world around me as my companions, I expect they will be my companions when they and I have crossed the flood into the great eternity. I have lived with them in this city, and I expect they will be my neighbors in the better city. I know all their trials and temptations; I know all their business perplexities; I know all their hardships; and I want to stand before them a few years, and tell them of that Christ who will be their security in every financial strait and their bondsman in every crisis, and who, when the nations are in a panic and the world ablaze, will declare everlasting dividends of light, and joy, and triumph to all those who have invested their affections in him.

Men and brethren, brothers and sisters in Christ, are you ready for such a work? That which three years ago I talked to you as a mere theory has become a matter of practical demonstration. The night before the old Tabernacle was burned down, the trustees of my church met together, reviewed the finances, looked at the income, looked at the outgo, and decided that the income exceeded the outgo, proving a free church practicable. That being demonstrated, it was enough for that church. We will take that principle, and develop it on a larger scale. God will this year let you strike a blow that will ring through eternal ages. The grandeur of the work to which you have put your hand no language can describe, no imagination can conceive, no plummet sound, no ladder scale. If you shall, in the strength of God, as I think you will, rise up to this work of giving a free Gospel to the masses of Brooklyn and the masses of this country, it will take eternal ages for you to count up the rewards of your faithfulness. If some may scoff at you, let them scoff; remembering that they scoffed at Nehemiah, and at Daniel, and at Christ, and pronounced them fools. Remember, besides, that there are tens of thousands of good people in this land, and in Britain, who are praying for our success as a Church. Above all, remember that we are under the benediction of Him in whose word we trust and in whose strength we go forward. The mountains may depart, the seas may burn, the stars may scatter, the heavens may double up like parchment, the sun may burn down in the socket, and all the worlds fly in the Judgment-day like thistle-down in a tempest; but God will back out of his promises, and betray his discipleship, and break his oath—never! NEVER!

## OBJECTIONS TO FREE CHURCHES ANSWERED.

"The rich and poor meet together: the Lord is the maker of them all."—*Proverbs* xxii., 2.

LAST Sabbath I discoursed to you from these words, arguing in behalf of a free Christian church. I showed you, as well as I could, that it was a Scriptural idea; that it was the only practicable mode of city evangelization; that it appealed to a class of persons who would not otherwise be met; that, so far as we ourselves were concerned, all the Providential indications were in that direction; and then, lastly, that such an organization would enlist the sympathies of men of the world, as no other organization could. I resume the subject where I then left it.

What do you suppose Christ thinks of the present mode of conducting church finances? If Jesus were now to alight upon earth and build a church and assume its pastorate, would it be necessary for men to pay money in order to have seats in that church? From what you know of Christ's treatment of the widow with two mites, and of Mary Magdalen, and of the poor man by the wayside, do you think that a man's position in that particular church of Christ would be regulated according to the number of dollars that he could pay? No, says every man, that idea would be abhorrent to Christ. Well, then, I say it ought to be abhorrent to us. Do you wonder that there have been so many troubles in the churches—that many of them have fought like beasts at Ephesus, fought about the site upon which to build, fought about the architecture, fought about the choir, fought about the minister, fought before church, fought after church, fought all the week? Some of you know that the greatest conflicts of the last fifty years have been church troubles. If our churches were all regulated by the principles of Christ's religion, do you not believe that there would be a cessation to such combat? "But," says some one, "we must stick to the old plan, lest we shall not get on successfully in our finances," as though the present mode in the churches of conducting church finances were a success. Far from it. Three-fourths of the churches of Christ in this land are in debt, and in three-fourths of them the income does not equal the outgo, and, at the end of the year, a few generous men have to come together and make up the deficit, or some general effort is made on the part of the congregation to regulate the indebtedness. Ay, the regulation of church finances by the past mode is a positive failure. Every body knows that churches are the poorest pay, and that if a bank or an insurance company were conducted in the same slip-shod manner, so thoroughly inefficient — that it would be discredited and wiped out of existence. If the old mode of conducting church finances in the religious organizations had been thoroughly successful, then we might be on our guard; but as the fact is, in nine cases out of ten, it has been a failure; I say there is no danger in floating off from it.

But this brings me to answer the first objection which can be made to a free church, and that is, that *it can not*

## OBJECTIONS TO FREE CHURCHES ANSWERED. 229

*be financially supported.* You say that there is a great deal of expensive machinery in a church; there is the coal bill, and the gas bill, and the insurance bill, and the expenses of sexton, and music, and minister, and, as free churches ought to be conducted on a large and generous scale, there will be extraordinary expenses. Ay, we admit all this. In a free church the music should be of the very best possible character, every hymn storming the very gates of heaven. The church architecture ought to be plain but imposing, the people seated face to face in the great congregation. The preaching ought to be earnest. Indeed, it is a great deal easier to preach in such a church than in any other. If a man has been for a long time at a banquet, and five or six courses of food have passed before him, then when plain bread is presented he rejects it; but if you take that plain bread to men who for forty-eight hours have had nothing to eat, how they will clutch for it! Now I simply say that a vast majority of the people who have been attending our Christian churches have been stuffed for these twenty years with the confections of religion, and when we present them the plain bread of the Gospel, they do not want it; but if we should gather into our churches the outside masses who are starving for this bread of life, with what earnestness and with what avidity they would seize upon it. "But," you say, "the support of a church with such music, and with such architecture, and earnest preaching, would be very expensive, and how will you meet the indebtedness?" I answer: by annual subscription and by Sabbath collections. "But," you say, "there will be mean men who will come and occupy the pews and pay nothing, and so the financial interests of the church will go overboard." I acknowledge that there are mean men in churches. There are men with souls so small that fifty of them might dance on the point of a needle and have room to turn around without touching their elbows! I had in my church at Syracuse, New York, a man of comfortable means who gave nothing for the support of the Gospel; but Friday night after Friday night I heard him pray that the pastor might be blessed in his basket and store, while all the time I was thinking, if I were dependent upon you, I would have a small basket and a very poor store! The man is gone to a better country, and where, I hope, he can live more economically. But while there are mean men in the Church, I want you to understand that the majority of people who come to the house of God are not of that class. In our tabernacle, which was conducted on the free principle, there were only three or four such persons.

My observation is, that if you take a common-sense principle and lay it before common-sense men, and say that is for the improvement of society and the bettering of the condition of the world, men will generously support it; and as nine-tenths of the people in a community can understand the free church principle when it is plainly set before them, I believe that plan may anywhere and everywhere be developed. I have as much doubt of the existence of God and of a future world, and of the blessedness of the Gospel, as I have of the willingness of the people to support a free church in any town or city in all this country; in other words, I have no doubt at all. Says some one, "Is it right to put ministers of the Gospel in a way where they shall have an uncertainty of livelihood?" I reply by saying that if a man have a million dollars, and he give you a check for twenty-five dollars, when you go to the bank and present that check you know there is such a large margin between the man's capacity and that small check, that you have no doubt that it will be promptly cashed. Now Christ says to his ministers, "Go and preach my Gospel; I am able to take care of you. I will take care of you. Lo, I am with you alway—even unto the end of the world. The cattle on a thousand hills are mine, all the treasures of the universe are at my feet. Go, work in my vineyard, and you shall want no good thing." Alas, then, if we who are in the ministry fold our hands and begin to tremble and say, "Dear Lord, that is a beautiful principle, but where is my salary to come from?" Besides that, I want you to remember that the young men who will be willing to connect themselves with the free churches of this country—though they may not have large means now with which to help you—still they are, after a while, to shoulder the great church enterprises. Who are your poor men to-day? Largely, they who twenty years ago were in affluence. Who are your rich men to-day? Those who twenty years ago were in poverty, struggling up from the very foot of the ladder. I say these young men who are clerks in our stores on five hundred dollars a year, or a thousand dollars, or fifteen hundred, will after a while, under God, be the mighty men on 'Change; and though now, when they connect themselves with your church, they may be of little or of no financial help, after they have made their fortunes, as they will, every dollar of those fortunes will be consecrated to Christ. So that we may look in that direction and feel that there will be help.

My friends, unless the great masses of the people can be brought into our churches, what is to become of our cities? Do you know the fact that crime, and debauchery, and every sort of abomination are triumphing in our great towns? Just take out your pencils and make a calculation; it is only a question in common arithmetic— How long, if evil influences continue to increase at the same ratio, how long before the religion of Christ in our cities will be discomfited and our churches destroyed? In less than a century, as certain as two and two make four, unless some other plan is tried. Yet we know that religion is to triumph, and that sin is to go down, and that Christ is to reign in all our cities; but it will be by some other plan; it will be when the churches of Christ are thrown wide open, and the people told to come in, without any regard to their financial qualifications, and hear the Gospel and get prepared for heaven. The possibility of establishing and sustaining such a church is strengthened by the idea that men will support home institutions rather than foreign. How many of you were ever kept awake at night because the Gospel does not prosper in Greenland? How many ever refused food because there is heathenism in Guatemala? None! But when you can bring before men the question, What is to become of Brooklyn? will the people who live over the way on our street, without the consolation of Jesus Christ, ever have his sympathy in their troubles? will those children who play on the sidewalk come up under the restraints of our holy religion? Then it is a question that appeals to every man's heart—it is a home question —he can understand it, and will be willing to support it. I will illustrate: During the last war, in my church in

Philadelphia, one Sabbath we took up a collection for foreign missions—a most important cause—and I urged it with all my might, asking God for help. The collection was not as large as it ought to have been. The next Sabbath night, while I was in the pulpit, a man handed me a telegram. I opened it, and I read it to the people. It was an appeal from the army before Richmond, saying, "There are three thousand men down here bleeding to death. Send us lint, send us bandages, send us cordials, send us Christian men and women to bind up the wounded." I had not long to speak. I read the telegram, and then I said, "Men and women, these are your fathers, and these are your brothers, dying before the gates of Richmond. Will you send them cordials? will you send them bandages? will you send them lint? Pass the baskets." The collection was gathered, and the baskets came back burdened with the trophies. People took off their gold rings and their breastpins, and threw them into the contribution. It was a home question; it struck every man's heart, every woman's conscience, and the treasures were poured forth. Now I say when you can make the people of this country understand that the religious question is a home question; when we can make them feel that, while we have moral responsibility for the salvation of Hong Kong, and Pekin, and Madras, and Constantinople, we have a mightier responsibility for Brooklyn; when we can make them feel that in the support of a free church they not only contribute toward the religious education of their own families, but of all who come within the house of God—the generosity of the people will exceed any thing you have ever anticipated.

Again, some have objected to a free church *because it destroys the home feeling*, and it is a forcible objection; it is so mighty an objection, that if I can not meet it, I will surrender the principle advocated. Destroy the home feeling! Father sitting here in the church, mother sitting there, children somewhere else; or if the church be crowded some Sabbath, you can not get in at all. "We want our families beside us in the house of God. Seated with them here, we hope to worship with them in heaven." To this objection my answer is, In every free church let the pews be formally assigned without reference to the dollar question, priority of application giving priority of choice, pew not to be forfeited except in the event of bad behavior or non-attendance. Then a man seated in it with his family has a home feeling—more so than in the other style of church. If disaster come to him, and his fortune is gone, and he can pay nothing, and he has to bring his children home from the school, and move from a fine house into a smaller one, and put on plainer apparel, he sits down in the house of God, and says, "Here is a house from which I am certain not to be turned out; here we will be prepared for heaven." If, in the one case, there is a home feeling when the pew-rent system is in force, and men may be driven out because they lose their fortune and can not pay their pew-rent, I ask you if there is not a better home feeling in that church where a man feels that no earthly disaster shall affect his occupancy? If home feeling is found in any church on earth, it will be found in a free church—the seats formally assigned and occupied.

But there are others who may oppose the free church principle on the ground that *it obliterates social distinction*.

It is an objection oftener thought than spoken, but it is a really solid objection. It is an important question, "What shall be the social influences amidst which my family will be placed if we go to that church?" I believe in good blood, and that there is such a thing as bad blood. I believe in royal blood. In some families the tide seems all in the wrong way; in other families the tide seems all in the right way. I have known a father and mother mean, and their children mean, and their grandchildren mean, and the rule going on to the tenth generation—perhaps for all eternity. In another family I have seen father and mother good, and their children good, and their grandchildren good—the tide of virtue and generosity going on through all generations. Therefore, I believe in family blood. I admit that God never calls a man, if he is intelligent, to associate with ignorance, or if he be elegant, to associate with boorishness, or if he be virtuous, to associate with vice.

"Why," says somebody, "I am afraid to go to such a church as you are describing, because there may be some that come to that church whom I would not like to associate with; and how would I feel if some of my family should marry a scavenger!" Ah, my friend, we might have the Board of Trustees resolve that no one need marry a scavenger unless she wants to! In every free church, just as in every pew-rental church, you will pick your own society. While your Christian heart will dictate kindness and courtesy to all whom you meet on Sabbaths, you will not be obliged to run to those who sit in the same church and tell them all your family affairs, or invite them to your house. That is not requisite. If there be in a pew-rental church fifty social circles, then in every free church there will be fifty social circles. I can think of only one class of persons that will be very much offended with that style of church. I admire a man who has made a large fortune honestly, and who holds it usefully. I admire the perseverance, and the pluck, and the ingenuity, and the tact. I rejoice in his success, and I pray to God that the hand of commercial disaster may never dethrone him. But men who, by some freak of good fortune, are thrown to the top, and who use their means for the purpose of fattening their own vanity, and of wounding the feelings of those who are not as fortunate as themselves, excite in me such unbounded loathing and contempt that I dare not trust myself to speak of them. They are in my nostrils like the stench of summer carrion, and if the hand of commercial disaster shall tear off from them their gold and their diamonds and their trinkets, it will take one of M'Allister's best and most powerful microscopic apparatus to make visible to the naked eye the noxious insects. Their wealth equaled by their stupidity and their ignorance—such men will abhor the idea of a free Christian church; but rich men and poor men, high and low men, educated men and ignorant men, who believe in the brotherhood of man and the fatherhood of God, will accept the principle laid down in the text, and rejoice when in any church it is illustrated: "The rich and the poor meet together: the Lord is the maker of them all."

Now, my friends, I have answered these objections to a free church, not because my own congregation make them—they do not make objections—but thinking that there might be some who are about to connect themselves with us who do not know the principles upon which our church is to be founded. I will say that my soul is absorbed in this idea. It has been a matter of personal sacrifice to me that I have pleaded for it, and I say to all ministers of the Gospel who may be in the house to-night, if their idea is a large salary and magnificent income, they had better never plead for a free church; but if, on the other hand, their idea is to bring the Gospel of Christ to the masses of the people who are without Christ and without God in the world, then it is a very satisfactory idea, and will give them a reward now in their own consciences and in the joys of heaven. I commit the principle first to God, and then I commit it to the masses of the people. I came out from among them. I know them altogether. I am in sympathy with them. My father and mother toiled with their hands until old age stooped their shoulders and made their eye-sight very dim, and then they died, leaving us a glorious legacy, not in dollars and cents, but in prayers and Christian example that this world will never rob us of. In the hand of the God that loved them, and that I love, I trust this principle. I tell you plainly to-night that I would rather fail in this attempt to give the Gospel to the masses than to succeed in any thing else. Living or dying, in prosperity or in sorrow, in good report or in evil report, in the name of my Lord Jesus Christ, my hope in life, my peace in death, my triumph in eternity, I consecrate to-night, body, mind, and soul to this one enterprise. Considering what God has done for us in the past, we would be cowards now to distrust him. Oh, young men of my church, buckle on the whole armor of God. Do you know that if you start life in the service of Jesus Christ, you start well? I point you to-night to a field of usefulness than which God never opened a grander. Do you know that into your hands are to come the mighty destinies of Christ's kingdom very soon; and I look you in the eye and I ask you if, when in this battle these older men shall fall, you will catch up the standard? Quit you like men! Be strong!

Then I see in this audience men in middle life, from thirty to fifty years of age. What think you of giving a free Gospel to the masses? If you want to make up for lost time, here is the chance to do it. You have been down in the world. You know what it is made of. You have deliberately concluded that it is a most unsatisfactory portion. Fall into line, oh ye men in mid-life— men between thirty and fifty years of age. The battle may be hot, but I am not afraid to lead you, and I wave the sword in front of the host, crying, Forward! Let cowards fly! Act ye like sons of God!

But there are others here who linger by the banks of the river. They know that because of old age they must soon go over. You have had many a good time. Every wrinkle in your face ought to be a hallelujah. By what blood you have been bought! By what mercy you have been defended! You can not sing these hymns with as firm a voice as once you sang them; and you came to this house to-night with trembling step—not as once you came to a religious assemblage — and you look around, and your comrades are gone, and your best friends are on the other side of the river, and you feel that soon you must go and join them. You feel just like a farmer on a summer-day in the harvest-field, who says, "Now, boys, it is almost night, and the wind is from the east, and it will storm before morning; let us get in a few more sheaves." For you the hour is coming in which no man can work, and what you do you must do now. There are yet two or three or four sheaves for you to reap for the Lord's garner. Oh, give us your prayers, aged men. Give us what strength there may be still remaining in your arm; and then, when you are gone, we will tell our children how well you served in the temple, and, like Elisha, we will cry as when Elijah went up, "My father, my father, the chariots of Israel, and the horsemen thereof!"

What I say to one I say to all—from those who sit beneath to those who rise above me in the galleries—what you do for Christ, do quickly. The field is white, the sickle is sharp, the reward is grand, the time is short, the judgment is near! What thy hand findeth to do, do it now.

Let me say that you ought to toil with great buoyancy. This whole earth is to be saved, and the cities are to be evangelized. I sometimes hear Christian people talk as though the Church of Christ is to be defeated; as though it were to be like one of those steamers, the *City of Boston* or the *President*, that went out with a large cargo and with many passengers, and has never come to port, and never will come to port. Some of you may have had friends on some of those steamers, and you waited and watched, and said, "I wonder on what iceberg they shivered! I wonder in what fire they burned! I wonder where they went down!" and you cried out in your soul, "Oh, treacherous sea, give back that ship! give her back! though it be with shivered mast and scarred bulk-head, and pumps all working to keep out the leak, and passengers with faces wan with hunger and eyes hollow with woe. Give her back!" The ocean answered not. It only moaned to the beach, and moaned to the sky. "Ah!" says some one, "it will be just like that with the Church. She will never come into harbor." I deny it. She has had a rough time, and been caught in many a hurricane, and driven against many a rock, and sometimes her commanders have been at their wits' end, and have cried out, "We shall go down! We shall go down!" Christ stands at the helm, and she shall outride the gale; and when she drops anchor on the beach of pearl, all heaven will throw out signals of delight, and the standards will wave and the bells will ring because the voyage is over, and "the wicked cease from troubling, and the weary are at rest." In that day of triumph, will you be one of the victors? Are your sins pardoned? Are you ready for Christian work? Will heaven be your home? As I was entering the gates of this building to-night, a man stopped me and said, "That man you saw last night at eight or nine o'clock is dead." I said, "It can not be possible." I was there at nine o'clock, and said, "I will soon see you again"—for he was here last Sabbath. Now they tell me he is gone! Are we all ready? We can not always be here. It can not be that all these people will meet each other again in this building.

When the *Atlantic* struck Mars Head, you read a good many telegrams, going all over the country through the associated press, but there was just one telegram that struck me as no other telegram I ever saw. It was sent by some man whose friends were in Detroit. He had escaped from the wreck, and, amidst all that gloom, and amidst the dead bodies that laid around him, he wrote out a telegram of one word, and it thrilled all through this land. That word was "Saved!" Oh! what good news it must have been when the friends got it. And I think there are some here to-night who have made shipwreck of their earthly prospects, and they have been driven against the rocks of disaster, and I cry out, Oh that now the strong hand of Christ might be reached down to pull them up on the eternal shore, and that the tidings might thrill to the throne, *Saved!* and that watchmen standing on the ramparts of heaven might cry to people in the temple, "*Saved!*" and the news run from street to street, until all the city of the sun shall ring with the glorious announcement, "*Saved!* SAVED!" for there is joy among the angels of God over one sinner that repenteth.

## WOMAN'S WAR AGAINST THE BOTTLE.

"Awake, awake, Deborah: awake, awake."—*Judges* v., 12.

A TEXT of five words, and four of them one and the same. It seems that the men of Israel had lost their courage. Trampled into the dust by their oppressors, the cowards had not spirit to rise. Their vineyards destroyed, their women dishonored, their children slain, the land was dying for a leader worthy of the cause. A holy woman by the name of Deborah saw the desolation, and, putting her trust in the Lord, sounded the battle-cry, and by the help of General Barak launched into the plain ten thousand armed men. The Canaanites, of course, came out with a larger force. They came out against Israel with nine hundred iron chariots, each of these iron chariots having attached to the sides of it long, sharp scythes, so that when these engines of war were driven down to battle, each one of the nine hundred was ready to cut two great swathes of death. But when God gives a mission to a woman, he gives her strength and grace to execute it. The nine hundred chariots of the Canaanites could not save them. They fly! they fly! horse and horseman, chariot and charioteer, officers and troops, in one wild and terrific overthrow. Sisera, their leader, is so frightened in the conflict, that he can not wait until his team turns round: he leaps from the chariot and starts, full run, for the mountains. Then this epic of the text was composed, to celebrate the grand womanly triumph: "Awake, awake, Deborah: awake, awake!"

My friends, an army of Canaanitish and infernal influences has come down to destroy this fair land. They come on, armed with decanter, and demijohn, and legislative enactment, and brewer's tank, and apothecary's bitters, and distiller's "worm" that never dieth. To meet these influences, some very brave men have gone out in battle, and have tried to break to pieces these iron chariots of destruction; but for the most part the land has slept. Indeed, it slept until a few weeks ago, at the West, when the Lord God uttered his voice until it rang through the churches, and the homes, and the gin-palaces, and off upon the prairie, saying, "Awake, awake, Deborah: awake, awake!" And now, while I speak, this great Austerlitz goes on, and earth, and heaven, and hell await the stupendous issue.

Before I proceed to discuss the modes and policies by which the great sin of drunkenness is to be assaulted, I want to tell you two or three things which I think will bear me out in the statement that something radical needs to be done. The first fact I want to put before you is this: that there are coming up a vast multitude of children in this country who have, from the day of their birth, a thirst for strong drink. Whether it be developed in early life or not, it is there—they have inherited it. Right along the ancestral line, how often goes the river of death! It seems as if their cradle is rocked by the rum-fiend. The father sits down to make his will. He says: "In the name of God, amen! I bequeath to my children my houses, and lands, and all my property. Share and share alike they must. Hereto I affix my hand and seal, in the presence of witnesses." But that father may at the same time be making a will that he does not realize. He may be really saying: "In the name of Disease, and Appetite, and Death, amen! I bequeath to my children my thirst for strong drink. My tankards shall be theirs, my condemnation shall be theirs. In the ruin that I have wrought for them, let them share and share alike. Hereto I put my hand and seal, in the presence of all the astonished host of heaven and all the jubilant harpies of hell." He does not know that he is making two wills at the same time. There are young men in this house to-day who have had two inheritances: one an inheritance of dollars — they have nearly spent that; the other an inheritance of thirst for strong drink — they have not spent that.

In addition to this, there is coming up from the lower haunts of society an uncounted throng of children who have been familiar with the odors of the whisky-jug and the ale-pitcher from the time they started into life. In every fibre of their soul they feel the sting of parental indulgences, and while your children to-day will be in the Sabbath-school singing "hosanna," there will be a vaster multitude — vaster by millions and millions — of little children, barefooted, imbruted in their countenances, filthy and uncombed, who will be singing the song of the drunkard. Their swaddling-clothes were torn off the winding-sheet of death. Their toy in infancy was a gin-bottle. They were baptized from the laver of woe. Obscene songs were their lullaby. Their inheritance has been a father's curse and a mother's beastliness. Are you surprised that they turn out badly?

Ay, if one out of ten thousand turns out any thing but badly, you ought to be surprised.

There is another fact I want to present, showing that there is a need of something radical on this subject, and that is the multiplicity of drinking-houses all over our cities. There never has been any lack of these establishments. There never has been much reason for a man's being thirsty a great while. But it was once only like an eruption on the body of the city; now it has become a multitude of carbuncles that threaten the very life of the community. You go down a beautiful street and see carpenters at work. You say, "I wonder what they are going to make there?" You go along a few days after, and you see they are painting an ale-pitcher on the sign, and see the red and blue light in the lamp at the door, as though kindled by a spark from the nether world to which it will decoy very many victims. In those places the villainies of your city are concocted. Those are the places where men whet their courage for arson, and for garroting, and for burglary, and for murder. I can remember the time when these saloons were chiefly on the street corners. Now they flame out from the heart of the block — a long line of fortifications leveling their enginery of death. Sometimes they call them "hotels." Sometimes they call them "wine-cellars." Sometimes they call them "restaurants." Sometimes they call them "retreats." Sometimes they call them "concert saloons," where music plays the march of death. Sometimes they call them "casinos," combining all the abominations of the theatre, grog-shop, and brothel. Sometimes they call them "lager-bier saloons," under which, I suppose, there are more villainies and more obscenities than under any other name. These institutions are springing up all around us. They come like some fabulous monster, taking at one swallow a hundred victims. They are plagues sweating on your great thoroughfares, and rotting away the life of Brooklyn and New York. They are on every avenue—Fulton Avenue, Atlantic Avenue, Lafayette Avenue, Gates Avenue—girding the city with a chain of eternal fire.

We can not even have the laws against them executed. All through this country it is against the law to sell liquor on the Sabbath-day. Where is the city that keeps that law? Where are the police? Where are the mayors? Where are the common councils? Where are the legislative assemblies? The fact is, that when the Republicans are in power they dare not execute the law lest they lose votes, and when the Democrats are in power they dare not execute the law lest they lose votes. Meanwhile, between these political parties who are struggling for the spoils of office, the virtue and the religion of the city die.

What chance is there for the morals of our city when these places are so easy of access, and when, if you want to get out of the smell of rum, you have to ride five or six miles out of town, and even the outskirts of the city are sometimes worse than the heart of it? What chance is there for that young man? Temptation before him, temptation behind him, in the loft above him, and in the cellar beneath him; and when our very best citizens patronize such places! They are cold, and they must go in and get something warm; they are warm, and they must get something to cool off. They lose money, and begin to drink to keep up their spirits; they gain something, and then they can afford to drink. And so the casks are filled, and the strychnine is poured in, and the leaks are stopped, and the faucets are drawn, and the intoxication is swilled down; and sometimes, standing before professed Christian men, their breath is so foul with drink that I feel tempted to bury my face in my pocket-handkerchief.

Look at another fact. Many of the drug-stores of our country, that ought to be the agencies of health, are becoming the means of dissipation and death. There are forms of disease that need a stimulus, and under a prudent and skillful physician I think that alcohol has an important work to do; but what have you to say about the deceptions practiced upon people in this day by bitters—bitters of all sorts—cordials, tonics, Hostetter Bitters, Golden Bitters, Plantation Bitters — Bitters that make a man's life bitter, and his death bitter, and his eternity bitter. Bitters! Now, I say, if you are going to blast a man for time and eternity, give him a fair chance. Put on the outside of the bottle what it is. But a man, maintaining, as he thinks, his sobriety, goes and gets a bottle of bitters and puts it on his desk. That bottle is soon gone. After a while he gets another, and another, and another; and one day, while he is seated in his room, the cork flies out of the black bottle of bitters, and with it a fiend that grapples the man by the throat, and says: "Ah! I have been chasing about for you fifteen years. I have got you now. Down with you to perdition!" If you propose to destroy a man, give him at least a fair fight.

Take two appalling statistics. In one year we spent in this country many million dollars more money in making, and selling, and buying intoxicating drinks than for the woolen goods, and cotton goods, and flour, and meal, and boots, and shoes, and clothing of the people. In other words, we pay in this country much more to kill the people than to make them live. Put that down in your memorandum-books for one item.

Then the other item is this: If we should take all the drunkards in this country and gather them in battle array, five men abreast, they would make a line a hundred miles long. So that, if you wanted to marshal that host, and look at the companies, and the regiments, and the battalions, and you wanted to review them, you would have to mount one horse and ride until he was exhausted, and then mount another horse and ride until he was exhausted, and another horse, until he was exhausted; and then if you wanted to marshal that great host, and had a voice loud enough to order them to "Forward, march!" their step would make the earth shake and the gates of hell tremble. That is the other item.

Now if all these things are so, is it not time that something great, something earnest, something radical be done? Revolution! Revolution! In the light of these things I come to consider this great movement which has attracted the attention of this whole land toward the West. You ask me, as I have often been asked in private—you ask me silently two questions. You say, in the first place, "Do you approve of that assault made by the women of the West upon the liquor business?" And in the second place, "Would you have the same assault and the same scenes enacted here at the East?" I take your questions separately and alone. I answer your first. You say, "Do you approve of the assault that has been made by the women of the West upon the grog-shops there?" I reply that there have been some things done there that I have no sympathy with, and I also assert that, so long as we have so many fools masculine, we ought to be willing to have a few fools feminine. Then I go further on, and aver that the campaign waged at the West by the women against the grog-shops of Ohio, and Illinois, and Indiana, and Michigan, is the grandest and most magnificent thing that has been on earth since the day when Deborah in the name of the Lord God Almighty hurled ruin and death on the armed oppressors of Israel. Why, it seems that by the force of prayer—certainly there can not be any thing wrong about that; and by the force of Christian song—certainly there can not be any thing wrong about that—there were in a little while three hundred saloons shut up, and in some villages all the drinking-places were abandoned. You tell me they will be open again very soon. I reply, is it nothing to shut up the fires of hell for six weeks? Why, it seems that these men engaged in that business did not know how to cope with this kind of warfare. They knew how to fight the Maine Liquor Law, and they knew how to fight the National Temperance Society, and they know how to fight the Sons of Temperance and Good Samaritans; but when Deborah appeared upon the scene, Sisera took to his feet and got to the mountains. It seems that they did not know how to contend against "Coronation," and "Old Hundred," and "Brattle Street," and "Bethany," they were so very intangible. These men found that they could not accomplish much against that kind of warfare, and in one of the cities a German regiment was brought out all armed to disperse the women. They came down in battle array; but, oh, what poor success! for that German regiment was made up of gentlemen, and gentlemen do not like to shoot women with hymn-books in their hands. Oh, they found that gunning for female prayer-meetings was a very poor business! No real damage was done, although there has been threat of violence after threat of violence all over the land. Let us give fair warning to all military companies, and to all mayors, and to all courts of law, that on the day that one of these Christian women engaged in this holy war shall, under the point of soldiers' bayonet, or under the stroke of police club, fall down wounded or slain, on that day there will be a fire kindled in this country, a fire of indignation and national wrath, that all the waters of the Mississippi and the Ohio and the Hudson can not put out; and the influence will keep on rolling over this whole country, until the last liquor shop, and the last distillery, and the last gin store, and the last brewery, shall be trampled out under the feet of an indignant people. I tell you that the curse of the Lord God Almighty is on that business forever and forever, amen!

They say that it was not dignified for these women—they ought to have been home crocheting, or watching the loaves of bread in the oven to see that they did not get too brown and hard. Oh, my soul, which would have been most dignified? to have staid in the homes already desolated by rum, shivering amidst half-clad children, waiting for the staggering step of the father, or brother, or son, or to put on the only hat and shawl that had not been pawned away by the companion, and go out under the leadership of some great-souled Deborah, and with the famished family at the back, attempt with the artillery of prayer and song to put an end to those institutions where the domestic ruin had originated? Who are you, that, seated in your homes of plenty and sobriety, you should be so severely critical of these women of the West, who not for personal display, not for a play spell, but because they wanted to get back the homes of which they had been robbed, and the children's inheritance, and the souls of the men who had been imperiled by strong drink, went forth to do their duty? When my voice shall, through the printing-press, reach those women at the West, I want to say to them, "God speed you in the work!" "Awake, awake, Deborah: awake, awake." Nine hundred chariots can not do you any harm. The Lord of Hosts is with you, and he is mightier than all that can be against you.

Now I come to answer the second question, "Would you have the same kind of war upon the liquor establishments made at the East, and in our midst, as at the West?" I say most emphatically, NO; but for different reasons from what I have ever heard given. It is not because I think that the women of the West were undignified or unchristian, it is not because I think that the women of Brooklyn are too good for such a holy iconoclasm; but it is because there seems to be no Deborah with sufficient faith in God to lead forth the host. Here at the East we are all watching to see what somebody else will say, and we are bound hand and foot by the conventionalities of society more than at the West; and at the flutter of a newspaper, we are so frightened that we are not fit for any great warfare of the kind of which I speak. I will, however, say, oh mothers, and sisters, and daughters of Brooklyn! I really think if you had as much faith in God as your sisters at the West have, and the same recklessness of human criticism, I really believe that in one month three-fourths of the grog-shops of Brooklyn would be closed, and there would be running through the gutters of the streets Burgundy, and Cognac, and Heidsick, and old Port, and Schiedam schnapps, and lager-bier, and you would save your fathers, and your husbands, and your sons, first, from a drunkard's grave, and, secondly, from a drunkard's hell!

But the time has not come. I have read the reports of the women who have assembled in this city in different churches, and I see that the time has not come. A woman can not do that which she thinks she can not, and you can not. There is no Deborah with enough faith in God and recklessness of human criticism to go forth in the work. I really think that, perhaps, things have got to be worse before they are any better. I do not know but that there must yet be one dead in each house, slain by this destroying angel, and that the piano that you brought into your parlor last week will have to go down under the sheriff's hammer, and some midnight your son be tossed into your front door dead-drunk, and the rose on your daughter's cheek fade under the breath of the rum-fiend as her father stoops over to kiss her "good-night," and this tornado of domestic desolation go on until our great cities shall be one wreck of dissipation and crime. I do not know but it will have to be that way before the women of the East are as brave as the women of the West.

But since we are not ready for that war, there is something in which all the women of my church are ready to engage, and in which all the women of this city are ready to be marshaled, and that is in some kind of war against the drinking usages of society. Oh, young woman, never give your hand in marriage to a man who tampers with strong drink, any more than you would take hold of a basilisk! You would reform him by marriage, would you? Never! I have seen the experiment tried too often, and the women who made the unsuccessful experiment, by marriage, of reforming a man, some of them are in suicides' graves, some are in the alms-house, and all the rest are wretched, without one exception. Reform him, will you? Why, where one woman has succeeded in that experiment, there are five hundred women buried in the ruins. Young woman, if a young man does not think enough of you to give up the wine-cup, tell him plainly that you will not contest for his affections with so vile a rival. Do not be hasty to leave your father's house in such an unseaworthy craft. They say that Captain Williams was drunk when he drove the *Atlantic* on Mars' Head, and look out how you trust your voyage of life in the hands of an inebriate. The rocks! the rocks!

Let the mothers teach their children from the very start what an accursed thing rum is. Give the lesson to them with "Brown's Shorter Catechism." Give every emphasis to the truth, and then pray, morning, noon, and night, and until the day of your death, that your sons—ay, your daughters, too, may be saved from these overwhelming temptations.

Let sisters make the home every evening bright, make it very bright. You do not know the allurements that are around your brother. You can not afford to stand by his bruised brow when he is dead, as I knew a sister who once did when the night before she had heard her brother howling in the delirium, while three men could not hold him down, for he arose in the couch and beat back imaginary demons, crying, "Begone! begone!" We are not ready for the crusade of the West here, but I want to marshal every woman in this house in one of three regiments. In the first place, we will have a regiment of mothers, their step not so strong as once it was, for they have come a great way; but their faith in God, mighty—the God who has never forsaken them. Alas! for the mother who bends over the son scorched with this fiery sirocco. O God! appease her agony for a little while.

In the second regiment, we will have all the wives of the country; some of their homes already invaded by this evil; their domestic joy somewhat shaken; the next ten years charged with a good deal of uncertainty.

The third regiment will be made up of the daughters of the land; their comfort and their respectability dependent upon the sobriety of their parents; their brow not yet clouded; their lips unacquainted with the acrid draught that a drunkard's child always has to drink.

A man said to a little girl going along the street, "Why, Jennie, I don't see you any more. You used to come to my house begging for cold victuals. I haven't seen you for weeks. Where have you been, Jennie?" "Oh!" she replied, "we don't want cold victuals any more. Papa don't drink now, and so we have warm victuals." God have mercy on the drunkard's child!

Now the three regiments are formed. Forward! ye

women baptized of the Holy Ghost. Forward! into the strife. Your ensigns shall not be stained with tears or blood. No skeleton will mark the line of your march; but in the wake of this great army there will smile a harvest of reformed inebriates, and there will be heard the shout of children at the return of their fathers from the captivity of the wine-cup. The mountains and the hills will break forth into singing, and all the trees of the wood will clap their hands. "Instead of the thorn shall come the fir-tree; instead of the brier shall come the myrtle-tree; and it shall be to the Lord for a name, for an everlasting sign that shall not be cut off."

Postponing until next Sabbath morning what I have to say to the men who are tampering with strong drinks, postponing until next Sabbath morning my counsel to all those who have already the shackles fastened upon them, postponing until next Sabbath morning the completion of the discourse that I have begun now, I will only say to the families of my congregation, banish the wine-cup from your table, dash the beaker from your lip, and in the strength of God resolve that you will no more have any thing to do with strong drink; for I tell you now that there is a multitude of you kept away from Christ by intoxicating liquor, and there are some of you who profess to be followers of Jesus, members of my church, who are drinking a little too much. Though you have not gone far on in sin, though you may never have been intoxicated, as I suppose you have not, I know some of you are drinking a little too much, and so I ask you all to abstain. Come out on the side of sobriety. Come out on the side of the Christian religion. Let me tell you now, no drunkard hath eternal life, and that some of you are running an awful risk of being drunkards. May the Lord God Almighty save you, and me, and our families, and this whole country from the scathing, scalding, blasting, damning influence of strong drink!

## THE PROUD RIDER UNHORSED.

"And as he journeyed, he came near Damascus: and suddenly there shined round about him a light from heaven: and he fell to the earth, and heard a voice saying unto him, Saul, Saul, why persecutest thou me? And he said, Who art thou, Lord? And the Lord said, I am Jesus whom thou persecutest."—*Acts* ix., 3–5.

THE Damascus of Bible times still stands, with a population of one hundred and thirty-five thousand. It was a gay city of white and glistering architecture, its minarets and crescents and domes playing with the light of the morning sun; embowered in groves of olive, and citron, and orange, and pomegranate; a famous river plunging its brightness into the scene; a city by the ancients styled "a pearl surrounded by emeralds."

A group of horsemen are advancing upon that city. Let the Christians of the place hide, for that cavalcade coming over the hills is made up of persecutors; their leader small and unattractive in some respects, as leaders sometimes are insignificant in person: witness the Duke of Wellington and Dr. Archibald Alexander. But there is something very intent in the eye of this man of the text, and the horse he rides is lathered with the foam of a long and quick travel of one hundred and thirty-five miles. He cries "Go 'long" to his steed, for those Christians must be captured and silenced, and that religion of the cross must be annihilated. Suddenly the horses shy off, and plunge until the riders are precipitated. Freed from their riders, the horses bound snorting away. You know that dumb animals, at the sight of an eclipse, or an earthquake, or any thing like a supernatural appearance, sometimes become very uncontrollable. A new sun had been kindled in the heavens, putting out the glare of the ordinary sun. Christ, with the glories of heaven wrapped about him, looked out from a cloud and the splendor was insufferable, and no wonder the horses sprang and the equestrians dropped. Dust-covered and bruised, Saul attempts to get up, shading his eyes with his hand from the severe lustre of the heavens, but unsuccessfully, for he is struck stone blind as he cries out, "Who art thou, Lord?" and Jesus answered him, "I am the one you have been chasing. He that whips and scourges those Damascine Christians, whips and scourges me. It is not their back that is bleeding; it is mine. It is not their heart that is breaking; it is mine. I am Jesus whom thou persecutest."

From that wild, exciting, and overwhelming scene there rises up the greatest preacher of all the ages—Paul, in whose behalf prisons were rocked down, before whom soldiers turned pale, into whose hand Mediterranean sea-captains put control of their shipwrecking craft, and whose epistles are the *avant courier* of a resurrection-day.

I learn first from this scene that a *worldly fall sometimes precedes a spiritual uplifting*. A man does not get much sympathy by falling off a horse. People say he ought not to have got into the saddle if he could not ride. Those of us who were brought up in the country remember well how the workmen laughed when, on our way back from the brook, we suddenly lost our ride. At the close of the war, when the army passed in review at Washington, if a general had toppled from the stirrups it would have been a national merriment. Here is Paul on horseback—a proud man, riding on with Government documents in his pocket, a graduate of a most famous school in which the celebrated Dr. Gamaliel had been a professor, perhaps having already attained two of the three titles of the school—Rab, the first; Rabbi, the second; and on his way to Rabbak, the third and highest title. I know from his temperament that his horse was ahead of the other horses. But without time to think of what posture he should take, or without any consideration for his dignity, he is tumbled into the dust. And yet that was the best ride Paul ever took. Out of that violent fall he arose into the apostleship. So it has been in all the ages, and so it is now.

You will never be worth any thing for God and the Church until you lose fifty thousand dollars, or have your reputation upset, or in some way, somehow, are thrown and humiliated. You must go down before you go up. Joseph finds his path to the Egyptian court through the pit into which his brothers threw him. Daniel would never have walked amidst the bronzed lions that adorned the Babylonish throne if he had not first walked amidst the real lions of the cave. And Paul marshals all the generations of Christendom by falling flat on his face on the road to Damascus. Men who have been always prospered may be efficient servants of the world, but will be of no advantage to Christ. You may ride majestically seated on your charger, rein in hand, foot in stirrup, but you will never be worth any thing spiritually until you fall off. They who graduate from the school of Christ with the highest honors have on their diploma the seal of a lion's muddy paw, or the plash of an angry wave, or the drop of a stray tear, or the brown scorch of a persecuting fire. In nine hundred and ninety-nine cases out of the thousand there is no moral or spiritual elevation until there has been a thorough worldly upsetting.

Again, I learn from the subject that the *religion of Christ is not a pusillanimous thing*. People in this day try to make us believe that Christianity is something for men of small calibre, for women with no capacity to reason, for children in the infant-class under six years of age, but not for stalwart men. Look at this man of the text! Do you not think that the religion that could capture such a man as that must have some power in it? He was a logician, he was a metaphysician, he was an all-conquering orator, he was a poet of the highest type. He had a nature that could swamp the leading men of his own day, and, hurled against the Sanhedrim, he made it tremble. He learned all he could get in the school of his native village; then he had gone to a higher school, and there mastered the Greek and the Hebrew, and perfected himself in *belles-lettres*, until in after years he astonished the Cretans, and the Corinthians, and the Athenians, by quotations from their own authors. I have never found any thing in Carlyle, or Goethe, or Herbert Spencer, that could compare in strength or beauty with Paul's Epistles. I do not think there is any thing in the writings of Sir William Hamilton that shows such mental discipline as you find in Paul's argument about justification and the resurrection. I have not found any thing in Milton finer in the way of imagination than I can find in Paul's illustrations drawn from the amphitheatre. There was nothing in Robert Emmet pleading for his life, or in Edmund Burke arraigning Warren Hastings in Westminster Hall, that compared with the scene in the court-room, when before robed officials Paul bowed and began his speech, saying, "I think myself happy, King Agrippa, because I shall answer for myself this day." I repeat, that a religion that can capture a man like that must have some power in it. It is time you stopped talking as though all the brain of the world were opposed to Christianity. Where Paul leads, we can afford to follow. I am glad to know that Christ has in the different ages of the world had in his discipleship a Mozart and a Handel in music; a Raphael and a Reynolds in painting; an Angelo and a Canova in sculpture; a Rush and a Harvey in medicine; a Grotius and a Washington in statesmanship; a Blackstone, a Marshall, and a Kent in law; and the time will come when the religion of Christ will conquer all the observatories and universities, and Philosophy will through her telescope behold the morning star of Jesus, and in her laboratory see "that all things work together for good," and with her geological hammer discover the "Rock of Ages." Oh, instead of cowering and shivering when the skeptic stands before you and talks of religion as though it were a pusillanimous thing—instead of that, take your New Testament from your pocket and show him the picture of the intellectual giant of all the ages, prostrated on the road to Damascus while his horse is flying wildly away; then ask your skeptic what it was that frightened the one and threw the other? Oh no, it is no weak Gospel. It is a glorious Gospel. It is an all-conquering Gospel. It is an omnipotent Gospel. It is the power of God and the wisdom of God unto salvation.

Again, I learn from the text a man *can not become a Christian* until he is unhorsed. The trouble is, we want to ride into the kingdom of God, just as the knight rode into castle gate on palfry, beautifully caparisoned. We want to come into the kingdom of God in fine style. No kneeling down at the altar, no sitting on "anxious seats," no crying over sin, no begging at the door of God's mercy. Clear the road, and let us come in all prancing in the pride of our soul. No, we will never get into heaven that way. We must dismount. There is no knight-errantry in religion, no fringed trappings of repentance, but an utter prostration before God, a going down in the dust, with the cry, " Unclean, unclean!"—a bewailing of the soul, like David from the belly of hell—a going down in the dust, until Christ shall by his grace lift us up as he lifted Paul. Oh, proud-hearted sinner, you must get off that horse. May a light from the throne of God brighter than the sun throw you! Come down into the dust and cry for pardon, and life, and heaven.

Again, I learn from this scene of the text that the *grace of God can overcome the persecutor.* Christ and Paul were boys at the same time in different villages, and Paul's antipathy to Christ was increasing. He hated every thing about Christ. He was going down then with writs in his pockets to have Christ's disciples arrested. He was not going as a sheriff goes, to arrest a man against whom he has no spite, but Paul was going down to arrest those people because he was glad to arrest them. The Bible says, "He breathed out slaughter." He wanted them captured, and he wanted them butchered. I hear the click, and clash, and clatter of the hoofs of the galloping steeds on the way to Damascus. Oh! do you think that

that proud man on horseback can ever become a Christian? Yes! there is a voice from heaven like a thunder-clap uttering two words, the second word the same as the first, but uttered with more emphasis, so that the proud equestrian may have no doubt as to who is meant, "*Saul!* SAUL! That man was saved, and he was a persecutor; and so God can by his grace overcome any persecutor. The days of sword and fire for Christians seem to have gone by. The bayonets of Napoleon I. pried open the "Inquisition" and let the rotting wretches out. The ancient dungeons around Rome are to-day mere curiosities for the travelers. The Coliseum, where wild beasts used to suck up the life of the martyrs while the emperor watched and Lolia Paulina sat with emerald adornments worth sixty million sesterces, clapping her hands as the Christians died under the paw and the tooth of the lion—that Coliseum is a ruin now. The scene of the Smithfield fires is a hay-market. No emperor again will lead the pope's mule through St. Mark's Square. The day of fire and sword for Christians seems to have gone by; but has the day of persecution ceased? No. Are you not caricatured for your religion? In proportion as you try to serve God and be faithful to him, are you not sometimes maltreated? That woman finds it hard to be a Christian, as her husband talks and jeers while she is trying to say her prayers or read the Bible. That daughter finds it hard to be a Christian with the whole family arrayed against her—father, mother, brother, and sister making her the target of ridicule. That young man finds it hard to be a Christian in the shop, or factory, or store, when his comrades jeer at him because he will not go to the gambling-hell or the house of shame. Oh no, the days of persecution have not ceased, and will not until the end of the world. But, oh! you persecuted ones, is it not time that you began to pray for your persecutors? They are no prouder, no fiercer, no more set in their way than was this persecutor of the text. He fell. They will fall, if Christ from the heavens grandly and gloriously look out on them. God can by his grace make a Renan believe in the divinity of Jesus, and a Tyndall in the worth of prayer. Robert Newton stamped the ship's deck in derisive indignation at Christianity only a little while before he became a Christian. "Out of my house," said a father to his daughter, "if you will keep praying;" yet before many months passed, the father knelt at the same altar with the child. And the Lord Jesus Christ is willing to look out from heaven upon that derisive opponent of the Christian religion, and address him not in glittering generalities, but calling him by name, "John! George! Henry!—Saul! Saul! why persecutest thou me?"

Again, I learn from this subject that there is *hope for the worst offenders*. It was particularly outrageous that Saul should have gone to Damascus on that errand. Jesus Christ had been dead only three years, and the story of his kindness and his generosity and his love filled all the air. It was not an old story as it is now. It was a new story. Jesus had only three summers ago been in these very places, and Saul every day in Jerusalem must have met people who knew Christ, people with good eyesight whom Jesus had cured of blindness, people who were dead, and who had been resurrected by the Saviour, and people who could tell Paul all the particulars of the crucifixion—just how Jesus looked in the last hour—just how the heavens grew black in the face at the torture. He heard that recited every day by people who were acquainted with all the circumstances, and yet in the fresh memory of that scene he goes to persecute Christ's disciples, impatient at the time it takes to feed the horses at the inn, not pulling at the snaffle, but riding with loose rein faster and faster. Oh, he was the chief of sinners. No outbreak of modesty when he said that. He was a murderer. He stood by when Stephen died, and helped in the execution of that good man. When the rabble wanted to be unimpeded in their work of destroying Stephen, and wanted to take off their coats, but did not dare to lay them down lest they be stolen, Paul said, "I'll take care of the coats," and they put them down at the feet of Paul, and he watched the coats, and he watched the horrid mangling of glorious Stephen. Is it a wonder that when he fell from the horse he did not break his neck—that his foot did not catch somewhere in the trappings of the saddle, and he was not dragged and kicked to death? He deserved to die miserably, wretchedly, and forever, notwithstanding all his metaphysics, and his eloquence, and his logic. He was the chief of sinners. He said what was true when he said that. And yet the grace of God saved him, and so it will you. If there is any man in this house who thinks he is too bad to be saved, and says, "I have wandered very grievously from God, I do not believe there is any hope for me," I tell you the story of this man in the text who was brought to Jesus Christ in spite of his sins and opposition. There may be some here who are as stoutly opposed to Christ as Paul was. There may be some here who are captive of their sins as much so as the young man who said in regard to his dissipating habits, "I will keep on with them. I know I am breaking my mother's heart, and I know I am killing myself, and I know that when I die I shall go to hell, but it is now too late to stop."

The steed on which you ride may be swifter, and stronger, and higher-mettled than that on which the Cilician persecutor rode, but Christ can catch it by the bridle, and hurl it back and hurl it down. There is mercy for you who say you are too bad to be saved. You say you have put off the matter so long. Paul had neglected it a great while. You say that the sin you have committed has been amidst the most aggravating circumstances. That was so with Paul's. You say you have exasperated Christ and coaxed your own ruin. So did Paul. And yet he sits to-day on one of the highest of the heavenly thrones; and there is mercy for you, and good days for you, and gladness for you, if you will only take the same Christ which first threw him down and then raised him up. It seems to me as if I can see Paul to-day rising up from the highway to Damascus and brushing off the dust from his cloak and wiping the sweat of excitement from his brow, as he turns to us and all the ages, saying, "This is a faithful saying, and worthy of all acceptation, that Christ Jesus came into the world to save sinners, *of whom I am chief.*"

Once more: I learn from this subject that there *is a tremendous reality in religion.* If it had been a mere optical delusion on the road to Damascus, was not Paul just the man to find it out? If it had been a sham and pretense, would he not have pricked the bubble? He was a man of facts and arguments, of the most gigantic intellectual nature, and not a man of hallucinations. And when I see him fall from the saddle, blinded and overwhelmed, I say there must have been something in it. And, my dear brother, you will find that there is something in religion in one of three places—either in earth, or in heaven, or in hell. We will wake up somewhere, somehow, sometime. The only question is, where? There was a man who rode from Stamford to London, ninety-five miles in five hours, on horseback. Very swift. There was a woman of Newmarket who rode on horseback a thousand miles in a thousand hours. Very swift. But there are those here, ay, all of us are speeding on at tenfold that velocity, at a thousand-fold that rate, toward a glad or a wretched eternity. That was a fearful fall Paul got; but Christ raised him up. Yet there is a fall from which there will be no rising. That was the fall the man got who in his last moments turned to his wife, who, by her worldliness, had kept him away from Jesus, and said, with his expiring breath, "Rebecca, you are the cause of my damnation!" That was the fall the man got who said, in his last moments, "I have sinned away my day of grace. Oh, I know when my day of grace ended. It was at the close of that religious service." That was the fall the man got who said, "I am dying unprepared. Great God!" That was the fall thousands have got. They perished while they were speeding on in their career of sin and folly; and at the moment they thought they were most firmly seated in the stirrups, and the girdle most firmly buckled, and the domes of future success were kindled before their vision, they were suddenly flung into shame and everlasting contempt. May Almighty God, from the opening heavens, flash upon your soul this day the question of your eternal destiny, and oh that Jesus, whom you have maltreated by your slights and your neglects, would this day overcome you with his pardoning mercy, as he stands here with the pathos of a broken heart and sobs into your ear, "I have come for thee. I come with my back raw from the beating. I come with my feet mangled with the nails. I come with my brow aching from the twisted bramble. I come with my heart bursting for your woes. I can stand it no longer. *I am* Jesus *whom thou persecutest.*"

## THE CHRISTIAN NEEDLE-WOMAN.

"Now there was at Joppa a certain disciple named Tabitha, which by interpretation is called Dorcas."—*Acts* ix., 36.

THERE is in Joppa, a sea-port town, a woman with her needle embroidering her name ineffaceably into the charities of the world. I see her sitting in the village home. In the door-way and around about the building, and in the room where she sits, are the pale faces of the poor. She listens to their plaint, she pities their woe, she makes garments for them, she adjusts the manufactured articles to suit the bent form of this invalid woman, and to the cripple that comes crawling on his hands and knees. She gives a coat to this one, she gives sandals to that one. With the gifts she mingles prayers and tears and Christian encouragement. Then she goes out to be greeted on the street corners by those whom she has blessed, and all through the street the cry comes, "Dorcas is coming!" The sick look up gratefully in her face as she puts her hand on the burning brow, and the lost and the abandoned start up with hope as they hear her gentle voice, as though an angel had addressed them: and as she goes out the lane, eyes half put out with sin think they see a halo of light about her brow, and a trail of glory in her pathway. That night a half-paid shipwright climbs the hill and reaches home, and sees his little boy well clad, and says, "Where did these clothes come from?" And they tell him, "Dorcas has been here." In another place a woman is trimming a lamp; Dorcas brought the oil. In another place, a family that had not been at table for many a week are gathered now, for Dorcas has brought bread.

But there is a sudden pause in that woman's ministry. They say, "Where is Dorcas? Why, we haven't seen her for many a day. Where is Dorcas?" And one of these poor people goes up and knocks at the door and finds the mystery solved. All through the haunts of wretchedness the news comes, "Dorcas is sick!" No bulletin flashing from the palace gate, telling the stages of a king's disease, is more anxiously awaited for than the news from this sick benefactress. Alas for Joppa! there is wailing, wailing. That voice which has uttered so many cheerful words is hushed; that hand which had made so many garments for the poor is cold and still; that star which had poured light into the midnight of wretchedness is dimmed by the blinding mists that go up from the river of death. In every God-forsaken place in that town; wherever there is a sick child and no balm; wherever there is hunger and no bread; wherever there is guilt and no commiseration; wherever there is a broken heart and no comfort, there are despairing looks, and streaming eyes, and frantic gesticulations as they cry, "Dorcas is dead!" They send for the apostle Peter. He urges his way through the crowd around the door, and stands in the presence of the dead. What expostulation and grief all about him! Here stand some of the poor people, who show the garments which this poor woman had made for them. Their grief can not be appeased. The Apostle Peter wants to perform a miracle. He will not do it amidst the excited crowd, so he kindly orders that the whole room be cleared. The door is shut against the populace. The apostle stands now with the dead. Oh, it is a serious moment, you know, when you are alone with a lifeless body! The apostle gets down on his knees and prays, and then he comes to the lifeless form of this one all ready for the sepulchre, and in the strength of him who is the resurrection, he exclaims, "*Tabitha, arise!*" There is a stir in the fountains of life; the heart flutters; the nerves thrill; the cheek flushes; the eye opens; she sits up!

We see in this subject Dorcas the disciple; Dorcas the benefactress; Dorcas the lamented; Dorcas the resurrected.

If I had not seen that word disciple in my text, I would have known this woman was a Christian. Such music as that never came from a heart which is not chorded and strung by Divine grace. Before I show you the needle-work of this woman, I want to show you her regenerated heart, the source of a pure life and of all Christian charities. I wish that the wives and mothers and daughters and sisters of this congregation would imitate Dorcas in her discipleship. Before you sit with the Sabbath-class, before you cross the threshold of the hospital, before you carry a pack of tracts down the street, before you enter upon the temptations and trials of tomorrow, I charge you, in the name of God, and by the turmoil and tumult of the Judgment-day, oh women! that you attend to the first, last, and greatest duty of your life—the seeking for God and being at peace with him. Now, by the courtesies of society, you are deferred to, and he were less than a man who would not oblige you with kind attentions; but when the trumpet shall sound, there will be an uproar, and a wreck of mountain and continent, and no human arm can help you. Amidst the rising of the dead, and amidst the boiling of the sea, and amidst the live, leaping thunders of the flying heavens, there will be no chance for courtesies. But on that day, calm and placid will be every woman's heart who hath put her trust in Christ; calm notwithstanding all the tumult, as though the fire in the heavens were only the gildings of an autumnal sunset, as though the peal of the trumpet were only the harmony of an orchestra, as though the awful voices of the sky were but a group of friends bursting through a gateway at eventime with laughter, and shouting "Dorcas the disciple!" Would God that every Mary and every Martha would this day sit down at the feet of Jesus!

Further, we see *Dorcas the benefactress*. History has told the story of the crown; the epic poet has sung of the sword; the pastoral poet, with his verses full of the redolence of clover-tops, and a-rustle with the silk of the corn, has sung the praises of the plow. I tell you the praises of the needle. From the fig-leaf robe prepared in the garden of Eden to the last stitch taken last night on the garment for the Tabernacle fair, the needle has wrought wonders of kindness, generosity, and benefaction. It adorned the girdle of the high-priest; it fashioned the curtains in the ancient tabernacle; it cushioned the chariots of King Solomon; it provided the robes of Queen Elizabeth; and in high places and in low places, by the fire of the pioneer's back-log and under the flash of the chandelier, everywhere, it has clothed nakedness, it has preached the Gospel, it has overcome hosts of penury and want with the war-cry of "Stitch, stitch, stitch!"

The operatives have found a livelihood by it, and through it the mansions of the employer have been constructed. Amidst the greatest triumphs in all ages and lands, I set down the conquests of the needle. I admit its crimes: I admit its cruelties. It has had more martyrs than the fire; it has butchered more souls than the Inquisition; it has punctured the eye; it has pierced the side; it has struck weakness into the lungs; it has sent madness into the brain; it has filled the potter's field; it has pitched whole armies of the suffering into crime and wretchedness and woe. But now that I am talking of Dorcas and her ministeries to the poor, I shall speak only of the charities of the needle.

This woman was a representative of all those women who make garments for the destitute, who knit socks for the barefooted, who prepare bandages for the lacerated, who fix up boxes of clothing for Western missionaries, who go into the asylums of the suffering and destitute bearing that Gospel which is sight for the blind, and hearing for the deaf, and which makes the lame man leap like a hart, and brings the dead to life, immortal health bounding in their pulses. What a contrast between the practical benevolence of this woman and a great deal of the charity of this day! This woman did not spend her time idly planning how the poor of Joppa were to be relieved; she took her needle and relieved them. She was not like those persons who sympathize with imaginary sorrows, and go out in the street and laugh at the boy who has upset his basket of cold victuals, or like that charity which makes a rousing speech on the benevolent platform, and goes out to kick the beggar from the step, crying, "Hush your miserable howling!" The sufferers of the world want not so much theory as practice; not so much tears as dollars; not so much kind wishes as loaves of bread; not so much smiles as shoes; not so much "God bless yous!" as jackets and frocks. I will put one earnest Christian man, hard working, against five thousand mere theorists on the subject of charity. There are a great many who have fine ideas about church architecture who never in their life helped to build a church. There are men who can give you the history of Buddhism and Mohammedanism, who never sent a farthing for their evangelization. There are women who talk beautifully about the suffering of the world, who never had the courage like Dorcas to take the needle and assault it.

I am glad that there is not a page of the world's history which is not a record of female benevolence. God says to all lands and people, come now and hear the widow's mite rattle down into the poor-box. The Princess of Conti sold all her jewels that she might help the famine-stricken. Queen Blanche, the wife of Louis VIII. of France, hearing that there were some persons unjustly incarcerated in the prisons, went out amidst the rabble and took a stick and struck the door as a signal that they might all strike it, and down went the prison door, and out came the prisoners. Queen Maud, the wife of Henry I., went down amidst the poor and washed their sores, and administered to them cordials. Mrs. Retson, at Matagorda, appeared on the battle-field while the missiles of death were flying around, and cared for the wounded. But why go so far back? Why go so far away? Is there a man or woman in this house who has forgotten the women of the Sanitary and Christian

Commissions, or the fact that, before the smoke had gone up from Gettysburg and South Mountain, the women of the North met the women of the South on the battlefield, forgetting all their animosities while they bound up the wounded, and closed the eyes of the slain? Have you forgotten? Dorcas the benefactress!

I come now to speak of Dorcas *the lamented*. When death struck down that good woman, oh, how much sorrow there was in Joppa! I suppose there were women there with larger fortunes; women, perhaps, with handsomer faces; but there was no grief at their departure like this at the death of Dorcas. There was not more turmoil and upturning in the Mediterranean Sea, dashing against the wharves of that sea-port, than there were surgings to and fro of grief in Joppa because Dorcas was dead. There are a great many who go out of life and are unmissed. There may be a very large funeral; there may be a great many carriages and a plumed hearse; there may be high-sounding eulogiums; the bell may toll at the cemetery gate; there may be a very fine marble shaft reared over the resting-place; but the whole thing may be a falsehood and a sham. The Church of God has lost nothing, the world has lost nothing. It is only a nuisance abated; it is only a grumbler ceasing to find fault; it is only an idler stopped yawning; it is only a dissipated fashionable parted from his wine-cellar; while, on the other hand, no useful Christian leaves this world without being missed. The Church of God cries out like the prophet: "Howl, fir-tree, for the cedar has fallen." Widowhood comes and shows the garments which the departed had made. Orphans are lifted up to look into the calm face of the sleeping benefactress.

Reclaimed vagrancy comes and kisses the cold brow of her who charmed it away from sin, and all through the streets of Joppa there is mourning—mourning because Dorcas is dead.

I suppose you have read of the fact that when Josephine was carried out to her grave there were a great many men and women of pomp and pride and position that went out after her; but I am most affected by the story of history that on that day there were ten thousand of the poor of France who followed her coffin, weeping and wailing until the air rang again, because, when they lost Josephine, they lost their last earthly friend. Oh, who would not rather have such obsequies than all the tears that were ever poured in the lachrymals that have been exhumed from ancient cities. There may be no mass for the dead; there may be no costly sarcophagus; there may be no elaborate mausoleum; but in the damp cellars of the city, and through the lonely huts of the mountain glen, there will be mourning, mourning, mourning, because Dorcas is dead. "Blessed are the dead who die in the Lord; they rest from their labors, and their works do follow them."

I speak to you of *Dorcas the resurrected*. The apostle came to where she was, and said, "Arise; and she sat up." In what a short compass the great writer put that—"She sat up!" Oh, what a time there must have been when the apostle brought her out among her old friends! How the tears of joy must have started! What clapping of hands there must have been! What singing! what laughter! Sound it all through that lane! Shout it down that dark alley! Let all Joppa hear it! Dorcas is resurrected!

You and I have seen the same thing many a time; not a dead body resuscitated, but the deceased coming up again after death in the good accomplished. If a man labors up to fifty years of age, serving God, and then dies, we are apt to think that his earthly work is done. No! His influence on earth will continue till the world ceases. Services rendered for Christ never stop. Here is a Christian woman. She toils for the upbuilding of a church through many anxieties, through many self-denials, with prayers and tears, and then she dies. It is fifteen years since she went away. Now the Spirit of God descends upon that church; hundreds of souls stand up and confess the faith of Christ. Has that Christian woman, who went away fifteen years ago, nothing to do with these things? I see the flowering out of her noble heart. I hear the echo of her footsteps in all these songs over sins forgiven, in all the prosperity of the church. The good that seemed to be buried has come up again. Dorcas is resurrected.

After a while all these womanly friends of Christ will put down their needle forever. After making garments for others, some one will make a garment for them: the last robe we ever wear—the robe for the grave. You will have heard the last cry of pain. You will have witnessed the last orphanage. You will have come in worn out from your last round of mercy. I do not know where you will sleep, nor what your epitaph will be; but there will be a lamp burning at that tomb and an angel of God guarding it, and through all the long night no rude foot will disturb the dust. Sleep on, sleep on! Soft bed, pleasant shadows, undisturbed repose! Sleep on!

"Asleep in Jesus! Blessed sleep!
From which none ever wake to weep."

Then one day there will be a sky-rending, and a whirl of wheels, and the flash of a pageant; armies marching, chains clanking, banners waving, thunders booming, and that Christian woman will arise from the dust, and she will be suddenly surrounded—surrounded by the wanderers of the street whom she reclaimed, surrounded by the wounded souls to whom she administered! Daughter of God, so strangely surrounded, what means this? It means that reward has come, that the victory is won, that the crown is ready, that the banquet is spread. Shout it through all the crumbling earth. Sing it through all the flying heavens. Dorcas is resurrected!

In 1855, when some of the soldiers came back from the Crimean war to London, the Queen of England distributed among them beautiful medals, called Crimean medals. I think of it just now, as I recently had a book presented me representing that beautiful Crimean medal. Galleries were erected for the two Houses of Parliament and the royal family to sit in. There was a great audience to witness the distribution of the medals. A colonel who had lost both feet in the battle of Inkermann was pulled in on a wheel-chair; others came in limping on their crutches. Then the Queen of England arose before them in the name of her Government, and uttered words of commendation to the officers and the men, and distributed these medals, inscribed with the four great battle-fields, Alma, Balaklava, Inkermann, and Sebastopol. As the Queen gave these to the wounded men and the wounded officers, the bands of music struck up the national air, and the people with streaming eyes joined in the song:

"God save our noble Queen!
Long live our gracious Queen!
God save the Queen!"

And then they shouted, "Huzza! huzza!" Oh, it was a proud day for those returned warriors! But a brighter, better, and gladder day will come, when Christ shall gather those who have toiled in his service, good soldiers of Jesus Christ. He shall rise before them, and in the presence of all the glorified of heaven he will say, "Well done, good and faithful servant!" and then he will distribute the medals of eternal victory, not inscribed with works of righteousness which we have done, but with those four great battle-fields, dear to earth and dear to heaven, *Bethlehem! Nazareth! Gethsemane! Calvary!*

12*

## HORACE GREELEY, LIVING AND DEAD.

"Howl, fir-tree, for the cedar is fallen."—*Zechariah* xi., 2.

WHEN the smaller growths of the forest topple, there is but little excitement in the wood. The stork does not so much as flutter a wing, nor does the hart lift its mouth dripping from the water-brooks. But when a cedar that has been standing for ages, the glory of the forest, touched with decay, or under the swoop of the hurricane begins to weigh its anchorage of root, and falls, the crash startles the eagle from its aerie, and sends the stag in wild plunge from the rock, and shakes the very foundation of the mountains.

A few hours ago a black and swarthy axeman went into the forests of men. He had hewn down many a tall and gigantic growth: he has been swinging his axe for six thousand years, and he knows how to cut. He aimed the sharp and fatal edge at one whom we all knew—stroke after stroke, stroke after stroke, until the cedar which had stood the blasts of trouble and trial, and abuse and toil, drops into the dust, two hemispheres resounding with the fall. "Howl, fir-tree, for the cedar is fallen!"

Horace Greeley is dead! and the caricaturist drops his pencil, the author his pen, the merchant his yard-stick, the laborer his pickaxe, the child its toy, and the world its eulogium. Taking it all in all, I think it is the saddest death of any public man in our whole history. Let neither pen nor tongue, by useless review or unbrotherly criticism, add one drop to the nation's cup of grief; it is brimful already. Be it ours the Christian duty of learning the lessons of this man, living and dead.

I think the life of this man ought to *kindle hope and enthusiasm in all the struggling.* There are a great many young men who tell me that they have no chance. They say, "Yonder is a young man who started with a large fortune, and here is a young man who married a fine estate, and here is another who has been through our best universities, and has finished his education in Edinburgh or Germany; but I have no education, I have no money, I have no chance." You have as good a chance as Horace Greeley the boy. See him in Vermont, in homespun, dyed with butternut-bark, helping his father get a living for the family out of very poor soil. I tell you that one who has, with bare feet and in tow shirt, helped a father to get out of poor soil a living for mother and sisters, has a right to publish fifty books concerning "What he knows about farming." See the lad stepping up from the Albany boat on the New York Battery, and then coming and sitting down on the steps of a printing-house, waiting for the boss to come in the morning. Then look at him sitting in the foremost editorial chair of all the world, and then tell me again you have no chance. If a young man starts from a good, honest, industrious Christian mother, he graduates from a university better than that of Berlin or Edinburgh, with a diploma in each hand. Every sound man starts life with a capital of at least one hundred thousand dollars—I say every man. You tell me to prove it. I will prove it. Your right arm—will you take five thousand dollars, and have it cut off? "No," you say. Then certainly it is worth five thousand dollars, and your left arm is worth as much, and your right foot as much, and your left foot as much. Twenty thousand dollars of capital to start with. Your mind; for how much would you go up and spend your life in Bloomingdale Asylum? Twenty thousand dollars for your intellect? You would refuse it. It is worth that, anyhow — forty thousand dollars of equipment. Then you have an immortal soul; for how much would you sell it? For sixty thousand dollars? No! you say, with indignation. Then certainly it is worth that much. And there are your one hundred thousand dollars—the magnificent outfit with which the Lord God Almighty started every one of you. And yet there are young men who are waiting for others to come and start them—to make them; waiting for institutions to make them; waiting for circumstances to make them. Fool! go and make yourself. Columbus was a weaver; Halley a soap-boiler; Arkwright a barber; Æsop a slave; the learned Bloomfield was a shoe-maker; Hogarth was an engraver of pewter-plate; Sixtus V. was a swine-herdsman; Homer was a beggar; and Horace Greeley started life in New York with ten dollars and seventy-five cents in his pocket, as well off as if he had the eleven full round dollars. But there are a great many young men who are waiting for the other twenty-five cents before they begin. "Oh!" you say, "it was his eccentricities that got him success." A great many men have supposed that, and they have aped him, and they got so far as the bad penmanship and the slouched hat, but they never got to be Horace Greeleys. So it was in the days of Lord Byron. Excessively admired he was, and there were many people in England who resolved that they would be Lord Byrons, and they got to be, so far as a very large shirt-collar went, but no nearer. It was not eccentricity that made Horace Greeley; it was hard work. Proverbs xxii., 29: "Seest thou a man diligent in his business? he shall stand before kings."

Again, my friends, there comes from this providence a *warning for all brain-workers.* Mr. Greeley, at my own table, ten days before his nomination at Cincinnati, told me that he had not had a sound sleep in fifteen years! I said to him, "Why do you sit in your room writing, with your hand up at that elevation, on a board raised to that point?" "Well," he said, "I have so much work to do that I must not have my chest cramped at all. I must keep all my faculties of body and mind in full play, or I can not get on." During the late war, in connection with his editorial duty, almost every evening you might have seen him on the rail-car going out to meet a lecturing engagement. He was writing articles for other journals besides his own. He was preparing a history of the war, which history might have taken the exclusive time of any other man for two or three years. And now people say it is political disappointment that killed him. I do not believe it, unless it is on the principle that it is the last straw that breaks the camel's back. A man with his magnificent cerebral development would not have been overthrown in that way; it was because for twenty years he had been giving the death-blow with his own pen — extreme work, work which he did conscientiously, but it was *over*work. Work is good, as I said in the former head of my discourse; but too much work is death.

Now, brethren of literary toil, you had better hold up. If you are going at the rate of sixty miles an hour, you had better stop and go no more than thirty. The temptations to overwork for literary men are multiplying all the time in increased newspapers and magazines, and lecturing platforms. The temptation to night-work is especially great—that kind of work which is most exhausting and ruinous. When the sun goes down, God puts his candle out, and says to the world, "My child, you had better go to sleep; I have put the candle out." The brass-headed nails of coffins are made out of gaslight! The money that a man makes by midnight toil he pays toward the expenses of his own funeral. When the devil can not stop a good man's work by making him lazy, then he comes into the editor's room, or into the minister's study, or into the artist's studio, and he says, "Go it! you ought to be doing five times the work you are doing. You ought to write two books this year. You ought to send out twenty or thirty additional articles. You ought to deliver fifty lectures at two hundred dollars a night." Then, when his health fails, there is satanic congratulation. The devil first tries to stop a useful man by making him lazy. Failing in that, he then puts on the lash and digs in the spurs, and drives him to death. I say, therefore, to the men who are toiling with their brain, you had better "slow up," as they say on the railroad lines. I hear somebody say, "You had better take your own advice." I will. I am being converted under my own sermon. God gives to every man a certain amount of work, and he does not want him to do any more than that. "Do thyself no harm," is advice no more appropriate to the jailer when the prison is tumbling around his ears, than it is appropriate to those the wards of whose health and the fastnesses of whose strength begin to tremble with the earthquake. Paul was very careful of his body; long before the days of expressage he sends hundreds of miles for his greatcoat to Troas. Oh, ye men of literary toil! you have been careful about keeping the candle snuffed and burning brightly; is it not almost time you began to look after the candlestick? The sharp sword will not make any execution unless you have a handle to it. Through all the editorial rooms, and through all the studies of this country, let the warning reverberate; let it come up tonight from the graves of Kirke White, of Henry J. Raymond, and of Horace Greeley.

Again, I have found since this calamity came to the nation, the great *law of brotherhood illustrated*. Have you not been surprised to see how every heart thrilled in sympathy with this trial? Take this in consideration of the fact that we are now at the close of the meanest and most dastardly chapter of personality, and vituperation, and scorn, and political calumny that has ever been written. It is most marvelous. If there is any word expressive of contempt, and of hatred, and of disgust, and of defamation that has not been used within the past six months, it is because the dictionaries have made the word obsolete. Why, the cylinders of the printing-presses have hardly cooled off from the fiery assault. But the very moment this death is announced, how every thing is hushed! And next Wednesday, when the nation follows Horace Greeley to his grave, in the vast procession you will not be able to tell who were Republicans and who were Liberal Republicans. All the States will vote for him now, and by the electoral college of the whole world he will be proclaimed, unanimously, President of the great reformatory movements of the last twenty years. Oh, how quickly the nation grounded arms! how quickly the sword clanked back into the scabbard! The drums that were beating the victory of his political opponent deepen now into the grand march for the dead! Oh, is it not beautiful! We are all brothers, after all. The sorrow reveals it. It is just as when two brothers have been fighting about father's property, and will not speak to each other. Mother dies, and they go home to the obsequies, and John stands on one side of the mother's coffin, and George on the other side, and, for the first time speaking in five years, say, "Wasn't she a good mother?" And then hands clasp, and they say, "Oh, we can't live this way any longer, can we?" And so the two great parties, after long and bitter strife, now clasp hands over the sepulchre of the dead, and promise new exertion for the welfare of this country. If there be in all this audience a base heart in which the serpent of bad feeling against the renowned man still lingers, next Wednesday let him take that serpent and fling it under the hoofs of the black-tasseled horses that shall draw out to their last resting-place this great man. But I am lion-hunting to-night, and I have no ammunition to waste on vultures that plunge their beaks into the bosoms of the dead.

I learn from this solemn providence that *newspaper men, like all other men, will have to come to an account before God.* Nothing could keep this man when the time came for him to go. God called; he went. The doctors could not hold him back; the prayers of a nation could not hold him back; even his own loving daughter, her hand in his, could not hold him back. Surely she had enough trouble. Mother gone, and father gone—all within a few weeks. God comfort that double anguish, and be to her more than father or mother. I say when God called him to meet his account, he had to go. It is a vast responsibility that rests upon people that set type or sit in editorial chairs. The audience is so large, the influence is so great, the results are so eternal, that I believe, in the day of judgment, amidst all the millions of men who will come up to render their account, the largest account will be rendered by newspaper men; and I will tell you why. Here is a paper that has, for instance, fifty thousand circulation. We will suppose that each of those papers is read by three men. There is an audience of one hundred and fifty thousand people. Now, suppose that in one of the issues of that paper there be a grand truth forcibly put, how magnificent the opportunity! Suppose there be a wrong thing projected in that paper, who can estimate the undoing of that one issue! Oh, if there is any man who needs to be a Christian, it is an editor! He needs more grace, more help, more wisdom than any other man. Now, in the columns, it is by custom that the editor writes "we" and "us;" in the last great day it will be "I" and "me." I congratulate you, newspaper men, on the splendor of your opportunity; but I charge you before God, who will judge the quick and the dead, that you be careful to use your influence in the right direction. How grand will be the result in the last day for the man who has consecrated the printing-press to high and holy objects! God will say to such a one,

"You broke off a million chains, you opened a million blind eyes, you gave resurrection to a million of the dead." But what shall become of those who have prostituted their press to blackmailing and the advocacy of that which is wrong, multiplying the numbers of their papers by pandering to the tastes of bad men and worse women, poisoning the air with a plague that killed a nation? Why, God will say to such men in the last day, "You were destroying angels, smiting the first-born of man and beast; you made the world horribly worse, when you might have made it gloriously better. Go down, and suffer with the millions you have damned! You knew your duty, and you did it not."

I remark, further, there ought to be, in consequence of this providence, a great arousal on the part of men engaged *in temperance reform*. Horace Greeley was the champion of temperance in this country. His pen wrote more and effected more than that of any other man. You remember how he spoke last winter in the Lay College on this subject. He was a hater of all intoxicating drinks, from the rye whisky that pitches the sot into the ditch, up to the wine-glass that makes a fool of the fine lady in the parlor. He had seen so much devastation of drunkenness amidst the brethren of his own occupation; he had heard the snapping of the heart-strings of widowhood and orphanage, robbed by the fiend that squats in the wine-cask and sweats in the brewery, the smoke of its torment ascending up forever and forever. I think that yesterday all the gin-bottles in the grog-shop rattled with gladness when it was told that Horace Greeley was dead, and that drunkenness, which "biteth like a serpent and stingeth like an adder," hissed for joy.

But boast not, O thou demon of the pit! If Horace Greeley is dead, the principles he advocated live. Elisha may be buried, but we will keep his grave open, and let down this inert cause until, touching his bones, it shall spring up with tenfold power, and go forth for the conquest of the world. Because Christ turned water into wine, men turn the pure juice of the grape into swill. Now that the standard-bearer of temperance has fallen, who will catch up the colors and carry them on to victory? I ask these fathers and mothers, before their sons wither under this hot simoon of hell, to come and join the standard. I ask men in all circumstances to deny their palates and save their souls. When next Wednesday the nation gathers around Horace Greeley's grave, I would like to have the little children whose fathers he redeemed from the cup, come and throw flowers all over that grave, and the woman whom he lifted up from the squalor of being a drunkard's wife come and pour her tears on the resting-place of him who has spoken his last word and written his last line in behalf of the reformation of the inebriate. "Howl, howl, fir-tree, for the cedar has fallen."

I learn, again, from this providence that the *last hours of a man's life are a poor time to prepare for eternity.* I do not know about Mr. Greeley's experience; I do not know whether in life he thought much about the things of eternity. I suppose he did; I hope he did. I read that in his last moments he said, "I know that my Redeemer liveth;" and a man who can say that is fit for any thing in time or any thing in eternity. But it is my belief, it is my hope that, in the days of his life, he thought much upon these great subjects, and did not leave until the last hour consecration to God. The last moments of his life were passed under mental aberration, and it is always true that the last hours of a man's life are a poor time in which to prepare for eternity. It is either delirium or some trouble about property, or it is the magnitude of world-changing, or it is bidding good-bye to friends—making it a very poor hour to prepare for heaven. The fact is, that if a man wants to get ready for eternity, he must do it while he is well. I do not suppose there were ten men in the United States with a stronger natural constitution than Horace Greeley; but Death is an old besieger, and he prides himself on the strength of the castle he takes. Be ye also ready. Do not wait until you see the *flambeau* of the bridegroom coming through the darkness before you begin to trim your lamps. You may wait for your last moment; but when your last moment comes, it will not wait for you. There are a great many doors through which you may get out of this world, but there is only one door into heaven. "*I am the door*," said One who threw out his hands in the gesticulation, showing the sacrificial blood clotted in the palm and dripping from the fingers. I can only with my voice reach those who hear it now; but ye men of the press who take the words I utter to-night, tell all the cities, tell all the world that Jesus died to save men; that the death-bed is a poor place to get ready for eternity; that it is appointed unto all men once to die, but after that—the judgment! the judgment!

Hush, all ye people! Let the nation uncover its head and bow lowly, and carry out the illustrious dead. Along the same streets where he trudged a poor boy, and afterward a weary man, let him be carried. Hang out signals, white and black—black for the woe, white for the resurrection. Bring him across the river into this city, where he always loved to come; then out toward Greenwood take him. Toll long and loud the bell at the gate. Put him down under the snow to rest—the only good rest he has had for thirty years; his right hand closed, for there are no more heroic words for it to write; his lips shut, for there are no more encouraging words for them to speak; his brow cool, for his head has stopped aching now; his heart quiet, for it never will break again. I put upon his grave not a single wreath, not a single daisy or a blossom; but I put upon his grave a scroll, plain and white, a scroll half open, that you may read it from both sides: "I am the resurrection and the life: he that believeth in me, though he were dead, yet shall he live." "Howl, howl, fir-tree, for the cedar is fallen."

## THE ARRIVAL OF AUTUMN.

"The summer is ended."—*Jeremiah* viii., 20.

THE text was occasioned by the departure of the glory of the Jews; but read on this first autumnal Sabbath, starts up in my mind more thoughts than the bang of a sportsman's gun ever routed quails out of the grass. "The summer is ended."

The soul of the intelligent Christian reflects the natural world from all sides. While there are those who have not enough beauty in their souls to speckle the wing of an insect, nor enough music to drown the buzz of a gadfly, to the intelligent Christian, river-wave, and cloud-bank, and tree-branch, and bird-song, are so many evangelists and apostles with their scroll of light to unwind, and their sermon to preach. He sees a cross in every tree, and Christ in every lily; beholds death descending on a falling leaf, and the resurrection foretold in every bud bursting. The year is to him a great temple of praise, on whose altar, as an offering, spring puts its blossoms, and summer its sheaf of grain, and autumn its branch of fruits; while winter, like a white-bearded priest, stands at the altar praising God with psalm of snow and hail and tempest.

The summer season is the perfection of the year. The trees are in full foliage. The rose—God's favorite flower, for he has made nearly five hundred varieties of it—flames with divine beauty. I do not wonder that Nero once paid one hundred and fifty thousand dollars for one wreath of roses with which to adorn his supper-table. The origin of the rose is suggested by the legend which says in the East a holy woman was burned at the stake, and when the executioner put the torch to the wood, it kindled into roses instead of fire, and so the world has had plenty of flowers ever since. Summer is the season of beauty. The world itself is only one drop from the overflowing cup of God's joy. All the sweet sounds ever heard are but one tone from the harp of God's infinite melody. When God made all things, he did not half try. To the work of man there is a wrong side, but there is no wrong side to the carpets which God hath nailed to the earth, or to the curtains he hath hung to the heavens. No thread ever snaps in God's loom. In your recent wanderings you have seen the beauty of the Lord, and the beauty of the summer.

The summer is also a season of exposure. Excursion trains come into collision, and the *Wawasset* perishes on the Potomac. The perils of the traveler were illustrated by the conductor on the Mount Washington Railroad this summer. When on the steepest place of that steepest rail-track in all the earth, a man was frightened, and said to the conductor: "Suppose the locomotive should give out, where would we go to?" "Ah," said the conductor, "there is a brake at the front of the car." "But," said the traveler, "suppose that should give out, where then would we go to?" Said the conductor, "There is another brake, you see, on the cars." "But," said the affrighted passenger, "suppose that also should give way, where then would we go to?" And the conductor replied, significantly, "That depends upon how you have lived."

Summer, a season of exposure! Many yield to the temptation, and eat forbidden fruit, the sin of our first parents, and die. Diseases that had their root in some cough of the winter, in the summer put forth the white blossom of death. Malaria floats on the August night air. Every bill of mortality is increased. Epidemics drive out their hundred hearses to Greenwood and Laurel Hill. Old age sinks down from exhaustion under the heat, and Death, like an old Herod, sends the messengers to Bethlehem for the massacre of the infants. In the week that ended last 19th of July, five hundred children died in the city of New York. Summer is a season of exposure as well as a season of harvest and a season of beauty.

But that summer wave of beauty is receding. The sap of the tree is halting in its upward current. The night is fast conquering the day. The populations of our great cities are flying homeward. Crowded rail-trains are full of returning tourists. You and I are buckling on the work of the cooler months. The sports of our recreating days are gone. Summer with fever heats has perished, and to-night we twist a wreath of scarlet sage and china-asters for her brow, and bury her under the scattered rose-leaves, while we beat amidst the woods and by the water-courses this solemn dirge, "*The summer is ended!*"

There are three or four classes of persons of whom the words of my text are descriptive. In the first place, *they are appropriate to the aged.* Those in this audience who are far advanced in years were once just like ourselves. There was a time when they could hardly bridle their exuberance. They laughed, they romped, they shouted, they sang. The world was as bright to them then as it is to us now. Though they are in the October of life now, it was June with them once. They take with placidity things that once would have made them blaze with indignation. Sometimes they may chide us because of our vivacity; but when two or three of the aged get together, I have overheard them talk in the next room about occurrences which make me believe that when they were of our age they were just like us. How fast they did drive! What strong wrestlers they brought to the earth! In what a willful mood they upset the sleigh, to see the victims crawl out of the snow-bank! How many "frolics" there were, and how many "quiltings!" The aged do not talk much to us about these things. They wonder why we are not as cool as they are. Ah! the dear souls forget that July is never as cool as November. Aged Christians used to be a great discouragement to me, when I heard of their great attainments, and viewed my own spiritual backwardness; but now they are great encouragement to me; for since I have found that they were about as I am, I have come to the conclusion that the same things which have favored them will favor me, and I get some hint of what a good man I will be in my ninetieth year.

But the aged feel life going away from them. They stop at the top of the stairs, all out of breath, and say, "I can't walk up stairs as well as I used to." They hold the book off on the other side of the light when they read. Their eye is not so quick to catch a sight, nor their ear a sound. Instead of the strong stride with which they once went along the street, they take short steps now, as though about to stop in the journey. Their

voice is tremulous, and their hand, that failed not to sen
the bullet to the mark, has lost its steadiness. Too feebl
even to walk out, on pleasant days the cushioned chair
is wheeled to the veranda. The bloom and verdure of
their life have drooped. June has melted into July.
July has fallen back into August. August has cooled
into September. "The summer is ended."

I have noticed that in this climate, in the latter part of
October or the first of November, there is a season of
beautiful weather called Indian summer. It is the gem
of all the year. A haziness is in the atmosphere, but
still every thing is pleasant and mild. And so I see before me to-night some who have come to that season.
There is a haziness on their vision, I know, but the
sweetness of heaven has melted into their soul. I congratulate those who have come to the Indian summer of
their life. Their grandchildren climb up on the back of
the chair, and run their fingers along the wrinkles which
time has for a long while been furrowing there. On sunny afternoons, grandfather goes out in the church-yard
and sees on the tombstones the names, the very names
that sixty years ago he wrote on his slate at school. He
looks down where his children sleep their last sleep, and
before the tears have fallen, says, "So much more in
heaven!" Patiently he awaits his appointed time, until
his life goes out gently as a tide, and the bell tolls him
to his last home under the shadow of the church that he
loved so long and loved so well. Blessed old age, if it
be found in the way of righteousness!

But I remark again, that my text is appropriate for
all *those whose fortunes have perished.* If a man lose his
property at thirty or forty years of age, it is only a sharp

discipline, generally, by which later he comes to larger success. It is all folly for a man to sit down in mid-life discouraged. The marshals of Napoleon came to their commander, and said, "We have lost the battle, and we are being cut to pieces." Napoleon took his watch from his pocket, and said, "It is only two o'clock in the afternoon. You have lost that battle, but we have time enough to win another. Charge upon the foe!" Though the meridian of life has passed with you, and you have been routed in many a conflict, give not up in discouragement. There are victories yet for you to gain. But sometimes monetary disaster comes to a man when there is something in his age, or something in his health, or something in his surroundings, which make him know well that he will never get up again. In 1857 it was estimated that for many years previous to that time, annually, there had been thirty thousand failures in the United States. Many of those persons never recovered from the misfortune. The leaves of worldly prosperity all scattered—the day-book, and the ledger, and the money-safe, and the package of broken securities crying out, "The summer is ended." But let me give a word of comfort in passing. The sheriff may sell you out of many things, but there are some things of which he can not sell you out. He can not sell out your health. He can not sell out your family. He can not sell out your Bible. He can not sell out your God. He can not sell out your heaven! You have left more than you have lost. A man of large wealth died; two men were talking over his death, and one said to the other, "How much did he leave?" The other man thoughtfully replied, "*Every dollar!*" So that if the ghost of Stephen Girard or John

Jacob Astor should come into a retail store on Canal Street, they could not get trusted for ten cents, and would not have money enough to ride in a car on Fulton Avenue! The poets always represent ghosts as walking. I suppose they can not afford to ride. Death is an auctioneer which sells us out of all our earthly possessions, and there is nothing left when once he drops his hammer of stone on the coffin-lid, crying, "Gone! gone!"

But, sons and daughters of God, mourn not when your property goes. The world is yours, and life is yours, and death is yours, and immortality is yours, and thrones of imperial grandeur are yours, and rivers of gladness are yours, and shining mansions are yours, and God is yours! The eternal God hath sworn it; and every time you doubt it, you charge the King of heaven and earth with perjury. Instead of complaining how hard you have it, go home to-night, take up your Bible full of promises, get down on your knees before God, and thank him for what you *have*, instead of spending so much time in complaining about what you have not.

Again, the words of the text are appropriate to all those *who have passed through luxuriant seasons of grace without improvement.* I know there are those who do not believe in revivals; but I think that if there had been no revivals there would not have been a single church in England or America to-day. It would have been impossible to withstand the flood of sin and wretchedness; had it not been for those large gatherings, the Church of God could not have maintained its ground. Suppose a foreign despotism should attack our country. Would we be afraid of having men come too plentifully to our standard? No! We would say, "Let them come, a million men from the North, a million men from the South, and a million men from the West, and let us go out and fight the foe." The quicker they come and the vaster the multitude, the gladder would be our huzza. Yet there are Christians who, when they see a sudden re-enforcement in the Church, are afraid. Alas! that they are so unwise. A revival that would bring all the twelve hundred millions of our race into the kingdom of God in one day ought not to frighten any honest Christian. But there are men in the house who have gone through revivals, and been unsaved. There are hundreds of men in this audience before me, to-night, who ought to have been saved in 1857. You felt the throb of that national upheaval. You remember the time—many of you do, at any rate—when the enginehouses were turned into prayer-meetings; when in one day, to one of our ports, there came five vessels with sea-captains, who had been brought to God in the last voyage. Religion broke out of church into places of business and amusement. Christian songs floated into the temple of mammon, while the devotees were counting their golden beads. A company of merchants on Chambers Street, New York, at their own expense, hired Burton's old theatre, and every day at twelve o'clock the place was filled with men crying after God. The telegrams flashed backward and forward from Fulton Street prayer-meeting, and Jaynes's Hall, in Philadelphia, "God is here! Fifty souls to-day borne into the kingdom. Seventy-five people stood up for prayers! One hundred souls rejoicing in the Gospel!" Oh, that was the healthiest excitement the world has ever felt since the day of Pentecost. Some of you went through all that, and are not saved. It required more resolution and determination for you not to be saved than, under God, would have made you a Christian. But all that process has hardened your soul. Through all these seasons of revival you have come, and you are to-night living without God, on the way to a death without hope. "The summer is ended!"

Again, the text is appropriate to all *those who expire after a wasted life.* There are two things that I do not want to bother me in my last hour. The one is, my worldly affairs. I want all those affairs so plain and disentangled that the most ignorant administrator could see what was right at a glance, and there could be no standing around about the office of the surrogate devouring widow's houses. The other thing I do not want to be bothered about in my last hour, is the safety of my soul. God forbid that I should crowd into that last, feeble, languishing, delirious hour questions enough momentous to swamp an archangel! The saddest thing on earth is a death-bed, with a wasted life standing on one side of it, and an overshadowing eternity standing on the other side of it, and no Jesus Christ anywhere in the room. Pull from under my head that pillow stinging with thorns, and put under it the hand of Jesus, on which many of my loved ones have died. Though the pillow may seem to the world as hard as the rock on which Jacob slept, still there will be let down to that Christian death-pillow a ladder reaching into the heaven, an angel on the lowest rung, an angel on the top rung, and an angel on every rung between, so that the soul ascending may mount upward, stepping from wing to wing into the skies. But the commonest thing in the world is for a man to die without hope. How we all were stunned when last summer, or last spring, the *Atlantic* struck a rock near Newfoundland; but hark to the crash of ten thousand immortal shipmates! If you have ever slept in a house on the prairie, where in the morning, without rising from your pillow, you could look off on the landscape, you could see it miles away, clear to the horizon: it is a very bewildering scene. But how much more intense the prospect, when from the last pillow a soul looks back on life, and sees one vast reach of mercies, mercies, mercies unimproved, and then gets upon one elbow, and puts the head on the hand to see beyond all that, but seeing nothing beyond but mercies, mercies, mercies unimproved. The bells of sorrow will toll through all the past, and the years of early life and mid-life wail with a great lamentation. A dying woman, after a life of frivolity, says to me: "Mr. Talmage, do you think that I can be pardoned?" I say, "Oh yes." Then gathering herself up in the concentred dismay of a departing spirit, she looks at me, and says, "Sir, *I know I shall not!*" Then she looks up as though she hears the click of the hoofs of the pale horse, and her long locks toss on the pillow as she whispers, "The summer is ended."

Again, the text is appropriate to all *those who wake up in a discomfited eternity*. I know there are those who say, "It don't make any difference how we live or what we believe. We will come out at the golden gate. They are all there together in glory—the Pauls and the Neros, and the Abraham Lincolns and the John Wilkes Booths, the Robespierres and the men who were destroyed by the guillotine, and the Court of Charles I. and

Louis XVI.—all together in glory. If I thought it were true that, whatever our belief or behavior in this world, we would go safely, I would preach that. It is a great deal pleasanter to offer congratulation than to offer warning. But that Bible tells us differently, and our own sense of what is right utters an overwhelming negative. Do you believe that your sister and your mother, who lived Christian lives and died holy deaths, are now in a world in the companionship of all the unrepentant libertines and debauchees that went out last year from Baxter Street? My soul abhors the idea. Let me say, if your belief leads you to that, so that you really do think that your Christian mother and your Christian sister are in such society, I want to tell you mine are not! mine are not!

No! No! The good must go up, and the bad must go down. I want no Bible to tell me that truth. There is something within my heart that says it is not possible that a man whose life has been all rotten can, in the future world, without repentance, be associated with men who have been consecrated to Christ. What does the Bible say? It says that "As we sow we shall reap." It says, "These shall go away into everlasting punishment, and the righteous into life eternal." Does that look as though they were coming out at the same place? "And there was a great gulf fixed." "And the smoke of their torment ascendeth up for ever and ever." If a man rejects the Bible I am not surprised that he believes any thing, or refuses to believe any thing; but how a man can believe in that Bible, and yet believe that all the good and all the unrepentant will go to the same place, I can not understand. Ah! you may ask me strange questions.

You may say, "Are the heathen lost?" I reply, God has not given us supervisal of the heathen. I simply know this, that if your soul and mine have had an offer of life from Christ the Lord, and reject it, and continue to reject it, we must go to the bad place, and not come out of it. I am not now discussing the state of the heathen, but discussing the state of my soul and yours.

Now suppose a man goes out from Brooklyn, a city in which there are as many religious advantages as in any city under the sun, and suppose he wakes up in a discomfited eternity—how will he feel? Having become a serf of darkness, how will he feel when he thinks that he might have been a prince of light? There are no words of lamentation sufficient to express that sorrow. You can take the whole group of sad words—pain, pang, convulsion, excruciation, torment, agony, woe—and they come short of the reality. The summer of gracious opportunity is all gone. The last clock has struck. The last bell rung. The last call has been rejected. Then looking up to a heaven that it can never reach, and looking down to a ruin it must always inhabit, and shivering with the chill of an unending horror, the soul will wring its hands and cry, "The summer is ended!"

I am glad that that hour of doom has not struck for any body here; and I mean to-night to launch a life-boat large enough to take off all the passengers. Shove off, my lads, and pull for the wreck! What is the use of dying, when the ten thousand voices of heaven cry, Live! live! Oh, there is enough mercy in the heart of my Lord Jesus Christ, in the flash of an instant, to take all this audience into the peace and the hope of the Gospel! If I point you out the peril, it is only because I want to tell you of the way of escape. Say! bondmen of sin and death, will you be free? Men and women bought out of eternal serfdom by your own Brother's blood, will you accept emancipation? The Lord Jesus waits for you. He stands on two torn feet, spreading out two mangled hands, with which He would press you to His broken heart; while heaven bends over, watching and waiting to see whether you will now repent and believe, lest the night drop, and the last chance of mercy be gone, and the door be shut, and the harvest is past, and the summer is ended.

# BLEATING SHEEP AND LOWING OXEN.

"And Samuel said, What meaneth then this bleating of the sheep in mine ears, and the lowing of the oxen which I hear?"—1 *Samuel* xv., 14.

THE Amalekites thought they had conquered God, and that he would not carry into execution his threats against them. They had murdered the Israelites *in* battle and *out* of battle, and left no outrage untried. For four hundred years this had been going on, and they say, "God either dare not punish us, or he has forgotten to do so." Let us see. Samuel, God's prophet, tells Saul to go down and slay all the Amalekites, not leaving one of them alive; also to destroy all the beasts in their possession — ox, sheep, camel, and ass. Hark! I hear the tread of two hundred and ten thousand men, with monstrous Saul at their head, ablaze with armor, his shield dangling at his side, holding in his hand a spear, at the waving of which the great host marched or halted. The sound of their feet shaking the earth, seems like the tread of the great God, as, marching in vengeance, he tramples nations into the dust. I see smoke curling against the sky. Now there is a thick cloud of it; and now I see the whole city rising in a chariot of smoke behind steeds of fire. It is Saul that set the city ablaze. The Amalekites and Israelites meet; the trumpets of battle blow peal on peal, and there is a death-hush. Then there is a signal waved; swords cut and hack; javelins ring on shields; arms fall from trunks, and heads roll into the dust. Gash after gash, the frenzied yell, the gurgling of throttled throats, the cry of pain, the laugh of revenge, the curse hissed between clenched teeth — an army's death-groan. Stacks of dead on all sides, with eyes unshut and mouths yet grinning vengeance. Huzza for the Israelites! Two hundred and ten thousand men wave their plumes and clap their shields, for the Lord God hath given them the victory.

Yet that victorious army of Israel are conquered by sheep and oxen. God, through the prophet Samuel, told Saul to slay all the Amalekites, and to slay all the beasts in their possession; but Saul, thinking that he knows more than God, saves Agag, the Amalekitish king, and five drove of sheep and a herd of oxen that he can not bear to kill. Saul drives the sheep and oxen down toward home. He has no idea that Samuel, the prophet, will find out that he has saved these sheep and oxen for himself. Samuel comes and asks Saul the news from the battle. Saul puts on a solemn face, for there is no one who can look more solemn than your genuine hypocrite, and he says, "I have fulfilled the commandment of the Lord." Samuel listens, and he hears the drove of sheep a little way off. Saul had no idea the prophet's ear would be so acute. Samuel says to Saul, "If you have done as God told you, and slain all the Amalekites and all the beasts in their possession, what meaneth the bleating of the sheep in mine ears, and the lowing of the oxen that I hear?" Ah, one would have thought that blushes would have consumed the cheek of Saul! No, no! He says the army—not himself, of course, but the army—had saved the sheep and oxen for sacrifice; and then they thought it would be too bad anyhow to kill Agag, the Amalekitish king. Samuel takes the sword and he slashes Agag to pieces; and then he takes the skirt of his coat, in true Oriental style, and rends it in twain, as much as to say, "You, Saul, just like that, shall be torn away from your empire, and torn away from your throne." In other words, let all the nations of earth hear the story that Saul, by disobeying God, won a flock of sheep but lost a kingdom.

I learn first from this subject that *God will expose hypocrisy.* Here Saul pretends he has fulfilled the divine commission by slaying all the beasts belonging to the Amalekites, and yet at the very moment he is telling the story, and practicing the delusion, the secret comes out, and the sheep bleat and the oxen bellow.

A hypocrite is one who pretends to be what he is not, or to do what he does not. Saul was only a type of a class. The modern hypocrite looks awfully solemn, whines when he prays, and during his public devotion shows a great deal of the whites of his eyes. He never laughs, or, if he does laugh, he seems sorry for it afterward, as though he had committed some great indiscretion. The first time he gets a chance, he prays twenty minutes in public, and when he exhorts, he seems to imply that all the race are sinners, with one exception, his modesty forbidding the stating who that one is. There are a great many churches that have two or three ecclesiastical Uriah Heeps.

When the fox begins to pray, look out for your chickens. The more genuine religion a man has, the more comfortable he will be; but you may know a religious impostor by the fact that he prides himself on the fact that he is uncomfortable. A man of that kind is of immense damage to the Church of Christ. A ship may outride a hundred storms, and yet a handful of worms in the planks may sink it to the bottom. The Church of God is not so much in danger of the cyclones of trouble and persecution that come upon it as of the vermin of hypocrisy that infests it. Wolves are of no danger to the fold of God unless they look like sheep. Arnold was of more damage to the army than Cornwallis and his hosts. Oh, we can not deceive God with a church certificate! He sees behind the curtain as well as before the curtain; he sees every thing inside out. A man may, through policy, hide his real character; but God will after a while tear open the whited sepulchre and expose the putrefaction. Sunday faces can not save him; long prayers can not save him; psalm-singing and church-going can not save him. God will expose him just as thoroughly as though he branded upon his forehead the word "Hypocrite." He may think he has been successful in the deception, but at the most unfortunate moment the sheep will bleat and the oxen will bellow.

One of the cruel bishops of olden time was going to excommunicate one of the martyrs, and he began in the usual form—"In the name of God, amen." "Stop!" says the martyr, "don't say, 'in the name of God!'" Yet how many outrages are practiced under the garb of religion and sanctity! When, in synods and conferences, ministers of the Gospel are about to say something unbrotherly and unkind about a member, they almost always begin by being tremendously pious, the venom of their assault corresponding to the heavenly flavor of the prelude. Standing there, you would think they were ready to go right up into glory, and that nothing kept them down but the weight of their boots and overcoat, when suddenly the sheep bleat and the oxen bellow.

Oh, my dear friends, let us cultivate simplicity of Christian character! Jesus Christ said, "Unless you become as this little child, you can not enter the kingdom of God." We may play hypocrite successfully now, but the Lord God will after a while expose our true character. You must know the incident mentioned in the history of Ottacas, who was asked to kneel in the presence of Randolphus I.; and when before him he refused to do it, but after a while he agreed to come in private when there was nobody in the king's tent, and then he would kneel down before him and worship; but the servants of the king had arranged it so that by drawing a cord the tent would suddenly drop. Ottacas after a while came in, and supposing he was in entire privacy, knelt before Randolphus. The servants pulled the cord, the tent dropped, and two armies surrounding looked down on Ottacas kneeling before Randolphus. If we are really kneeling to the world while we profess to be lowly subjects of Jesus Christ, the tent has already dropped, and all the hosts of heaven are gazing upon our hypocrisy. God's universe is a very public place, and you can not hide hypocrisy in it.

Going out into a world of delusion and sham, pretend to be no more than you really are. If you have the grace of God, profess it; profess no more than you have. But I want the world to know that where there is one hypocrite in the Church there are five hundred outside of it, for the reason that the field is larger. There are men in all circles who will bow before you, and who are obsequious in your presence and talk flatteringly, but who all the while in your conversation are digging for bait and angling for imperfections. In your presence they imply that they are every thing friendly, but after a while you find they have the fierceness of a catamount, the slyness of a snake, and the spite of a devil. God will expose such. The gun they load will burst in their own hands; the lies they tell will break their own teeth; and at the very moment they think they have been successful in deceiving you and deceiving the world, the sheep will bleat and the oxen will bellow.

I learn further from this subject *how natural it is to try to put off our sins upon other people.* Saul was charged with disobeying God. The man says it was not he; he did not save the sheep; the army did it—trying to throw it off on the shoulders of other people. Human nature is the same in all the ages. Adam, confronted with his sin, said, "The woman tempted me, and I did it." And the woman charged it upon the serpent; and if the serpent could have spoken, it would have charged it upon the devil. I suppose the real state of the case was that Eve was eating the apple, and that Adam saw it, and begged and coaxed until he got a piece of it. I suppose that Adam was just as much to blame as Eve was. You can not throw off the responsibility of any sin upon the shoulders of other people.

Here is a young man who says, "I know I am doing wrong, but I have not had any chance. I had a father who despised God, and a mother who was a disciple of godless fashion. I am not to blame for my sins—it is my bringing up." Ah no! that young man has been out in the world long enough to see what is right, and to see what is wrong, and in the great day of eternity he can not throw his sins upon his father or mother, but will have to stand for himself and answer before God. You have had a conscience, you have had a Bible, and the influence of the Holy Spirit. Stand for yourself, or fall for yourself.

Here is a business man. He says, "I know I don't do exactly right in trade, but all the dry-goods men do it, and all the hardware men do this, and I am not responsible." You can not throw off your sin upon the shoulders of other merchants. God will hold you responsible for what you do, and them responsible for what they do. I want to quote one passage of Scripture for you—I think it is in Proverbs: "If thou be wise, thou shalt be wise for thyself; but if thou scornest, thou alone shalt bear it."

I learn further from this subject what *God meant by extermination.* Saul was told to slay all the Amalekites, and the beasts in their possession. He saves Agag, the Amalekite king, and some of the sheep and oxen. God chastises him for it. God likes nothing done by halves. God will not stay in the soul that is half his and half the devil's. There may be more sins in our soul than there were Amalekites. We must kill them. Woe unto us if we spare Agag! Here is a Christian. He says, "I will drive out all the Amalekites of sin from my heart. Here is jealousy—down goes that Amalekite. Here is backbiting—down goes that Amalekite;" and what slaughter he makes among his sins, striking right and left! What is that out yonder, lifting up his head? It is Agag—it is worldliness. It is an old sin he can not bear to strike down. It is a darling transgression he can not afford to sacrifice. Oh, my brethren, I appeal this morning for entire consecration! Some of the Presbyterians call it the "higher life." The Methodists, I believe, call it "perfection." I do not care what you call it; without holiness no man shall see the Lord. I know men who are living with their soul in perpetual communion with Christ, and day by day are walking within sight of heaven. How do I know? They tell me so. I believe them. They would not lie about it. Why can not we all have this consecration? Why slay some of the sins in our soul, and leave others to bleat and bellow for our exposure and condemnation. Christ will not stay in the same house with Agag. You must give up Agag, or give up Christ. Jesus says, "All of that heart or none." Saul slew the poorest of the sheep and the meanest of the oxen, and kept some of the finest and the fattest, and there are Christians who have slain the most unpopular of their transgressions, and saved those which are most respectable. It will not do. Eternal war against all the Amalekites; no mercy for Agag.

I learn further from this subject that *it is vain to try to defraud God*. Here Saul thought he had cheated God out of those sheep and oxen; but he lost his crown, he lost his empire. You can not cheat God out of a single farthing. Here is a man who has made ten thousand dollars in fraud. Before he dies every dollar of it will be gone, or it will give him violent unrest. Here is a Christian who has been largely prospered. He has not given to God the proportion that is due in charities and benevolences. God comes to the reckoning, and he takes it all away from you. Do you suppose, if a man has an income of ten thousand dollars, and he gives only five hundred dollars of it to God, that God is going to let him keep it? No. Do you suppose that if a man have one hundred thousand dollars in capital or in estate, and gives only two thousand of it to the Lord God in a year, that God is going to let him keep any? Or, keeping it, it will curse him to the bone. You can not cheat God. How often it has been that Christian men have had a large estate, and it is gone. The Lord God came into the counting-room and said, "I have allowed you to have all this property for ten, fifteen, or twenty years, and you have not done justice to my poor children. When the beggar called upon you, you hounded him off your steps; when my suffering children appealed to you for help, you had no mercy. I only asked for so much, or so much, but you did not give it to me, and now I will take it all."

God asks of us one-seventh of our time in the way of Sabbath. Do you suppose we can get an hour of that time successfully away from its true object? No, no. God has demanded one-seventh of your time. If you take one hour of that time that is to be devoted to God's service, and instead of keeping his Sabbath, use it for the purpose of writing up your accounts or making worldly gains, God will get that hour from you, if he chases you into hell to get it. God says to Jonah, "You go to Nineveh." He says, "No, I wont. I'll go to Tarshish." He starts for Tarshish. The sea raves, the winds blow, and the ship rocks. Come, ye whales, and take this passenger for Tarshish! No man ever gets to Tarshish whom God tells to go to Nineveh. The sea would not carry him; it is God's sea. The winds would not waft him; they are God's winds. Let a man attempt to do that which God forbids him to do, or to go into a place.

where God tells him not to go, the natural world as well as God is against him. The lightnings are ready to strike him, the fires to burn him, the sun to smite him, the waters to drown him, and the earth to swallow him. Those whose princely robes are woven out of heart's strings; those whose fine houses are built out of skulls; those whose springing fountains are the tears of oppressed nations—have they successfully cheated God? The last day will demonstrate—it will be found out on that day that God vindicated not only his goodness and his mercy, but his power to take care of his own rights and the rights of his Church, and the rights of his oppressed children. Come, ye martyred dead, awake! and come up from the dungeons where folded darkness hearsed you, and the chains like cankers peeled loose the skin, and wore off the flesh, and rattled on the marrowless bones. Come, ye martyred dead, from the stakes where you were burned, where the arm uplifted for mercy fell into the ashes, and the cry of pain was drowned in the snapping of the flame and the howling of the mob; from valleys of Piedmont and Smithfield Square, and London Tower, and the Highlands of Scotland. Gather in great procession, and together clap your bony hands, and together stamp your mouldy feet, and let the chains that bound you to dungeons all clank at once, and gather all the flames that burned you in one uplifted arm of fire, and plead for a judgment. Gather all the tears ye ever wept into a lake, and gather all the sighs ye ever breathed into a tempest, until the heaven-piercing chain-clank, and the tempest-sigh, and the thunder-groan, announces to earth and hell and heaven a judgment! a judgment! Oh, on that day God will vindicate his own cause, and vindicate the cause of the troubled and the oppressed! It will be seen in that day that though we may have robbed our fellows, we never have successfully robbed God.

My Christian friends, as you go out into the world, exhibit an open-hearted Christian frankness. Do not be hypocritical in any thing; you are never safe if you are. At the most inopportune moment, the sheep will bleat and the oxen bellow. Drive out the last Amalekite of sin from your soul. Have no mercy on Agag. Down with your sins; down with your pride; down with your worldliness. I know you can not achieve this work by your own arm, but Almighty grace is sufficient—that which saved Joseph in the pit; that which delivered Daniel in the den; that which shielded Shadrach in the fire; that which cheered Paul in the shipwreck.

# DIFFICULT ROWING.

"The men rowed hard to bring it to the land; but they could not: wherefore they cried unto the Lord."—*Jonah* i., 13, 14.

NAVIGATION in the Mediterranean Sea always was perilous, especially so in early times. Vessels were propelled partly by sail and partly by oar. When, by reason of great stress of weather, it was necessary to reef the canvas or haul it in, then the vessel was entirely dependent upon the oars, sometimes twenty or thirty of them on either side the vessel. You would not venture outside Sandy Hook with such a craft as my text finds Jonah sailing in; but he had not much choice of vessels. He was running away from the Lord; and when a man is running away from the Lord, he has to run very fast.

God had told Jonah to go to Nineveh, to preach about the destruction of that city. Jonah disobeyed. That always makes rough water, whether in the Mediterranean, or the Atlantic, or the Pacific, or the Caspian Sea, or in the Hudson, or the East River. It is a very hard thing to scare sailors. I have seen them, when the prow of the vessel was almost under water, and they were walking the deck knee-deep in the surf, and the small boats by the side of the vessel had been crushed as small as kindling-wood, whistling as though nothing had happened; but the Bible says that these mariners of whom I speak were frightened. That which sailors call "a lump of a sea" had become a blinding, deafening, swamping fury. How mad the wind can get at the water, and the water can get at the wind, you do not know unless you have been spectators. I have in my house a piece of the sail of a ship, no larger than the palm of my hand: that piece of canvas was all that was left of the largest sail of the ship *Greece*, that went into the storm five hundred miles off Newfoundland, last September a year. Oh, what a night that was! I suppose that it was in some such storm as this that Jonah was caught.

He knew that the tempest was on his account, and he asked the sailors to throw him overboard. Sailors are a generous-hearted race, and they resolved to make their escape, if possible, without resorting to such extreme measures. The sails are of no use, and so they lay hold on their oars. I see the long bank of shining blades on either side the vessel. Oh! how they did pull, the bronzed seamen, as they laid back into the oars. But rowing on the sea is very different from rowing upon a river; and as the vessel hoists, the oars skip the wave and miss the stroke, and the tempest laughs to scorn the flying paddles. It is of no use, no use. There comes a wave that crashes the last mast, and sweeps the oarsmen from their places, and tumbles every thing in the confusion of impending shipwreck, or, as my text has it, "The men rowed hard to bring it to the land; but they could not: wherefore they cried unto the Lord."

This scene is very suggestive to me, and I pray God I may have grace and strength enough to represent it before this dying yet immortal auditory. Two years ago I preached you a sermon on another phase of this very subject, and I got a letter some weeks ago from Houston, Texas, the writer saying that the reading of that sermon in London had led him to God. And last night I received another letter from South Australia, saying that the reading of that sermon in Australia had brought several souls to Christ. And then, I thought, why not now take another phase of the same subject, for perhaps that God who can raise in power that which is sown in weakness may this night, through another phase of the same subject, bring salvation to the people who shall hear, and salvation to the people who shall read. Men and women, who know how to pray, lay hold of the Lord God Almighty to-night, and wrestle for the blessing.

Bishop Latimer would stop sometimes in his sermon, in the midst of his argument, and say, "Now, I will tell you a fable;" and to-night I would like to bring the scene of the text as an illustration of a most important religious truth. As those Mediterranean oarsmen trying to bring Jonah ashore were discomfited, I have to tell you that they were not the only men who have broken down on their paddles, and have been obliged to call on the Lord for help. I want to say that the unavailing efforts of those Mediterranean oarsmen has a counterpart in the efforts *we are making to bring souls to the shore of safety and set their feet on the Rock of Ages.* You have a father, or mother, or husband, or wife, or child, or near friend, who is not a Christian. There have been times when you have been in agony about their salvation. A minister of Christ, whose wife was dying without any hope in Jesus, walked the floor, wrung his hands, cried bitterly, and said, "I believe I shall go insane, for I know she is not prepared to meet God." And there may have been days of sickness in your household, when you feared it would be a fatal sickness; and how closely you examined the face of the doctor as he came in and scrutinized the patient, and felt the pulse, and you followed him into the next room, and said, "There isn't any danger, is there, doctor?" And the hesitation and the uncertainty of the reply made two eternities flash before your vision. And then you went and talked to the sick one about the great future. Oh, there are those here who have tried to bring their friends to God! They have been unable to bring them to the shore of safety. They are no nearer that point than they were twenty years ago. You think you have got them almost to the shore, when you are swept back again. What shall you do? Put down the oar? Oh no! I do not advise that; but I do advise that you appeal to that God to whom the Mediterranean oarsmen appealed—the God who could silence the tempest and bring the ship in safety to the port. I tell you, my friends, that there has got to be a good deal of praying before our families are brought to Christ. Ah! it is an awful thing to have half a household on one side the line, and the other part of the household on the other side of the line! Oh, the possibility of an eternal separation! One would think that such a thought would hover over the pillow, and hover over the arm-chair, and hover over the table, and that each clatter at the door would cause a shudder as though the last messenger had come. To live together in this world five years, or ten years, or fifty years, and then afterward to live away from each other millions, millions, millions, millions of years, and to know and feel that between us and eternal separation there is only one heart-beat! When our Christian friends go out of this life into glory, we are comforted. We feel we shall meet them again in the good land. But to have two vessels part on the ocean of eternity, one going to the right and the other to the left—farther apart, and farther apart—until the signals cease to be recognized, and there are only two specks on the horizon, and then they are lost to sight forever!

I have to tell you that the unavailing efforts of these Mediterranean oarsmen has a counterpart in the efforts some of us are making to bring our children to the shore of safety. There never were so many temptations for young people as there are now. The literary and the social influences seem to be against their spiritual interests. Christ seems to be driven almost entirely from the school and the pleasurable concourse, yet God knows how anxious we are for our children. We can not think of going into heaven without them. We do not want to leave this life while they are tossing on the waves of temptation and away from God. From which of them could we consent to be eternally separated? Would it be the son? Would it be the daughter? Would it be the eldest? Would it be the youngest? Would it be the one that is well and stout, or the one that is sick? Oh, I hear some parent saying to-night, "I have tried my best to bring my children to Christ. I have laid hold of the oars until they bent in my grasp, and I have braced myself against the ribs of the boat, and I have pulled for their eternal rescue; but I can't get them to Christ." Then I ask you to imitate the men of the text, and cry mightily unto God. We want more importunate praying for children, such as the father indulged in when he had tried to bring his six sons to Christ, and they had wandered off into dissipation. Then he got down in his prayers, and said, "O God! take away my life, if through that means my sons may repent and be brought to Christ;" and the Lord startlingly answered the prayer, and in a few weeks the father was taken away, and through the solemnity the six sons fled unto God. Oh, that father could afford to die for the eternal welfare of his children! He rowed hard to bring them to the land, but could not, and then he cried unto the Lord. There are parents here who are almost discouraged about their children. Where is your son to-night? He has wandered off, perhaps, to the ends of the earth. It seems as if he can not get far enough away from your Christian counsel. What does he care about the furrows that come to your brow; about the quick whitening of the hair; about the fact that your back begins to stoop with the burdens? Why, he would not care much if he heard you were dead! The black-edged letter that brought the tidings he would put in the same package with other letters telling the story of his shame. What are you going to do? Both paddles broken at the middle of the blade, how can you pull him ashore? I throw you one oar to-night with which I believe you can bring him into harbor. It is the glorious promise: "I will be a God to thee, and to thy seed after thee." Oh, broken-hearted father and mother, you have tried every thing else, now make an appeal for the help and omnipotence of the covenant-keeping God! and perhaps at your next family gathering—perhaps on Thanksgiving-day, perhaps next Christmas-day—the prodigal may be home; and if you crowd on his plate more luxuries than on any other plate at the table, I am sure the brothers will not be jealous, but they will wake up all the music in the house, "because the dead is alive again, and because the lost is found." Perhaps your prayers have been answered already. The vessel may be coming homeward, and by the light of this night's stars that absent son may be pacing the deck of the ship, anxious for the time to come when he can throw his arm around your neck and ask for forgiveness for that he has been wringing your old heart so long. Glorious reunion! that will be too sacred for outsiders to look upon; but I would just like to look through the window when you have all got together again, and are seated at the banquet.

> "Though parents may in covenant be,
> And have their heaven in view;
> They are not happy till they see
> Their children happy too."

Again, I remark that the unavailing effort of the Mediterranean oarsmen has a counterpart in the effort which *we are making to bring this world back to God, his pardon, and safety*. If this world could have been saved by human effort, it would have been done long ago. John Howard took hold of one oar, and Carey took hold of another oar, and Adoniram Judson took hold of another oar, and Luther took hold of another oar, and John Knox took hold of another oar, and they pulled until they fell back dead from the exhaustion. Some dropped in the ashes of martyrdom, some on the scalping-knives of savages, and some into the plague-struck room of the lazaretto; and still the chains are not broken, and still the despotisms are not demolished, and still the world is unsaved. What then? Put down the oars and make no effort? I do not advise that. But I want you, Christian brethren, to understand that the church, and the school, and the college, and the missionary society are only the instrumentalities; and if this work is ever done at all, God must do it, and he *will* do it, in answer to our prayer. "They rowed hard to bring it to the land; but they could not: wherefore they cried unto the Lord."

Again, the unavailing effort of those Mediterranean oarsmen has a counterpart in every man that is *trying to row his own soul into safety*. When the Eternal Spirit flashes upon us our condition, we try to save ourselves. We say, "Give me a stout oar for my right hand, give me a stout oar for my left hand, and I will pull myself into safety." No. A wave of sin comes and dashes you one way, and a wave of temptation comes and dashes you in another way, and there are plenty of rocks on which to founder, but seemingly no harbor into which to sail. Sin must be thrown overboard, or we must perish. There are men in this house, in all these galleries, who have tried for ten years to become Christians. They believe all I say in regard to a future world. They believe that religion is the first, the last, the infinite necessity. With it, heaven! Without it, hell! They do every thing but *trust* in Christ. They make sixty strokes in a minute. They bend forward with all earnestness, and they lay back until the muscles are distended, and yet they have not made one inch in ten years toward heaven. What is the reason? That is not the way to go to work. You might as well take a frail skiff, and put it down at the foot of Niagara, and then head it up toward the churning thunder-bolt of waters, and expect to work your way up through the lightning of the foam into calm Lake Erie, as for you to try to pull yourself through the surf of your sin into the hope, and pardon, and placidity of the Gospel. You can not do it in that way. Sin is a rough sea, and long-boat, yawl, pinnace, and gondola go down unless the Lord deliver; but if you will cry to Christ and lay hold of divine mercy, you are as safe from eternal condemnation as though you had been twenty years in heaven.

I wish I could put before this audience, unpardoned, their own helplessness. You will be lost as sure as you sit there if you depend upon your own power. You can not do it. No human arm was ever strong enough to unlock the door of heaven. No foot was ever mighty enough to break the shackle of sin. No oarsman swarthy enough to row himself into God's harbor. The wind is against you. The tide is against you. The Law is against you. Ten thousand corrupting influences are against you. Helpless and undone. Not so helpless a sailor on a plank, mid-Atlantic. Not so helpless a traveler girded by twenty miles of prairie on fire. Prove it, you say. I will prove it. John vi., 44: "No man can come to me, except the Father which hath sent me draw him."

But while I have shown your helplessness, I want to put by the side of it the power and willingness of Christ to save you. I think it was in 1686 a vessel was bound for Portugal, but it was driven to pieces on an unfriendly coast. The captain had his son with him, and with the crew they wandered up the beach, and started on the long journey to find relief. After a while, the son fainted by reason of hunger and the length of the way. The captain said to the crew, "Carry my boy for me on your shoulders." They carried him on; but the journey was so long, that after a while the crew fainted from hunger and from weariness, and could carry him no longer. Then the father rallied his almost wasted energy, and took up his own boy, and put him on his shoulder, and carried him on mile after mile, mile after mile, until, overcome himself by hunger and weariness, he too fainted by the way. The boy laid down and died, and the father, just at the time rescue came to him, also perished, living only long enough to tell the story—sad story, indeed! But glory be to God that Jesus Christ is able to take us up out of our shipwrecked and dying condition, and put us on the shoulder of his strength, and by the omnipotence of his Gospel bear us on through all the journey of this life, and at last through the opening gates of heaven! He is mighty to save. Hear it, ye dying men and women! Though your sin be long, and black, and inexcusable, and outrageous, the very moment you believe I will proclaim pardon—quick, full, grand, unconditional, uncompromising, illimitable, infinite. Oh the grace of God! I am overwhelmed when I come to think of it. Give me a thousand ladders, lashed fast to each other, that I may scale the height. Let the line run out with the anchor until all the cables of earth are exhausted, that we may touch the depth. Let the archangel fly in circuit of eternal ages in trying to sweep around this theme. Oh the grace of God! It is so high. It is so broad. It is so deep. Glory be to my God, that where man's oar gives out, God's arm begins! Why will ye carry your sins and your sorrows any longer when Christ offers to take them? Why will you wrestle down your fears when this moment you might give up and be saved? Do you not know that every thing is ready?

> "See, Jesus stands with open arms;
> He calls, he bids you come.
> Sin holds you back, and fear alarms;
> But still there yet is room."

Oh! men and women, bought by the blood of Jesus, how can I give you up? Will you turn away this plea, as you have turned away so many? Have you deliberately chosen to die? Do you want to be lost? Do you turn your back on heaven because you do not want to see Christ, nor your own loved ones whom he has taken into his bosom? Can not some of these fathers and mothers hear the voices of their children in glory calling to-night, saying,

> "Steer this way, father,
> Steer straight for me;
> Here safe in heaven
> I am waiting for thee."

Do you not see the hands of mercy, the hands of loved ones, let down now from the skies, beckoning you to the pardoning Jesus, beckoning you up to heaven and to glory? Can it be that it is all in vain? Calvary in vain? Death-bed warnings in vain? Ministering spirits in vain? The opening gates of heaven in vain? The importuning of God's eternal Spirit all in vain? To your knees, oh dying soul! before it be too late to pray. I hear the creaking of the closing door of God's mercy. To some of you the last chance has come. The tongue in the great bell begins to swing for the death-knell of thy soul immortal! And in an hour in which ye think not your disembodied spirit may go shrieking out toward the throne of an offended God, and—what then? Has not God been calling to you, my dear brother, during the past week? In the shaking down of fortunes, has he not shown you the uncertainty of this world's treasures? Do you not feel to-night as if you would like to have God and Jesus, and all the precious promises of his Gospel? I remember that after the great crisis of 1857, when the whole land was rocked with commercial sorrow, the Spirit of God descended, and there were two hundred and seventy thousand souls in one year who found the peace of Christ. Oh, I would that the rocking in New York and Brooklyn to-day—the commercial rocking—might rouse up men to the consideration of the interests of their immortal souls! As I asked you this morning, I ask you now, "What shall it profit a man if he gain the whole world, and lose his soul?" Come back, oh wanderer! I do not ask where you came from to-night. Though you may have come from places of sin, I shall not be partial in my offer of salvation. I offer it to every one who sits before me. "Whosoever will, let him come," and let him come now.

Plenty of room at the feast. Jesus has the ring of his love all ready to put upon your hand. Come now and sit down, ye hungry ones, at the banquet. Ye who are in rags of sin, take the robe of Christ. Ye who are swamped by the breakers around you, cry to Christ to pilot you into smooth, still waters. On account of the peculiar phase of the subject, I have drawn my illustrations, you see, chiefly, to-night, from the water. I remember that a vessel went to pieces on the Bermudas a great many years ago. It had a vast treasure on board. But the vessel being sunk, no effort was made to raise it. After many years had passed, a company of adventurers went out from England, and after a long voyage they reached the place where the vessel was said to have sunk. They got into a small boat and hovered over the place. Then the divers went down, and they broke through what looked like a limestone covering, and the treasures rolled out—what was found afterward to be, in our money, worth one million five hundred thousand dollars, and the foundation of a great business house. At that time the whole world rejoiced over what was called the luck of these adventurers. Oh ye who have been rowing toward the shore, and have not been able to reach it, I want to tell you to-night that your boat hovers over infinite treasure! All the riches of God are at your feet. Treasures that never fail, and crowns that never grow dim. Who will go down now and seek them? Who will dive for the pearl of great price? Who will be prepared for life, for death, for judgment, for the long eternity? Many who hear my voice hear it for the last time, and I shall meet them not again until the heavens be rolled up as a scroll, and the books be open. Flee the wrath to come! The Lord help you! I am clear of the blood of souls. See two hands of blood stretched out toward thy dying soul, as Jesus says, "Come unto me, all ye that labor and are heavy laden, and I will give you rest."

## THE BURNING OF THE BROOKLYN TABERNACLE.

(ANNIVERSARY DISCOURSE.)

"He shall baptize you with the Holy Ghost and with fire."—*Matthew* iii., 11.

MEN had better listen when God speaks in wave, or wind, or storm, or earthquake, or conflagration. God spoke to Job out of the hurricane; to Lisbon, out of the earthquake; to both continents by the burning of the *Austria* in mid-ocean, the driving against Mars Head of the *Atlantic*, the awful going down of the *Ville du Havre;* while he spoke to our own congregation last December, through the burning of the Brooklyn Tabernacle. God's most vehement utterances are in flames of fire. The most tremendous lesson he ever gave to New York was in the conflagration of 1835; to Chicago, in the conflagration of 1871; to Boston, in the conflagration of 1872; to our own congregation, in the fiery downfall of our beloved place of worship.

The day was full of merciless frost. Things cracked with the cold. Man and beast felt it was a day to have warm shelter. The bell had rung for religious service, and the families of our congregation had started for the accustomed place of worship, some with thanksgivings that they must needs offer, some with sorrows that they must needs have healed, all of them with souls that needed more preparation for the judgment-day. A black flag of smoke against the sky, and the rush of the hose-carriages made us ask, "Where is it? what ward? Horrible to be turned out of house and home on such a day as this!" Some one says, "It is in the direction of the Tabernacle. Ay, it is the church!" and there is a rush past the streets crying, "Fire! fire!" And instead of sitting down in placid worship that day, our congregation, joined by other congregations on the streets, stood in the presence of God before the altar of a burning church. Many wrung their hands and thought of the sacred scenes in which there they had mingled—the baptisms, the weddings, the burials, the communion-days, the scenes of revival, the deliverances, and the victories. All efforts at extinguishment seemed to fail. The great organ, as the flames roared through its pipes, played its own requiem, and the walls came down with a crash that made the earth tremble. Some saw in that nothing but unmitigated disaster, while others of us heard the voice of God as from heaven, sounding through the crackling thunder of that awful day, saying, "He shall baptize you with the Holy Ghost and with fire!" The Lord has fulfilled the prophecy. That which threatened to be entire extinguishment has really been an unmistakable benediction.

Through many self-denials, and through kindness and practical help on all sides, our building hastens toward completion. Through a panic that has staggered the land, and made some of the noblest enterprises come to a dead halt, the work has gone gradually but surely on, and we shall soon have a house to dedicate to the Lord, a house marvelous for capacity, and for beauty, and for strength, in which men and women for many generations will assemble to worship God. Added to that, while we were in the wilderness, the Lord has descended mightily in a pentecostal blessing, and a great multitude have cried out after God, and there has been a rush for the cross, and a wailing over sin, and a jubilant shout over pardon such as you and I have never before heard. "Oh, give thanks unto the Lord, for he is good, for his mercy endureth forever!" Out of darkness he brings light. Out of trouble he brings assurance. Out of defeat he brings victory. Out of smoking, crackling, roaring, devastating calamity, "he baptizes us with the Holy Ghost, and with fire."

I propose this morning, so far as God may help me, to draw out the analogy between these two baptisms—the baptism of last December and the baptism of this December.

First, I remark they were *both sudden*. We all felt that whatever else might go down, that Tabernacle never could. We thought it fire-proof. When on that cold December day that building was in flames, there was on every countenance in the street amazement. Sudden as sudden could be! So has it been with the other baptism — the baptism of the Holy Ghost. The spiritual fire broke out here on Sabbath night, and, while hundreds were rising and asking for prayers, there was a look of amazement on the faces of the people, and some aged Christians wondered what it all meant. The first baptism—suddenly. The next baptism—suddenly. So nearly always does the Spirit come. So it came when Jonathan Edwards preached in Northampton, and John Livingstone in Scotland, and William Tennant preached in Monmouth, and Dr. Finlay preached in Baskinridge, and Nettleton, and Daniel Baker, and Truman Osborne, and Mr. Earle, and Edward Payson Hammond preached everywhere. Almost always the blessing came suddenly. It has been especially so in our midst. In a night family altars have been reared in houses where before there was no prayer; infidels persuaded of the truth of Christianity in five minutes; children going at three o'clock to the Sabbath-schools unsaved coming home Christians at five o'clock; men coming into these services to make merry with the anxiety of those who were seeking after God, themselves at the close rising for prayer; and many of the old passages of Scripture that seemed to lie dormant in the hearts of God's people have flashed up with unwonted and overwhelming power.

Whitefield was once preaching on Blackheath, and a man and his wife coming from market saw the crowd and went up to hear. Whitefield was saying something about what happened eighteen hundred years ago, and the man said to his wife, "Come, Mary, we will not stop any longer. He is talking about something that took place more than eighteen hundred years ago. What's that to us?" But they were fascinated. They could not get away. The truth of God came to their hearts. When they were home, they took down the Bible and said, "Is it possible that these old truths have been here so long and we have not known it?" Ah! it was in the flash of God's Spirit on Blackheath that they were saved — the Spirit coming mightily, and suddenly, and overwhelmingly upon them. So it was that God's Spirit came to Andrew Fuller, and James Hervey, and the Earl of Rochester, and Bishop Latimer — suddenly. So it came to multitudes in this assemblage, both the baptism of fire and the baptism of the Holy Ghost. A father was enraged whose child was interested in religious things many years ago, because she would go to the place of worship. He forbade her going; but she slipped out when he was not watching. He said, "There now, she has gone to the meeting;" and he went to the meeting. She was kneeling at the altar. He put his arms around her with indignation to carry her out, when she cried, "Father, you are too late; I HAVE FOUND JESUS!" And so there have been those among us who would like to have kept Christ out of their families, but they came not soon enough to succeed. It is too late, father; your child has already found Jesus.

But I remark again, the analogy between these two baptisms — the baptism of fire and the baptism of the Holy Ghost—is in the fact that they were *both irresistible.* Notwithstanding all our boasted machinery and organization for putting out fires, the efforts that were made did not repulse the flames last December one single instant. Having begun, they kept on more and more triumphantly, clapping their hands over the destroyed building. There was a great sound of fire-trumpets and brave men walking on hot walls; but the flames were balked not an instant. So it has been with the Holy Spirit moving through the hearts of this people. Why, there have been aged men who for forty or fifty years resisted the truth who have surrendered! There have been men here who have sworn that the religion of Jesus Christ should never come into their households; they and their children kneel now at the same altar. We have all felt it. Formalists trying to put out the spiritual fire have only had their trouble for their pains. It has gone on.

It is going on now, conquering pride, and worldliness, and sin; and I pray it may keep on until it has swept everything before it, and there shall be in every household an altar, and in every heart a throne for the blessed Jesus. Go on, great baptism of the Holy Ghost as with fire!

In the days of revival in England, when John Wesley was preaching, everywhere scoffers would mimic his preaching, and one man thought it was very smart to gather an audience, and stand up with a Bible, and take John Wesley's favorite text, "Except ye repent, ye shall all likewise perish;" and he preached—he, the scoffer—to an audience of scoffers, until the truth rebounded on his own heart and he cried for mercy, and the truth overwhelmed the hearts of his hearers, and they cried for mercy, and instead of being an audience of mockers it became an audience of seekers. Oh! this is the power of God, this is the wisdom of God unto salvation. Both baptisms—the one of fire and the one of the Holy Ghost —irresistible.

I remark again, that I find the analogy in the fact that both baptisms *were consuming.* Did you ever see any more thorough work than was done by that fire last December? The strongest beams turned to ashes. The iron cracked, curled up, and was destroyed. The work of the flames consummate. So it has been with the Holy Ghost: it has been a consuming fire amidst the sins and the habits of those who despise God. How many have had their transgressions utterly consumed! Some who were victims of bad habits have had their chains broken off. Down at the club-room and down at the saloon, they wonder why these people do not come any more. Ah! instead of the laughter of fools, which is like the crackling of thorns under a pot, they have come to that religion which is joy here and hosanna forever; and after a man has set down once at the Lord's banquet, he has no more patience with the swine's diet. When the revival, two years ago, swept through the city of Lawrence, at the West, it was stated to be a fact that the gin saloons lost fifty per cent. of their business. So may it always be—the Spirit of God consuming the dissipations of men! That Spirit has gone through the hearts and lives of many who sit before me, like fire through stubble. They have been swept by the purifying flames. Both baptisms have been consuming.

Again, I find an analogy in the two baptisms, because they both *were melting*. If you examined the bars and bolts, and plumbing work of the Tabernacle after it went down, you know it was a melting process. The things that seemed to have no relation to each other adjoined—flowed together. So it has been with the Spirit of God, melting down all asperities and unbrotherliness. Heart has flowed out toward heart. It has been a melting process. If there is any thing that our city churches need, it is melting. There are a thousand icicles hanging to the eaves of our city churches where there are two icicles hanging to the eaves of the country churches. We are so afraid we will get acquainted with somebody that will not do us honor! The great want of the Church to-day is a thaw—a thaw. Oh, that the Lord God would rise up and melt down the freezing conventionalities of his Church! I think that that fire of last December and this spiritual fire of this December have melted us until we flow together in Christian sympathy, and harmony, and love, and that we can now join hands in one great family circle as a church, and sing as we never sang before:

> "Before our Father's throne
> We pour our ardent prayers;
> Our fears, our hopes, our aims are one,
> Our comforts and our cares.
>
> "The glorious hope revives
> Our courage by the way,
> While each in expectation lives,
> And longs to see the day."

But I have, on this anniversary of the burning of the Brooklyn Tabernacle, to say that we have not, as a church, yet entered upon the mission for which God has baptized us—first with fire, and now with the Holy Ghost. We need to put forth on a more earnest mission than we have ever entered upon. God evidently does not intend us for smooth work. He has rocked us in a very rough cradle. Ofttimes has this church been assaulted in various ways, and if there are any who expect to have a smooth time and an easy pathway, they had better wake up from the delusion and get out of this church. If God baptized us with fire, it is because he means to fit us for hot and tremendous work. If you are afraid of fatigue, and afraid of persecution, and afraid of opposition, you had better not train in this battalion, for I have no quiet encampment to offer you by still waters; but rather to tell you of a forced march, hard fighting, and a bayonet charge. I believe God means us to go forth and proclaim an earnest, uncompromising, out and out, straightforward, revolutionary, old-fashioned Gospel, that believes in repentance and regeneration, in glory and in perdition. But, my friends, in order to enter upon that work we want still more vigorous baptism of the Holy Ghost. We want that Spirit to come down in all our families with his arousing, melting, illuminating, saving presence; and I believe that then the influences which we have already had in the way of a blessing will be only as a spark compared with the great conflagration of religious enthusiasm and zeal we shall feel here.

But, my friends, when is this work to begin? If you, as a private Christian, and I, as a minister of the Lord Jesus Christ, have some work to do, when shall we begin it? Now, and here. Oh, men and women of the world! do you not feel to-day the baptism of the Holy Ghost? Is there not something in the passing of the seasons, something in this last Sabbath of the year, something in the tramp of your pulses, something in the solemn surroundings of this morning, something in the wave of influence that comes in upon your soul, to make you realize that this may be your last chance for heaven? Miss it now, and you miss it forever. Do you not see how swiftly your Sabbaths are going? Do you not see how the years of your life are rushing into a great eternity? The year 1873 has already landed thousands and tens of thousands of souls beyond the reach of all mercy. The book with twelve chapters made up of the twelve months is about finished by the recording angel, and he has his hands on the lids of that book, about to close it for the last reckoning. Oh, my hearer! if you turn your back upon your best interests, if your final opportunity for redemption disappear, if the rushing wing that passes us is the wing of the retreating spirit, if this be the moment of awful calamity — the downfall of an immortal soul—then you will see a conflagration compared with which that of last December was child's play. It will be when the Lord shall be revealed from heaven with flaming fire, to take vengeance upon those who know not God and obey not the Gospel of our Lord Jesus Christ! From that conflagration of last December we shall recover; but the soul that goes down into that final conflagration shall never recuperate. That fire in December last continued only three or four hours, and on the following day even the smoke ceased to curl up in the frosty air; but that soul that rejects Christ shall go into a fire that shall never be quenched, "and the smoke of *its* torment ascendeth up forever and forever." May God Almighty through Jesus Christ keep us out of that! Whatever misfortune and disaster may come upon us in this world, let it come; but God forbid that any of us should lose heaven! We can not afford to lose our soul. Save that, we have saved every thing. Lose that, we have lost every thing. Instead of the baptism that consumes, oh that we might this morning, penitently, believingly, prayerfully, joyfully receive the baptism that saves! I suppose that some of you know there were persons who stood in the presence of that burning church last December who for the first time sought after God. They said then to themselves; indeed they arose in the prayer-meetings afterward, and said it: "When I stood in the presence of that building, I was reminded as never before that there was nothing fire-proof, that there was nothing on earth certain, and there and then, in the presence of that devastation and ruin, I resolved that I would be the Lord's, and I have kept my promise. I have given my heart to Jesus." Oh! if that was the result in some souls on that cold Sabbath day, now, when this morning I rehearse the scene, shall it not be, under God's Spirit, the means of bringing some of you to Christ? You have tried this world. You have been drinking out of the fountains of its pleasure. You have tried in January, February, March, April, May, June, July, August, September, October, November, and now nearly to the close of December, and tell me frankly, oh man of the world! is there any thing this side Christ and heaven that can give solace, and peace, and contentment to your immortal nature? No; you know there is nothing. You have tried the world, and it has failed you. It is a cheating world. It is a lying world. It is a dying world. Oh, seek after God to-day, and be at peace with him!

# THE BRIGHTEST OF DAYS.

"And call the Sabbath a delight."—*Isaiah* lviii., 13.

THERE is an element of gloom striking through all false religions. Paganism is a brood of horrors. The god of Confucius frowned upon its victims with blind fate. Mohammedanism promises nothing to those exhausted with sin in this world but an eternity of the same passional indulgences. The papacy prostrates its devotees with fastings and kneelings and merciless taxation of the poor man's wages, and tugs until it sweats, from January to December, in trying to pull its dead priests and archbishops out of purgatory. But God intended that our religion should have the grand characteristic of cheerfulness. St. Paul struck the key-note when he said, "Rejoice evermore; and again I say, rejoice." This religion has no spikes for the feet; it has no hooks for the shoulder; it has no long pilgrimages to take; it has no funeral-pyres upon which to leap; it has no Juggernauts before which to fall. Its good cheer is symbolized in the Bible by the brightness of waters, and the redolence of lilies, and the sweetness of music, and the hilarities of a banquet. A choir of seraphim chanted at its induction, and pealing trumpet, and waving palm, and flapping wing of archangel are to celebrate its triumphs. It began its chief mission with the shout, "Glory to God in the highest!" and it will close its earthly mission with the ascription, "Hallelujah, for the Lord God omnipotent reigneth!"

But men have said that our religion is not cheerful, because we have such a doleful Sabbath. They say, "You can have your religious assemblages, and your long faces, and your sniffling cant, and your psalm-books, and your Bibles. Give us the Sunday excursion, and the horse-race, and the convivial laughter. We have so much joy that we want to spread it all over the seven days of the week, and you shall not have one of our days of worldly satisfaction for religious dolefulness." I want to show these men—if there are any such in the house this morning—that they are under a great delusion, and that God intended the fifty-two Sundays of the year to be hung up like bells in a tower, beating a perpetual chime of joy and glory and salvation and heaven; for I want you to carry out the idea of the text, "and call the Sabbath a delight."

I remark, in the first place, we are to find in this day *the joy of healthy repose.* In this democratic country we all have to work—some with hand, some with brain, some with foot. If there is in all this house a hand that has not, during the past year, been stretched forth to some kind of toil, let it be lifted. Not one, not one. *You* sell the goods. *You* teach the school. *You* doctor in the sick-room. *You* practice at the bar. *You* edit a newspaper. *You* tan the hides. *You* preach the Gospel. *You* mend the shoes. *You* sit at the shuttle. *You* carry the hod of bricks up the ladder on the wall. And the one occupation is as honorable as the other, provided God calls you to it. I care not what you do, if you only do it well. But when Saturday night comes, you are jaded and worn. The hand can not so skillfully manufacture; the eye can not see as well; the brain is not so clear; the judgment is not so well balanced. A prominent manufacturer told me that he could see a difference between the goods which went out of his establishment on Saturday from the goods that went out on Monday. He said, "They were very different indeed. Those that were made in the former part of the week, because of the rest that had been previously given, were better than those that were made in the latter part of the week, when the men were tired out." The Sabbath comes, and it bathes the soreness from the limbs, quiets the agitated brain, and puts out the fires of anxiety that have been burning all the week. Our bodies are seven-day clocks, and unless on the seventh day they are wound up, they run down into the grave. The Sabbath was intended as a savings-bank; into it we are to gather the resources upon which we are to draw all the week. That man who breaks the Sabbath robs his own nerve, his own muscle, his own brain, his own bones. He dips up the wine of his own life, and throws it away. He who breaks the Lord's day gives a mortgage to disease and death upon his entire physical estate, and at the most unexpected moment that mortgage will be foreclosed, and the soul ejected from the premises. Every gland, and pore, and cell, and finger-nail demands the seventh day for repose. The respiration of the lungs, the throb of the pulse in the wrist, the motion of the bone in its socket declare, "Remember the Sabbath-day, to keep it holy." There are thousands of men who have had their lives dashed out against the golden gates of the Sabbath. A prominent London merchant testifies that thirty years ago he went to London.

He says, "I have during that time watched minutely, and I have noticed that the men who went to business on the Lord's day, or opened their counting-houses, have, without a single exception, come to failure." A prominent Christian merchant in Boston says, "I find it don't pay to work on Sunday. When I was a boy, I noticed out on Long Wharf there were merchants who loaded their vessels on the Sabbath-day, keeping their men busy from morning till night, and it is my observation that they themselves came to nothing—these merchants—and their children came to nothing. It doesn't pay," he says, "to work on the Sabbath."

I appeal to your own observation. Where are the men who twenty years ago were Sabbath-breakers, and who have been Sabbath-breakers ever since? Without a single exception, you will tell me, they have come either to financial or to moral beggary. I defy you to point out a single exception, and you can take the whole world for your field. It has either been a financial or moral defalcation in every instance. Six hundred and forty physicians in London petition Parliament, saying: "We must have the Sabbath obeyed. We can not have health in this city and in this nation unless the Sabbath is observed." Those in our own country have given evidence on the same side. The man who takes down the shutters of his store on the Sabbath takes down the curse of Almighty God. That farmer who cultures his ground on the Sabbath-day raises a crop of neuralgia, and of consumption, and of death. A farmer said, "I defy your Christian Sabbath. I will raise a Sunday crop." So he went to work and plowed the ground on Sunday, and harrowed it on Sunday, and he planted corn on Sunday, and he reaped the corn on Sunday, and he gathered it into the barn on Sunday. "There," he says, "I have proved to you that all this idea about a fatality accompanying Sabbath work is a perfect sham. My crop is garnered, and all is well." But before many weeks passed the Lord God struck that barn with his lightnings, and away went the Sunday crop.

So great is the moral depression coming upon those who toil upon the Sabbath-day, that you may have noticed (if you have not, I call your attention to the fact) that in cases where the public interest demands Sabbath toil the moral depression is so great that there are but very few who can stand it. For instance, the police service, without which not one of our houses would be safe —there are very few who can stand the pressure and temptation of it. In London, where there are five thousand policemen, the statistic is given that in one year nine hundred and twenty-one of that five thousand were dismissed, five hundred and twenty-three were suspended, and two thousand four hundred and ninety-two were fined. Now, if the moral depression be so great in occupations that are positively necessary for the peace and prosperity of society, I ask you what must be the moral depression in those cases where there is no necessity for Sabbath work, and where a man chooses worldly business on the Lord's day just because he likes it, or wants to add to his emoluments? During the last war, it was found out that those public works which paused on the seventh day turned out more war material than those which worked all the seven days. Mr. Bagnall, a prominent iron merchant, gives this testimony: "I find we have fewer accidents in our establishment and fewer interruptions, now we observe the Lord's day; and at the close of the year, now that we keep the Sabbath, I find we turn out more iron and have larger profits than any year when we worked all the seven days." The fact is, Sabbath-made ropes will break, and Sabbath-made shoes will leak, and Sabbath-made coats will rip, and Sabbath-made muskets will miss fire, and Sabbath occupations will be blasted. A gentleman said, "I invented a shuttle on the Lord's day. I was very busy, so I made the model of that new shuttle on the Lord's day. So very busy was I during the week that I had to occupy many Sabbaths. It was a great success. I enlarged my buildings; I built new factories, and made hundreds of thousands of dollars; but I have to tell you that all the result of that work on the Sabbath has been to me ruin. I enlarged my buildings, I made a great many thousands of dollars, but I have lost all, and I charge it to the fact of that Sunday shuttle." I will place in two companies the men in this community who break the Sabbath and the men who keep it, and then I ask you who are the best friends of society? Who are the best friends of morals? Who have the best prospects for this world? Who have the best for the world that is to come?

Sabbath morning comes in the household. I suppose that the mere philosopher would say that the Sabbath light comes in a wave current, just like any other light; but it does not seem so to me. It seems as if it touched the eyelids more gently, and threw a brighter glow on the mantel ornaments, and cast a better cheerfulness on the faces of the children, and threw a supernatural glory over the old family Bible. Hail! Sabbath light! We rejoice in it. Rest comes in through the window, or it leaps up from the fire, or it rolls out in the old arm-chair, or it catches up the body into ecstasy, and swings open before the soul the twelve gates which are twelve pearls. The bar of the unopened warehouse, the hinges of the unfastened store-window, the quiet of the commercial warehouse seem to say, "This is the day the Lord hath made." Rest for the sewing-woman, with weary hands, and aching side, and sick heart. Rest for the overtasked workman in the mine, or out on the wall, or in the sweltering factory. Hang up the plane, drop the adze, slip the band from the wheel, put out the fire. Rest for the body, for the mind, and for the soul.

> "Welcome, sweet day of rest,
> That saw the Lord arise;
> Welcome to this reviving breast,
> And these rejoicing eyes."

Again I remark, we ought to have in the Sabbath the *joy of domestic reunion and consecration.* There are some very good parents who have the faculty of making the Sabbath a great gloom. Their children run up against the wall of parental lugubriousness on that day. They are sorry when Sunday comes, and glad when it goes away. They think of every thing bad on that day. It is the worst day to them, really, in all the week. There are persons who, because they were brought up in Christian families where there were wrong notions about the Sabbath, have gone out into dissipation and will be lost. A man said to me, "I have a perfect disgust for the Sabbath-day. I never saw my father smile on Sunday. It was such a dreadful day to me when I was a boy, I never got over it, and never will." Those parents did not "call the Sabbath a delight;" they made it a gloom. But there are houses represented here this morning where the children say through the week, "I wonder when Sunday will come!" They are anxious to have it come. I hear their hosanna in the house; I hear their hosanna in the school. God intended the Sabbath to be especially a day for the father. The mother is home all the week. Sabbath-day comes, and God says to the father, who has been busy from Monday morning to Saturday night at the store, or away from home, "This is your day. See what you can do in this little flock in preparing them for heaven. This day I set apart for you." You know very well that there are many parents who are mere sutlers of the household; they provide the food and raiment; once in a while, perhaps, they hear the child read a line or two in the new primer; or if there be a case of especial discipline, and the mother can not manage it, the child is brought up in the court-martial of the father's discipline and punished. That is all there is of it. No scrutiny of that child's immortal interests, no realization of the fact that the child will soon go out in a world where there are gigantic and overwhelming temptations that have swamped millions. But in some households it is not that way; the home, beautiful on ordinary days, is more beautiful now that the Sabbath has dawned. There is more joy in the "good-morning," there is more tenderness in the morning prayer. The father looks at the child, and the child looks at the father. The little one dares now to ask questions without any fear of being answered, "Don't bother me—I must be off to the store." Now the father looks at the child, and he sees not merely the blue eyes, the arched brow, the long lashes, the sweet lip. He sees in that child a long line of earthly destinies; he sees in that child an immeasurable eternity. As he touches that child, he says, "I wonder what will be the destiny of this little one? I wonder if on this brow will come the coronet of God's redemption or the iron crown of despair? I wonder if I will clasp this little one after all my Sabbaths have passed, and the doom of eternity has been announced? Will that little hand at last wave a palm or rattle a chain?" And while this Christian father is thinking and praying, the sweet promise flows through his soul, "of such is the kingdom of heaven." And he feels a joy, not like that which sounds in the dance, or is wafted from the froth of the wine-cup, or that which is like the "crackling of thorns under a pot," but the joy of domestic reunion and consecration.

Have I been picturing something that is merely fanciful, or is it possible for you and for me to have such a home as that? I believe it is possible. If we *can* have such a halo of grace and light and love and parental faithfulness around about our homes, we can expect for our little ones, when they go out in the world, a life of great usefulness, and finally a home in heaven.

I have a statistic that I would like to give you. A great many people, you know, say there is nothing in the Christian discipline of a household. In New Hampshire there were two neighborhoods — the one of six families, the other of five families. The six families disregarded the Sabbath. In time, five of these families were broken up by the separation of husbands and wives; the other by the father becoming a thief. Eight or nine of the parents became drunkards, one committed suicide, and all came to penury. Of some forty or fifty descendants, about twenty are known to be drunkards and gamblers and dissolute. Four or five have been in State-prison. One fell in a duel. Some are in the almshouse. Only one became a Christian, and he after first having been outrageously dissipated. The other five families that regarded the Sabbath were all prospered. Eight or ten of the children are consistent members of the church. Some of them became officers in the church; one is a minister of the Gospel; one is a missionary to China. No poverty among any of them. The homestead is now in the hands of the third generation. Those who have died have died in the peace of the Gospel. Oh, is there nothing in a household that remembers God's holy day? Can it be possible that those who disregard this holy commandment can be prospered for this life, or have any good hope of the life that is to come?

Again, we ought to have in the Sabbath the *joy of Christian assemblage.* Where are all those people going on the Sabbath? You see them moving up and down the street. Is it a festal day? people might ask. Has there been some public edict commanding the people to come forth? No, they are only worshipers of God who are going to their places of religious service. In what delicate scale shall I weigh the joy of Christian convocation? It gives brightness to the eye, and a flush to the cheek, and a pressure to the hand, and a thrill to the heart. You see the aged man tottering along on his staff through the aisle. You see the little child·led by the hand of its mother. You look around and rejoice that this is God's day, and this·the communion of saints. "One Lord, one faith, one baptism." Some familiar tune sets all the soul a-quiver and a-quake with rapture.

We plunge into some old hymn, and all our cares and anxieties are bathed off. The glorious Gospel transports us, the Spirit descends, Jesus appears, and we feel the bounding, spreading, electric joy of Christian convocation.

I look upon the Church of God as one vast hosanna. Joy dripping from the baptismal font, joy glowing in the sacramental cup, joy warbling in the anthem, joy beating against the gate of heaven with a hallelujah like the voice of mighty thunderings. Beautiful for situation! The joy of the whole earth is Mount Zion. It is the day and the place where Christ reviews his troops, bringing them out in companies and regiments and battalions, riding along the line, examining the battle-torn flags of past combat, and cheering them on to future victories. Oh the joy of Christian assemblage!

I remark also, we are to have in this day the *joy of eternal Sabbatism*. I do not believe it possible for any Christian to spend the Lord's day here without thinking of heaven. There is something in the gathering of people in church on earth to make one think of the rapt assemblage of the skies. There is something in the song of the Christian Church to make one think of the song of the elders before the throne, the harpists and the trumpeters of God accompanying the harmony. The light of a better Sabbath gilds the tops of this, and earth and heaven come within speaking distance of each other, the song of triumph waving backward and forward, now tossed up by the Church of earth, now sent back by the Church of heaven.

" Day of all the week the best,
Emblem of eternal rest."

The Christian man stands radiant in its light. His bereft heart rejoices at the thought of a country where there is neither a coffin nor grave; his weary body glows at the idea of a land where there are no burdens to carry, and no exhaustive journeys to take. He eats the grapes of Eshcol. He stands upon the mountain top and looks off upon the Promised Land. He hears the call of the eternal towers, and the tramp of the numberless multitude with sins forgiven. This is the day which the Lord hath made. Let us rejoice and be glad in it. Oh ye who have been hunting for Sunday pleasures in the street, and on the river-bank, and in the houses of sin, I commend to you this holy day and holy service! I do not invite you to swallow a great bitterness, or to carry a heavy yoke; but I invite you to feel in body, mind, and soul the thrill of joy which God has handed down in the chalices of the golden Sabbath.

With what revulsion and with what pity we must look out on that large class of persons in our day who would, by legislative enactment, and by newspaper and magazine, and by their own personal example, throw discredit upon the Lord's day. There are two things which Protestants ought never to give up: the one is the Bible, the other is the Sabbath. Take away one, and you take both. Take either, and farewell to Christianity in this country, farewell to our civil and religious liberties. When they go, all go. He who has ever spent Sunday in Paris, or Antwerp, or Rome, if he be an intelligent Christian, will pray God that the day will never come when the Sabbath of continental Europe shall put its foot upon our shores. I had a friend in Syracuse who lived to be one hundred years of age. He said to me, in his ninety-ninth year, "I went across the mountains in the early history of this country. Sabbath morning came. We were beyond the reach of civilization. My comrades were all going out for an excursion. I said, 'No, I won't go; it is Sunday.' Why, they laughed. They said, 'We haven't any Sunday here.' 'Oh yes,' I said, 'you have. *I brought it with me over the mountains.*'"

There are two or three ways in which we can war against Sabbath-breaking usages in this day; and the first thing is to get our children right upon this subject, and teach them that the Sabbath-day is the holiest of all the days, and the best and the gladdest. Unless you teach your child under the parental roof to keep the Lord's day, there are nine hundred and ninety chances out of a thousand it will never learn to keep the Sabbath. You may think to shirk responsibility in the matter, and send your child to the Sabbath-school and the house of God; that will not relieve the matter. I want to tell you, in the name of Christ, my Maker and my Judge, that your example will be more potential than any instruction they get elsewhere; and if you disregard the Lord's day yourself, or in any wise throw contempt upon it, you are blasting your children with an infinite curse. It is a rough truth, I know, told in a rough way; but it is God's truth, nevertheless. Your child may go on to seventy or eighty years of age, but that child will never get over the awful disadvantage of having had a Sabbath-breaking father or a Sabbath-breaking mother. It is the joy of many of us that we can look back to an early home where God was honored, and when the Sabbath came it was a day of great consecration and joy. We remember the old faces around the table that Sabbath morning. Our hearts melt when we think of those blessed associations, and we may have been off and committed many indiscretions and done many wrong things; but the day will never come when we forget the early home in which God's day was regarded, and father and mother told us to keep holy the Sabbath.

There is another way in which we can war against the Sabbath-breaking usages of the country at this time, and that is by making our houses of worship attractive and the religious services inspiriting. I plead not for a gorgeous audience-chamber; I plead not for groined rafters or magnificent fresco; but I do plead for comfortable churches, home-like churches—places where the church-going population behave as they ought to. Make the church welcome to all, however poorly clad they may be, or whatever may have been their past history; for I think the Church of God is not so much made for you who could have churches in your own house, but for the vast population of our great cities, who are treading on toward death, with no voice of mercy to arrest them. Ah! when the prodigal comes into the church, do not stare at him as though he had no right to come. Give him the best seat you can find for him. Sometimes a man wakes up from his sin, and he says, "I'll go to the house of God." Perhaps he comes from one motive, perhaps from another. He finds the church dark and the Christian people frigid (and there are no people on earth who can be more frigid than Christian people when they try), and the music is dull, and he never comes again. Suppose one of these men enters the church. As he comes in he hears a song which his mother sang when he was a boy; he remembers it. He sits down, and some one hands him a book, open at

> "Jerusalem, my happy home,
> Name ever dear to me."

"Yes," he says, "I have heard that many times." He sees cheerful Christian people there, every man's face a psalm of thanksgiving to God. He says, "Do you have this so every Sunday? I have heard that the house of God was a doleful place, and Christians were lugubrious and repelling! I have really enjoyed myself!" The next Sabbath the man is again in the same place. Tears of repentance start down his cheek; he begins to pray; and when the communion-table is spread, he sits at it, and some one reaches over and says, "I am surprised to find *you* here. I thought you didn't believe in such things." "Ah!" he says, "I have been captured. I came in one day, and found you were all so loving and cheerful here that I concluded I would come among you. Where thou goest I will go; thy people shall be my people, and thy God my God. Where thou diest will I die, and there will I be buried."

Ah! you can't drive men out of their sins, but you can coax them out—you can charm them out.

I would to God that we could all come to a higher appreciation of this Sabbath heritage! We can not count the treasures of one Christian Sabbath. It spreads out over us the two wings of the archangel of mercy. Oh, blessed Sabbath! blessed Sabbath! They scoff a great deal about the old Puritanic Sabbaths, and there is a wonderful amount of wit expended upon that subject now—the Sabbaths they used to have in New England.

I never lived in New England, but I would rather trust the old Puritanic Sabbath, with all its faults, than this modern Sabbath, which is fast becoming no Sabbath at all. If our modern Sabbatism shall produce as stalwart Christian character as the old New England Puritanic Sabbatism, I shall be satisfied, and I shall be surprised.

Oh, blessed day! blessed day! I should like to die some Sabbath morning when the air is full of church music and the bells are ringing. Leaving my home group with a dying blessing, I should like to look off upon some Christian assemblage chanting the praises of God as I went up to join the one hundred and forty and four thousand and the thousands of thousands standing around the throne of Jesus. Hark! I hear the bell of the old kirk on the hill-side of heaven. It is a wedding-bell, for behold the Bridegroom cometh. It is a victor's bell, for we are more than conquerors through Him who hath loved us. It is a Sabbath-bell, for it calls the nations of earth and heaven to everlasting repose.

> "Oh when, thou city of my God,
>   Shall I thy courts ascend?
> Where congregations ne'er break up,
>   And Sabbaths have no end."

## THE WORLD GOING.

"The fashion of this world passeth away."—1 *Corinthians* vii., 31.

THERE are many who find in this subject only an element of sadness. I find in it chiefly an element of joy. As Paul sometimes used figures drawn from the theatre, I think that I have a right to say that as the shifting scenes at the end of an act do not indicate that the play is ended, but only that it is developing, so all the changes on earth are but the shifting scenes in the great drama of God's providence, which will come to a glorious and successful completion. I want, to-night, to take a Christian and manly view of this subject, and not the view of a sickly sentimentalist. I am glad that the fashion of the world, and that the world itself, is passing away, for it is only making room for something better. In the same procession in which march the manners, and the customs, and the institutions of the world, march the dispensations of God's providence by which the Church is to be made mightier, and society purer. Roll on, oh wheel of the ages! Though institutions fall, though governments be crushed, though empires be depopulated, though the world be destroyed, roll, great wheel of the ages! Let all crowns melt, if our King gets his dominions! Let all armies be routed, if from the ruins Christ shall marshal his armies with banners! Let this earth burn, if out of the leaping flames there shall spring the new heaven and new earth in which dwelleth righteousness!

I propose to talk to you about the transitory nature of all earthly things, and then to guard you against some wrong applications of the subject.

I suppose you have all noticed *the changes in families.* Where are the prominent families of forty years ago? They ruled society as with a sceptre. The cut and the style of their dress decided the apparel of the city. They walked with an air of opulence, or dashed down behind well-groomed steeds clattering on the pavements. As they passed, all hats were lifted; as they entered a room, all conversation was hushed or turned upon them. Poets, rulers, millionaires, sat at their table. They drank their wine from chalices that had glittered in the banquets of a century. They sat in antique chairs, in which lordly men had lounged, looking at the walls papered with the many scenes of the chase, in which their ancestors had mingled with sounding horn, and baying hounds, and broken antlers. They were praised—they were sought after. Other vehicles halted to let theirs pass, and to their haughty look men bowed obsequiously, and danced around them with flattering attentions. Where are those families now? Some of them, I am glad to say, their name mighty on 'Change, and mighty in social circles, untouched of disaster. But where are the most of them? Shall I tell you the story? The coat of arms is lost. The pictures and the golden urn long ago went to the auctioneer's room. Halls, so airy and grand, have become a nest of brokers' shops. He goes along the street, broken down with dissipations, buttons off, and rum-blossoms on—the last relic of that great house. In that old arm-chair, that went down into the rookery; in the pictures, whose torn canvas was pitched into the garret rubbish; in those halls that have exchanged the lordly step of the proprietor for the shuffling feet of bargain makers, I hear a voice, loud and deep, sounding above cartman's dray and auctioneer's mallet, "The fashion of this world passeth away!"

So, likewise, has it been with all *human achievements.* The bridge, that taxed the brain of the architect, no more crosses the stream; but the romantic school-boy sits on the crumbling abutments making rhymes about the mutation of all earthly things. To the structure that once caused the mill-wright many sleepless nights, the farmer no more brings his grist. The old wheel, broken and covered with weeds, no more dashes the mountain stream to foam. The fine house, that overshadowed all the others on the block, now crumbles; the small window-panes, and old-time roof, and outlandish stairs, seeming in sorrow to say, oh for those days when people passing here would exclaim, "Who lives there?" Many of the books that were popular in the libraries forty years ago are gone now—gone down into the cellar, gone into the garret, or stand begging on the book-stand on the street corner, or sleep their last sleep in the antiquarian's library. Not knowing where they tread, the Tennysons, and Longfellows, and Bancrofts, walk over the graves of historians and poets, taking by storm the libraries of the world; mounting up on ladders of shelves until they plant their batteries of light and truth on the very heights of knowledge. The great libraries at the Vatican, and in Munich and Dresden, are only the Westminster Abbeys in which royal books have been buried. The tooth of Time is gnawing away at reputations that it was supposed could never be damaged or lost. Book-worms are boring down through the passage that was expected to be immortal, while those old ambitious authors or their spirits seem wandering up and down the aisles of the national library, unable to find their way out into the sunlight, with skeleton fingers fumbling the venerable pages, with trembling voice seeming to say, "Gone and forgotten!" The old philosophers, who spent much of their time in tinkering with electricity, are mostly forgotten, while Morse lassoes the lightning, and Cyrus W. Field with it lashes fast two hemispheres. Time follows right after Old Mortality, but with sharper chisel and stronger hand, battering to pieces the monuments, and the sarcophagus, and the Pyramids. Lord and squire, duke and duchess, earl and viscount, baron and knight, are sharing the same fate with Lowell operative, and Nantucket whaleman, and Scranton coal-heaver. Feather and crest, star and epaulet, and cockade sharing the same fate with shoe-maker's last and blacksmith's apron.

So has it also been with great cities. Where is Nineveh, the blossoming splendor of the Assyrian empire, all nations driving their caravans into her streets? City of precious stones—jasper, and chrysoprasus, and chalcedony; her fountains tossing up into basins of alabaster, and amidst exquisite statuary; the wealth and pomp of the world passing through her streets, strolling through her galleries of art, shouting in her amphitheatres, mingling in her scenes of splendor and triumph. Alas for Nineveh! The antiquarian plunges his crow-bar into the grave of all that buried splendor, and the broken pillars respond, and the slabs of gypsum speak out, and the engraved cylinders break the silence, and all the ground sends up rumbling, rueful, and woeful voices: "The fashion of this world passeth away!" Where is Tadmor, the city of palms, built by the munificent hand of King Solomon? Warlike tribes dashed back from her walls as a wave splits into foam upon a rocky beach. Palm trees grew along all her streets, and overshadowed many of her buildings, until the city was a bower of beauty. The wealth of all nations unpacked and unrolled in her markets. Her Temple of the Sun, with three hundred and ninety columns, on double rows, heaving up toward heaven, on shoulders of marble, the worship, and the pomp, and the genius, and the wealth of a great nation. Oh, Tadmor! the cup of mirth to thy lip, the crown of greatness on thy brow, where art thou? The huts that cluster around her ruins make no answer. The broken tombs, and the defaced sculpture, and the mutilated frieze respond not; but the sands of the desert drift across the place, and in the low, mournful moan of the desert wind I hear it: "The fashion of this world passeth away!"

So, also, my friends, has it been with all *earthly authority*. Of how much worth now is the crown of Cæsar? Who bids for it? Who cares now any thing about the Amphictyonic Council or the laws of Lycurgus? Who trembles now because Xerxes crossed the Hellespont on a bridge of boats? Who fears because Nebuchadnezzar thunders at the gates of Jerusalem? Who cares now whether or not Cleopatra marries Antony? Who crouches before Ferdinand, or Boniface, or Alaric? Can Cromwell dissolve the English Parliament now? Is William, prince of Orange, king of the Netherlands? No; no! However much Elizabeth may love the Russian crown, she must pass it to Peter, and Peter to Catherine, and Catherine to Paul, and Paul to Alexander, and Alexander to Nicholas. Leopold puts the German sceptre into the hand of Joseph, and Philip comes down off the Spanish throne to let Ferdinand go on. House of Aragon, house of Hapsburg, house of Stuart, house of Bourbon, quarreling about every thing else, but agreeing in this: "The fashion of this world passeth away." But have all these dignitaries gone? Can they not be called back? I have been in assemblages where I have heard the roll called, and many distinguished men have answered. If I should call the roll to-night of some of those mighty ones who have gone, I wonder if they would not answer. I will call the roll. I will call the roll of the kings first: Alfred the Great! William the Conqueror! Frederick II.! Louis XVI.! No answer. I will call the roll of the poets: Robert Southey! Thomas Campbell! John Keats! George Crabbe! Robert Burns! Lord Byron! No answer. I call the roll of the artists: Michael Angelo! Paul Veronese! William Turner! Christopher Wren! No answer. Eyes closed. Ears deaf. Lips silent. Hands palsied. Sceptre, pencil, pen, sword, put down forever. In literature, in art, in government, "The fashion of this world passeth away."

But I find a more striking illustration of my subject (at any rate, it is more impressive to my own mind) when I look *at the changing shape of this physical earth.* Do you know that even the mountains on the back of a thousand streams are leaping into the valley? The Alleghanies are dying! The dews, with crystalline mallet, are hammering away the rocks. (So when you say any thing is "as firm as a rock," you say nothing.) Frosts, and showers, and lightnings are sculpturing Mount Washington and the Catskills. Niagara every year is digging for itself a quicker plunge. The sea all around the earth on its shifting shores is making mighty changes in bar, and bay, and frith, and promontory. Some of the old sea-coasts are midland now. Off Nantucket, eight feet below low-water mark, are found now the stumps of trees, showing that the waves are conquering the land. Parts of Nova Scotia are sinking. Ships to-day sail over what, only a little while ago, was solid ground. Near the mouth of the St. Croix River is an island which, in the movements of the earth, is slowly but certainly rotating. All the face of the earth changing —changing. In 1831, an island springs up in the Mediterranean Sea. In 1866, another island comes up under the observation of the American consul as he looks off from the beach. The earth all the time changing, the columns of a temple near Bizoli show that the water has risen nine feet above the place it was when those columns were put down. Changing! Our Colorado River, once vaster than the Mississippi, flowing through the great American desert, which was then an Eden of luxuriance, has now dwindled to a small stream creeping down through a gorge. The earth itself, that was once vapor, afterward water—nothing but water—afterward molten rock, cooling off through the ages until plants might live, and animals might live, and men might live, changing all the while, now crumbling, now breaking off. The sun, burning down gradually in its socket. Changing! changing! an intimation of the last great change to come over the world even infused into the mind of the heathen who has never seen the Bible. The Hindoos believe that Bramah, the creator, once made all things. He created the water, then moved over the water, out of it lifted the land, grew the plants, and animals, and men on it. Out of his eye went the sun. Out of his lips went the fire. Out of his ear went the air. Then Bramah laid down to sleep four thousand three hundred and twenty million years. After that, they say, he will wake up, and then the world will be destroyed, and he will make it over again, bringing up land, bringing up creatures upon it; then lying down again to sleep four thousand three hundred and twenty million years, then waking up and destroying the world again—creation and demolition following each other, until after three hundred and twenty sleeps, each one of these slumbers four thousand three hundred and twenty million years long, Bramah will wake up and die, and the universe will die with him—an intimation, though very faint, of the great change to come upon this physical earth spoken of in the Bible. But while Bramah may sleep, our God never slumbers nor sleeps; and the heavens shall pass away with a great noise, and the elements shall melt with fervent heat, and the earth and all things that are therein shall be burned up.

"Well," says some one in the audience, "if that is so; if the world is going from one change to another; if the fashion of this world is passing away, then what is the use of my toiling for its betterment?" That is the point on which I want to guard you. I do not want you to become misanthropic. It is a great and glorious world. If Christ could afford to spend thirty-three years on it for its redemption, then you can afford to toil and pray for the betterment of the nations, and for the bringing on of that glorious time when all people shall see the salvation of God. While, therefore, I want to guard you against misanthropic notions in respect to this subject I have presented, I want you to take this thought home with you: *This world is a poor foundation to build on.* It is a changing world, and it is a dying world. The shifting scenes and the changing sands are only emblems of all earthly expectation. Life is very much like this day through which we have passed. To many of us it is storm and darkness, then sunshine, storm and darkness, then afterward a little sunshine, now again darkness and storm. Oh, build not your hopes upon this uncertain world! Build on God. Confide in Jesus. Plan for an eternal residence at Christ's right hand. Then, come sickness or health, come joy or sorrow, come life or death, all is well, all is well, though the fashion of this world does pass away.

## WEAPONS CAPTURED.

"There is none like that; give it me."—1 *Samuel* xxi., 9.

DAVID fled from his pursuers. The world runs very fast when it is chasing a good man. The country is trying to catch David, and to slay him. David goes into the house of a priest, and asks him for a sword or spear with which to defend himself. The priest, not being accustomed to use deadly weapons, tells David that he can not supply him; but suddenly the priest thinks of an old sword that had been carefully wrapped up and laid away—the very sword that Goliath formerly used, and he takes down that sword, and while he is unwrapping the sharp, glittering, memorable blade, it flashes upon David's mind that this is the very sword that was used against himself when he was in the fight with Goliath, and David can hardly keep his hand off of it until the priest has unwound it. David stretches out his hand toward that old sword, and says, "There is none like that; give it me." In other words, "I want in my own hand the sword which has been used against me, and against the cause of God." So it was given him. Well, my friends, that is not the first or the last sword once used by giant and Philistine iniquity which is to come into the possession of Jesus Christ, and of his glorious Church. I want, as well as God may help me, to show you that many a weapon which has been used against the armies of God is yet to be captured and used on our side; and I only imitate David when I stretch out my hand toward that blade of the Philistine, and cry, "There is none like that; give it me!"

I remark, first, that this is true *in regard to all scientific exploration.* You know that the first discoveries in astronomy, and geology, and chronology were used to battle Christianity. Worldly philosophy came out of its laboratory, and out of its observatory, and said, "Now, we will prove, by the very structure of the earth, and by the movement of the heavenly bodies, that the Bible is a lie, and that Christianity, as we have it among men, is a positive imposition." Good men trembled. The telescope, the Leydenjars, the electric batteries, all in the hands of the Philistines. But one day, Christianity, looking about for some weapon with which to defend itself, happened to see the very old sword that these atheistic Philistines had been using against the truth, and cried out, "There is none like that; give it me!" And Copernicus, and Galileo, and Kepler, and Isaac Newton came forth and told the world that, in their ransacking of the earth and heavens, they had found overwhelming presence of the God whom we worship; and this old Bible began to shake itself from the Koran, and Shaster, and Zendavesta with which it had been covered up, and lay on the desk of the scholar, and in the laboratory of the chemist, and in the lap of the Christian, unharmed and unanswered, while the tower of the midnight heavens struck a silvery chime in its praise.

Worldly philosophy said, "Matter is eternal. The world always was. God did not make it." Christian philosophy plunges its crow-bar into rocks, and finds that the world was gradually made, and if gradually made, there must have been some point at which the process started; then, who started it? And so that objection was overcome, and in the first three words of the Bible we find that Moses stated a magnificent truth when he said, "*In the beginning.*"

Worldly philosophy said, "Your Bible is a most inaccurate book; all that story in the Old Testament, again and again told, about the army of the locusts—it is preposterous. There is nothing in the coming of the locusts like an army. An army walks, locusts fly. An army goes in order and procession, locusts without order." "Wait!" said Christian philosophy; and in 1868, in the south-western part of this country, Christian men went out to examine the march of the locusts. There are men right before me who must have noticed in that very part of the country the coming up of the locusts like an army; and it was found that all the newspapers unwittingly spoke of them as an army. Why? They seem to have a commander They march like a host. They halt like a host. No arrow ever went in straighter flight than the locusts come —not even turning aside for the wind. If the wind rises, the locusts drop, and then rise again after it has gone down, taking the same line of march, not varying a foot. The old Bible right every time when it speaks of locusts coming like an army; worldly philosophy wrong.

Worldly philosophy said, "All that story about the light 'turned as clay to the seal,' is simply an absurdity." Old-time worldly philosophy said, "The light comes straight." Christian philosophy says, "Wait a little while," and it goes on and makes discoveries, and finds that the atmosphere curves and bends the rays of light around the earth, literally "as the clay to the seal."

The Bible right again; worldly philosophy wrong again. "Ah," says worldly philosophy, "all that allusion in Job about the *foundations* of the earth is simply an absurdity. 'Where wast thou,' says God, 'when I set the foundations of the earth?' The earth has no foundation!" Christian philosophy comes, and finds that the word as translated "foundations" may be better translated "sockets." So now see how it will read if it is translated right: "Where wast thou when I set the sockets of the earth?" Where is the socket? It is the hollow of God's hand—a socket large enough for any world to turn in.

Worldly philosophy said, "What an absurd story about Joshua making the sun and moon stand still. If the world had stopped an instant, the whole universe would have been out of gear." "Stop," said Christian philosophy, "not quite so quick." The world has two motions—one on its own axis, and the other around the sun. It was not necessary, in making them stand still, that both motions should be stopped—only the one turning the world on its own axis. There was no reason why the halting of the earth should have jarred and disarranged the whole universe. Joshua right and God right; infidelity wrong every time. I knew it would be wrong. I thank God that the time has come when Christians need not be scared at any scientific exploration. The fact is that Religion and Science have struck hands in eternal friendship, and the deeper down geology can dig, and the higher up astronomy can soar, all the better for us. The armies of the Lord Jesus Christ have stormed the observatories of the world's science, and from the highest towers have flung out the banner of the cross; and Christianity to-night, from the observatories at Albany and Washington, stretches out its hand toward the opposing scientific weapon, crying, "There is none like that; give it me!" I was reading this afternoon of Herschel, who was looking at a meteor through a telescope, and when it came over the face of the telescope it was so powerful he had to avert his eyes. And it has been just so that many an astronomer has gone into an observatory and looked up into the midnight heavens, and the Lord God has, through some swinging world, flamed upon his vision, and the learned man cried out, "Who am I? undone! unclean! Have mercy, Lord God!"

Again, I remark that the *traveling disposition of the world*, which was adverse to morals and religion, is to be brought on our side. The man that went down to Jericho and fell amidst thieves, was a type of a great many travelers. There is many a man who is very honest at home who, when he is abroad, has his honor filched, and his good habits stolen. There are but very few men who can stand the stress of an expedition. Six weeks at a watering-place has damned many a man. In the olden times God forbade the traveling of men for the purposes of trade, because of the corrupting influences attending it. A good many men now can not stand the transition from one place to another. Some men who seem to be very consistent in Brooklyn, in the way of keeping the Sabbath, when they get into Spain, on the Lord's day always go out to see the bull-fights. Plato said that no city ought to be built nearer to the sea than ten miles, lest it be tempted to commerce. But this traveling disposition of the world, which was adverse to that which is good, is to be brought on our side. These mail trains, why, they are to take our Bibles; these steamships, they are to transport our missionaries; these sailors, rushing from city to city all around the world, are to be converted in Christian heralds, and go out and preach Christ among the heathen nations. The gospels are infinitely multiplied in beauty and power since Robinson, and Thompson, and Burckhardt have come back and talked to us about Siloam, and Capernaum, and Jerusalem, pointing out to us the lilies about which Jesus preached, the beach upon which Paul was shipwrecked, the fords at which Jordan was passed, the Red Sea bank on which were tossed the carcasses of the drowned Egyptians. A man said, "I went to the Holy Land an infidel; I came back a Christian. I could not help it."

I am not shocked at the idea recently proposed, of building a railroad to the Holy Land. I wish that all the world might go and see Golgotha and Bethlehem. If we can not afford to pay for muleteers now, perhaps when the rail train goes we can afford to buy a ticket from Constantinople to Joppa, and so we will get to see the Holy Land. Then let Christians travel! God speed the rail trains, and guide the steamships this night panting across the deep, in the phosphorescent wake—of the shining feet of him who from wave-cliff to wave-cliff trod bestormed Tiberius. The Japanese come across the water and see our civilization, and examine our Christianity, and go back and tell the story, and keep that empire rocking till Jesus shall reign

"Where'er the sun
Does his successive journeys run."

And the fire-arms, with which the infidel traveler brought

down the Arab horseman and the jackals of the desert, have been surrendered to the Church, and we reach forth our hand, crying, "There is none like that; give it me!"

So it has also been with the learning and the eloquence of the world. People say, "Religion is very good for women, it is very good for children, but not for men." But we have in the roll of Christ's host Mozart and Handel in music; Canova and Angelo in sculpture; Raphael and Reynolds in painting; Harvey and Boerhaave in medicine; Cowper and Scott in poetry; Grotius and Burke in statesmanship; Boyle and Leibnitz in philosophy; Thomas Chalmers and John Mason in theology. The most brilliant writings of a worldly nature are all aglow with Scriptural allusions. Through senatorial speech and through essayist's discourse, Sinai thunders, and Calvary pleads, and Siloam sparkles.

Samuel L. Southard was mighty in the court-room and in the Senate Chamber; but he reserved his strongest eloquence for that day when he stood before the literary societies at Princeton Commencement and plead for the grandeur of our Bible. Daniel Webster won not his chief garlands while he was consuming Hayne, nor when he opened the batteries of his eloquence on Bunker Hill, that rocking Sinai of the American Revolution; but on that day when, in the famous Girard Will case, he showed his affection for the Christian religion, and eulogized the Bible. The eloquence and the learning that have been on the other side came over to our side. Where is Gibbon's historical pen? Where is Robespierre's sword? Captured for God. "There is none like that; give it me!"

So, also, has it been with the *picture-making of the*

*world.* We are very anxious on this day to have the printing-press and the platform on the side of Christianity; but we overlook the engraver's knife and the painter's pencil. The antiquarian goes and looks at pictured ruins, or examines the chiseled pillars of Thebes, and Nineveh, and Pompeii, and then comes back to tell us of the beastliness of ancient art; and it is a fact now, that many of the finest specimens—merely artistically considered—of sculpture and painting that are to be found amidst those ruins are not fit to be looked at, and they are locked up. How Paul must have felt when, standing amidst those impurities that stared on him from the walls and the pavements and the bazars of Corinth, he preached of the pure and holy Jesus. The art of the world on the side of obscenity, and crime, and death.

In later days the Vatican and the cathedrals were crowded with religious pictures. The Titians, and Raphaels, and Giottos of the world put on canvas and cathedral walls the "Baptism of Jesus Christ," and the "Last Supper," and the "Crucifixion," and the "Resurrection," and the "Last Judgment;" but all those pictures were prostituted by superstition. Poor devotees come and cross themselves. They count their beads; they take the wafers; they glance at the pictured walls, and they go out unblessed and unsaved. What to unclean Henry VIII. was a beautiful picture of the Madonna? What to Lord Jeffries, the unjust judge, the picture of the "Last Judgment?" What to Nero, the unwashed, a picture of the baptism in the Jordan? The art of the world still on the side of superstition and death. But that is being changed now. The Christian artist goes over to Rome, looks at the pictures, and brings back to his American studio much of the power of those old masters. The Christian minister goes over to Venice, looks at the "Crucifixion of Christ," and comes back to his American pulpit to talk as never before of the sufferings of the Saviour. The private tourist goes to Rome and looks at Raphael's picture of the "Last Judgment." The tears start, and he goes back to his room in the hotel, and prays God for preparation for that day when

>"Shriveling like a parched scroll,
>The flaming heavens together roll."

Our Sunday-school newspapers and walls are adorned with pictures of Joseph in the court, Daniel in the den, Shadrach in the fire, Paul in the shipwreck, Christ on the cross. Oh that we might, in our families, think more of the power of Christian pictures! One little sketch of Samuel kneeling in prayer will mean more to your children than twenty sermons on devotion. One patient face of Christ by the hand of the artist will be more to your child than fifty sermons on forbearance. The art of the world is to be taken for Christ. What has become of Thorwaldsen's chisel and Ghirlandajo's crayon? Captured for the truth. "There is none like that; give it me!"

So, I remark, it is *with business acumen and tact*. When Christ was upon earth, the people that followed him, for the most part, had no social position. There was but one man naturally brilliant in all the apostleship. Joseph of Arimathea, the rich man, risked nothing when he offered a hole in the rock for the dead Christ. How many of the merchants in Asia Minor befriended Jesus? I think of only one. Lydia. Howmany of the castles on the beach of Galilee entertained Christ? Not one. When Peter came to Joppa, he stopped with one Simon, a tanner. What power had Christ's name on the Roman Exchange, or in the bazars of Corinth? None. The prominent men of the day did not want to risk their reputation for sanity by pretending to be one of his followers. Now that is all changed. Among the mightiest men in our great cities to-day are the Christian merchants and the Christian bankers; and if to-morrow, at the Board of Trade, any man should get up and malign the name of Jesus, he would be quickly silenced or put out. In the front rank of all our Christian workers to-day are the Christian merchants; and the enterprises of the world are coming on the right side. There was a farm willed away some years ago, all the proceeds of that farm to go for spreading infidel books. Somehow matters have changed, and now all the proceeds of that farm go toward the missionary cause. One of the finest printing-presses ever built was built for the express purpose of publishing infidel tracts and books. Now it does nothing but print Holy Bibles. I believe that the time will come when, in commercial circles, the voice of Christ will be the mightiest of all voices, and the ships of Tarshish will bring presents, and the Queen of Sheba her glory, and the wise men of the East their myrrh and frankincense. I look off to-night upon the business men of this city, and rejoice at the prospect that their tact, and ingenuity, and talent will, after a while, be brought into the service of Christ. It will be one of the mightiest of weapons. "There is none like that; give it me!"

Now, if what I have said be true, away with all downheartedness! If science is to be on the right side, and the traveling disposition of the world on the right side, and the learning of the world on the right side, and the picture-making on the right side, and the business acumen and tact of the world on the right side—thine, O Lord, is the kingdom! Oh, fall into line, all ye people! It is a grand thing to be in such an army, and led by such a commander, and on the way to such a victory. If what I have said is true, then Christ is going to gather up for himself out of this world every thing that is worth any thing, and there will be nothing but the scum left. We have been rebels, but a proclamation of amnesty goes forth now from the throne of God, saying, "Whosoever will, let him come." However long you may have wandered, however great your crimes may have been, "whosoever will, let him come." Oh, that to-night I could marshal all this audience on the side of Christ, and feel that there would go out of these doors not one enemy of Jesus! Oh, he is a loving Jesus! He is the best friend a man ever had. He is so kind—he is so loving, so sympathetic. I can not see how you can stay away from him. Come now, and accept his mercy. Behold him as he stretches out the arms of his salvation, saying, "Look unto me, all ye ends of the earth, and be ye saved; for I am God." Make final choice now. You will either be willows planted by the watercourses or the chaff which the wind driveth away.

## THE PILE OF STONES SPEAKING.

"What mean ye by these stones?"—*Joshua* iv., 6.

YOU are wiser than most people if you have not mixed in your mind the passage of the Red Sea and the passage of the Jordan. The scenery is different, and the lessons to be learned from them are different. The Jordan, like the Mississippi, has bluffs on the one side and flats on the other. Here and there a sycamore shadows it; here and there a willow dips into it. In the months of April and May the snows on Mount Lebanon thaw and flow down into the valley, and then Jordan overflows its banks. Then it is wide, deep, raging, and impetuous. At this season of the year I hear the tramp of forty thousand armed men coming down to cross the river. You say, "Why do they not go up nearer the rise of the river at the old camel ford?" Ah! my friends, it is because it is not safe to go around when the Lord tells us to go ahead. The Israelites had been going around forty years, and they had enough of it. I do not know how it is with you, my brethren, but I have always got into trouble when I went around, but always got into safety when I went ahead.

There spreads out the Jordan, a raging torrent, much of it snow-water just come down from the mountain top; and I see some of the Israelites shivering at the idea of plunging in, and one soldier says to his comrade, "Joseph, can you swim?" And another says, "If we get across this stream we will get there with wet clothes and with damaged armor, and the Canaanites will slash us to pieces with their swords before we get up the other bank." But it is no time to halt. The great host marches on. The priests, carrying the ark, go ahead; the people follow. I hear the tramp of the great multitude. The priests have now come within a stone's-throw of the water. Yet still there is no abatement of the flood. Now they have come within four or five feet of the stream; but there is no abatement of the flood. Bad prospect! It seems as if these Israelites who have crossed the desert are now going to be drowned in sight of Canaan. But "Forward!" is the cry. The command rings all along the line of the host. "Forward!" Now the priests have come within one step of the river. This time they lift their feet from the solid ground and put them down into the raging stream. No sooner are their feet there than Jordan flies. On the right hand, God piles up a great mountain of floods; on the left, the water flows off toward the sea. The great river, for hours, halts and rears. The backwaters, not being able to flow over the passing Israelites, pile wave on wave, until perhaps a seabird would find some difficulty in scaling the water cliff. Now the priests and all the people have gone over on dry land. The water on the left-hand side by this time has reached the sea; and now that the miraculous passage has been made, stand back and see the stupendous pile of waters leap. God takes his hand from that wall of floods, and, like a hundred cataracts, they plunge and roar in thunderous triumph to the sea.

How are they to celebrate this passage? Shall it be with music? I suppose the trumpets and cymbals were all worn out before this. Shall it be with banners waving? Oh no, they are all faded and torn. Joshua cries out, "I will tell you how to celebrate this: build a monument here to commemorate the event;" and every priest puts a heavy stone on his shoulder, and marches out, and drops that stone in the divinely-appointed place. I see the pile growing in height, in breadth, in significance; and in after years men went by that spot and saw this monument, and cried out one to another, in fulfillment of this prophecy of the text, "What mean ye by these stones?"

Blessed be God, he did not leave our church—I mean this particular church—down in the wilderness! We wandered about for a while, and some people said we had better take this route; and others, that route. Some said we had better go back, and some said there were sons of Anak in the way that would eat us up; and before the smoke had cleared away from the sky after our Tabernacle had been consumed, people stood on the very site of the place, and said, "This church will never again be built." Our enemies laughed among themselves, and said, "Aha, aha!" Meanwhile the rubbish was being cleared away, the foundation was being laid, and the pillars were being lifted; and instead of the temporary structure in which we worshiped, we have this building, in which we hope the people of God will worship him for hundreds and hundreds of years. We came down to the bank of the Jordan; we looked off upon the waters. Some of the sympathy that was expressed turned out to be snow-water melted from the top of Lebanon. Some said, "You had better not go in; you will get your feet wet" But we waded in, pastor and people, farther and farther, and in some way, the Lord only knows how, we got through; and to-night I go all around about this great house, erected by your prayers, and sympathies, and sacrifices, and cry out in the words of my text, "What mean ye by these stones?"

It is an outrage to build a house like this, occupying so much room in a crowded thoroughfare, and with such vast toil and outlay, unless there be some tremendous reasons for doing it; and so, my friends, I pursue you tonight with the question of my text, and I demand of these trustees, and of these elders, and of all who have assisted in the building of this structure, "What mean ye by these stones?"

In the first place, we mean that they shall be *an earthly residence for Christ.* Poor Jesus! He did not have much of a home when he was here. Who and where is that child crying? It is Jesus, born in an outhouse. Where is that hard breathing? It is Jesus, asleep on a rock. Who is that in the back part of the fishing-smack, with a sailor's rough overcoat thrown over him? It is Jesus, the worn-out voyager. Oh Jesus! is it not time that thou hadst a house? We give thee this. Thou didst give it to us first, but we give it back to thee. It is too good for us, but not half good enough for thee. Oh, come in and take the best seat here! Walk up and down all these aisles. Speak through these organ-pipes. Throw thine arm over us in these arches. In the flaming of these chandeliers speak to us, saying, "I am the light of the world." O King! make this thine audience-chamber. Here proclaim righteousness and make treaties. We clap our hands, we uncover our heads, we lift our ensigns, we cry with multitudinous acclamation, until the place rings, and the heavens listen, "O King! live forever!"

Is it not time that he who was born in a stranger's house and buried in a stranger's grave should have an earthly house? Come in, O Jesus! not the corpse of a buried Christ, but a radiant and triumphant Jesus, conqueror of earth, and heaven, and hell.

> "He lives, all glory to his name,
> He lives, my Jesus, still the same;
> Oh, the sweet joy this sentence gives:
> I know that my Redeemer lives!"

Blessed be his glorious name forever!

Again, if you ask the question of the text, "What mean ye by these stones?" I reply that *we mean the communion of saints.* Do you know that there is not a single denomination of Christians in Brooklyn that has not contributed something toward the building of this house? And if ever, standing in this place, there shall be a man who shall try by any thing he says to stir up bitterness between different denominations of Christians, may his tongue falter, and his cheek blanch, and his heart stop! My friends, if there is any church on earth where there is a mingling of all denominations, it is our church. I just wish that John Calvin and Arminius, if they are not too busy, would come out on the battlements and see us. Sometimes in our prayer-meetings I have heard brethren use phrases of a liturgy, and we knew where they came from; and in the same prayer-meetings I have heard brethren make audible ejaculation, "Amen!" "Praise ye the Lord!" and we did not have to guess twice where they came from. When a man knocks at our church door, if he comes from a sect where they will not give him a certificate, we say, "Come in by confession of faith." While Adoniram Judson, the Baptist, and John Wesley, the Methodist, and John Knox, the glorious old Scotch Presbyterian, are shaking hands in heaven, all churches on earth can afford to come into close communion. "One Lord, one faith, one baptism." Oh, my brethren, we have had enough of Big Bethel fights— Fourteenth New York Regiment fighting the Fifteenth Massachusetts Regiment. Now let all those who are for Christ, and stand on the same side, go shoulder to shoulder, and the church, instead of having a sprinkling of the divine blessing, go clear under the wave, in one glorious immersion, in the name of the Father, and of the Son, and of the Holy Ghost. I saw a little child once, in its dying hour, put one arm around its father's neck, and the other arm around its mother's neck, and bring them close down to its dying lips and give a last kiss. Oh, I said, those two persons will stand very near to each other always after such an interlocking. The dying Christ puts one arm around this denomination of Christians, and the other arm around that denomination of Christians, and he brings them down to his dying lips, while he gives them this parting kiss: "My peace I leave with you, my peace I give unto you."

"How swift the heavenly course they run,
Whose hearts and faith and hopes are one!"

I heard a Baptist minister once say that he thought in the millennium it would be all one great Baptist church; and I heard a Methodist minister say that he thought in the great millennial day it would be all one great Methodist church; and I have known a Presbyterian minister who thought that in the millennial day it would be all one great Presbyterian church. Now I think they are all mistaken. I think the Millennial Church will be a composite church; and just as you may take the best parts of five or six tunes, and under the skillful hands of a Handel, Mozart, or Beethoven, entwine them into one grand and overpowering symphony, so, I suppose, in the latter days of the world, God will take the best parts of all denominations of Christians, and weave them into one great ecclesiastical harmony, broad as the earth and high as the heavens, and that will be the Church of the future. Or, as mosaic is made up of jasper and agate and many precious stones cemented together—mosaic a thousand feet square in St. Mark's, or mosaic hoisted into colossal seraphim in St. Sophia—so I suppose God will make, after a while, one great blending of all creeds, and all faiths, and all Christian sentiments, the amethyst and the jasper and the chalcedony of all different experiences and beliefs, cemented side by side in the great mosaic of the ages; and while the nations look upon the columns and architraves of that stupendous Church of the future, and cry out, "What mean ye by these stones?" there shall be innumerable voices to respond, "We mean the Lord God omnipotent reigneth."

I remark again, *we mean by these stones the salvation of the people*. We did not build this church for mere worldly reforms, or for an educational institution, or as a platform on which to read essays and philosophical disquisitions; but a place for the tremendous work of soul-saving. Oh, I had rather be the means in this church of having one soul prepared for a joyful eternity than five thousand souls prepared for mere worldly success! All churches are in two classes, all communities in two classes, all the race in two classes—believers and unbelievers. Those going into light, these going into darkness. To augment the number of the one and subtract from the number of the other, we built this church; and toward that supreme and eternal idea we dedicate all our sermons, all our songs, all our prayers, all our Sabbath hand-shakings. We want to throw defection into the enemies' ranks. We want to make them either surrender unconditionally to Christ, or else fly in rout, scattering the way with canteens, blankets, and knapsacks. We want to popularize Christ. We would like to tell the story of his love here, until men would feel that they had rather die than live another hour without his sympathy and love and mercy. We want to rouse up an enthusiasm for him greater than was felt for Nathaniel Lyon when he rode along the ranks—greater than was exhibited for Wellington when he came back from Waterloo—greater than was expressed for Napoleon when he stepped ashore from Elba. We really believe in this place Christ will enact the same scenes that were enacted by him when he landed in the Orient; and there will be such an opening of blind eyes and unstopping of deaf ears, and casting out of unclean spirits—such silencing bestormed Gennesarets, as shall make this house memorable five hundred years after you and I are dead and forgotten. Oh, my friends, we want but one revival in this church: that beginning now and running on to the day when the chisel of Time, that brings down even St. Paul's and the Pyramids, shall bring this house into the dust. We want the host of newly-converted souls who shall next Sabbath morning pass in review by this sacramental table—we want them only the first regiment of a great army that will take this place on their way to glory.

But since there are so many uncertainties ahead, perhaps we had better begin now the work of salvation. Oh that this day of dedication might be the day of emancipation to all imprisoned souls! My friends, do not make the blunder of the ship-carpenters in Noah's time, who helped to build the ark, but did not get into it! God forbid that you who have been so generous in building this church should not get under its saving influence! "Come, thou and all thy house, into the ark." Do you think a man is safe out of Christ? Not one day, not one hour, not one minute, not one second. Three or four years ago, you remember, a rail train broke down a bridge on the way to Albany, and after the catastrophe they were looking around among the timbers of the crushed bridge and the fallen train, and found the conductor. He was dying, and had only strength to say one thing, and that was, "Hoist the flag for the next train." So there come up to us to-night voices from the eternal chasm of darkness, and sin, and death, telling us, "You can not save me, but save those who come after me. Lift the warning. Blow the trumpet. Give the alarm. Hoist the flag for the next train."

Oh that to-night my Lord Jesus would sweep his arm around this great audience, and take you all to his holy heart! You will never see so good a time for personal consecration as now. "What mean ye by these stones?" We mean your redemption from sin, and death, and hell, by the power of an omnipotent Gospel. Lord God Almighty, with thy presence now shake this house from foundation to cap-stone! Stretch out thine arm. Here is the sacrifice. Lord God of Elijah, answer as by fire.

Well, the Brooklyn Tabernacle is erected again. The Sabbath after the old Tabernacle was burned, in the Academy of Music, in December, 1872, I prophesied this building. I said it would be dedicated in 1873. I made a mistake of only two months. Would God that had been the largest mistake I had ever made! But now that it is done, it more than pleases us. We came here to-night not to dedicate it. That was done this morning by an illustrious company of Christian ministers of every name; and that eloquent and thrilling sermon still rings through and through our soul, telling us that "the glory of the second house shall be greater than that of the first." God grant it! But I am here to preach the dedication sermon of all your hearts. In the Episcopal and Methodist churches they have a railing around the altar, and the people come and kneel down at that railing and get the sacramental blessing. Well, my friends, it would take more than a night to gather you in circles around this altar. Then just bow where you are for the blessing. Aged men, this is the last church you will ever dedicate. May the God who comforted Jacob the patriarch, and Paul the aged, make this house to you the gate of heaven; and when, in your old days, you put on your spectacles to read the hymn or the Scripture lesson, may you get preparation for that land where you shall no more see through a glass darkly! May the warm sunshine of heaven thaw the snow off your foreheads!

Men in mid-life, do you know that this is the place where you are going to get your fatigues rested, and your sorrows appeased, and your souls saved? Do you know that at this altar your sons and daughters will take upon themselves the vows of the Christian, and from this place you will carry out, some of you, your precious dead? Between this baptismal font and this communion-table you will have some of the tenderest of life's experiences. God bless you, old and young and middle-aged! The money you have given to this church to-day will be, I hope, the best financial investments you have ever made. Your worldly investments may depend upon the whims of Wall Street or the honesty of business associates; but the money you have given to the house of the Lord shall yield you large percentage, and declare eternal dividends in the day when, instead of being the story of one burning church, it shall be the tragedy of a world on fire!

## CHRIST OUR SONG.

"The Lord is my strength and song."—*Psalm* cxviii., 14.

THE most fascinating theme for a heart properly attuned is the Saviour. There is something in the morning light to suggest him, and something in the evening shadow to speak his praise. The flower breathes him, the star shines him, the cascade proclaims him, all the voices of nature chant him. Whatever is grand, bright, and beautiful, if you only listen to it, will speak his praise. So now, when I come in the summer-time and pluck a flower, I think of Him who is "the Rose of Sharon and the Lily of the Valley." When I see in the fields a lamb, I say, "Behold the Lamb of God that taketh away the sin of the world." When, in very hot weather, I come under a projecting cliff, I say,

"Rock of Ages, cleft for me,
Let me hide myself in thee!"

Over the old-fashioned pulpits there was a sounding-board. The voice of the minister rose to the sounding-board, and then was struck back again upon the ears of the people. And so the ten thousand voices of earth rising up find the heavens a sounding-board which strikes back to the ear of all the nations the praises of Christ. The heavens tell his glory, and the earth shows his handywork. The Bible thrills with one great story of redemption. Upon a blasted and faded paradise it poured the light of a glorious restoration. It looked upon Abraham from the ram caught in the thicket. It spoke in the bleating of the herds driven down to Jerusalem for sacrifice. It put infinite pathos into the speech of uncouth fishermen. It lifted Paul into the seventh heaven; and it broke upon the ear of St. John with the brazen trumpets and the doxology of the elders, and the rushing wings of the seraphim.

Instead of waiting until you get sick and worn out before you speak the praise of Christ, while your heart is happiest, and your step is lightest, and your fortunes smile, and your pathway blossoms, and the overarching heavens drop upon you their benediction, speak the praises of Jesus.

The old Greek orators, when they saw their audiences inattentive and slumbering, had one word with which they would rouse them up to the greatest enthusiasm. In the midst of their orations, they would stop and cry out "Marathon!" and the people's enthusiasm would be unbounded. My hearers, though you may have been borne down with sin, and though trouble, and trials, and temptation may have come upon you, and you feel tonight hardly like looking up, methinks there is one grand, royal, imperial word that ought to rouse your soul to infinite rejoicing, and that word is "Jesus!"

Taking the suggestion of the text, I shall speak to you of Christ our Song. I remark, in the first place, that Christ *ought to be the cradle-song.* What our mothers sang to us when they put us to sleep is singing yet. We may have forgotten the words; but they went into the fibre of our soul, and will forever be a part of it. It is not so much what you formally teach your children as what you sing to them. A hymn has wings, and can fly everywhither. One hundred and fifty years after you are dead, and "Old Mortality" has worn out his chisel in re-cutting your name on the tombstone, your great-grandchildren will be singing the song which this afternoon you sang to your little ones gathered about your knee. There is a place in Switzerland where, if you distinctly utter your voice, there come back ten or fifteen distinct echoes; and every Christian song sung by a mother in the ear of her child shall have ten thousand echoes coming back from all the gates of heaven. Oh, if mothers only knew the power of this sacred spell, how much oftener the little ones would be gathered, and all our homes would chime with the songs of Jesus!

We want some counteracting influence upon our children. The very moment your child steps into the street, he steps into the path of temptation. There are foul-mouthed children who would like to besoil your little ones. It will not do to keep your boys and girls in the house and make them house-plants; they must have fresh air and recreation. God save your children from the scathing, blasting, damning influence of the streets! I know of no counteracting influence but the power of Christian culture and example. Hold before your little ones the pure life of Jesus; let that name be the word that shall exorcise evil from their hearts. Give to your instruction all the fascination of music, morning, noon, and night; let it be Jesus, the cradle-song. This is important if your children grow up; but perhaps they may not. Their pathway may be short. Jesus may be wanting that child. Then there will be a soundless step in the dwelling, and the youthful pulse will begin to flutter, and little hands will be lifted for help. You can not help. And a great agony will pinch at your heart, and the cradle will be empty, and the nursery will be empty, and the world will be empty, and your soul will be empty. No little feet standing on the stairs. No toys scattered on the carpet. No quick following from room to room. No strange and wondering questions. No upturned face, with laughing blue eyes, come for a kiss; but only a grave, and a wreath of white blossoms on the top of it; and bitter desolation, and a sighing at night-fall with no one to put to bed, and a wet pillow, and a grave, and a wreath of white blossoms on the top of it. The heavenly Shepherd will take that lamb safely anyhow, whether you have been faithful or unfaithful; but would it not have been pleasanter if you could have heard from those lips the praises of Christ? I never read any thing more beautiful than this about a child's departure. The account said: "She folded her hands, kissed her mother good-bye, sang her hymn, turned her face to the wall, said her little prayer, and then died."

Oh, if I could gather up in one paragraph the last words of the little ones who have gone out from all these Christian circles, and I could picture the calm looks, and the folded hands, and sweet departure, methinks it would be grand and beautiful as one of Heaven's great doxologies! In my parish, in Philadelphia, a little child was departing. She had been sick all her days, and a cripple. It was noonday when she went, and, as the shadow of death gathered on her eyelid, she thought it was evening and time to go to bed, and so she said, "Good-night, papa! Good-night, mamma!" And then she was gone! It was "good-night" to pain, and "good-night" to tears, and "good-night" to death, and "good-night" to earth; but it was "good-morning" to Jesus—it was "good-morning" to heaven. I can think of no cradle-song more beautiful than Jesus.

I next speak of *Christ as the old man's song.* Quick music loses its charm for the aged ear. The school-girl asks for a schottisch or a glee; but her grandmother asks for "Balerma" or the "Portuguese Hymn." Fifty years of trouble have tamed the spirit, and the keys of the music-board must have a solemn tread. Though the voice may be tremulous, so that grandfather will not trust it in church, still he has the psalm-book open before him, and he sings with his soul. He hums his grandchild asleep with the same tune he sang forty years ago in the old country meeting-house. Some day the choir sings a tune so old that the young people do not know it; but it starts the tears down the cheek of the aged man, for it reminds him of the revival scene in which he participated, and of the radiant faces that long since went to dust, and of the gray-haired minister leaning over the pulpit, and sounding the good tidings of great joy.

I was one Thanksgiving-day in my pulpit, in Syracuse, New York, and Rev. Daniel Waldo, at ninety-eight years of age, stood beside me. The choir sang a tune. I said, "I am sorry they sang that new tune; nobody seems to know it." "Bless you, my son," said the old man, "I heard that seventy years ago!"

There was a song to-day that touched the life of the aged with holy fire, and kindled a glory on their vision that our younger eye-sight can not see. It was the song of salvation—Jesus, who fed them all their lives long;

Jesus, who wiped away their tears; Jesus, who stood by them when all else failed; Jesus, in whose name their marriage was consecrated, and whose resurrection has poured light upon the graves of their departed. "Do you know me?" said the wife to her aged husband who was dying, his mind already having gone out. He said "No." And the son said, "Father, do you know me?" He said "No." The daughter said, "Father, do you know me?" He said "No." The minister of the Gospel standing by, said, "Do you know Jesus?" "Oh yes," he said, "I know him, 'chief among ten thousand, the one altogether lovely!'" Blessed the Bible in which spectacled old age reads the promise, "I will never leave you, never forsake you!" Blessed the staff on which the worn-out pilgrim totters on toward the welcome of his Redeemer! Blessed the hymn-book in which the faltering tongue and the failing eyes find Jesus, the old man's song! When my mother had been put away for the resurrection, we, the children, came to the old homestead, and each one wanted to take away a memento of her who had loved us so long, and loved us so well. I think I took away the best of all the mementoes; it was the old-fashioned, round-glass spectacles, through which she used to read her Bible, and I put them on, but they were too old for me, and I could not see across the room. But through them I could see back to childhood, and forward to the hills of heaven, where the ankles that were stiff with age have become limber again, and the spirit, with restored eye-sight, stands in rapt exultation, crying, "This is heaven!"

I speak to you again of *Jesus as the night-song*. Job speaks of him who giveth songs in the night. John

Welch, the old Scotch minister, used to put a plaid across his bed on cold nights, and some one asked him why he put that there. He said, "Oh, sometimes in the night I want to sing the praise of Jesus, and to get down and pray; then I just take that plaid and wrap it around me, to keep myself from the cold." Songs in the night! Night of trouble has come down upon many of you. Commercial losses put out one star, slanderous abuse put out another star, domestic bereavement has put out a thousand lights, and gloom has been added to gloom, and chill to chill, and sting to sting, and one midnight has seemed to borrow the fold from another midnight to wrap itself in more unbearable darkness; but Christ has spoken peace to your heart, and you can sing,

> "Jesus, lover of my soul,
> Let me to thy bosom fly,
> While the billows near me roll,
> While the tempest still is high.
> Hide me, oh, my Saviour! hide
> Till the storm of life is past,
> Safe into the haven guide;
> Oh, receive my soul at last."

Songs in the night! Songs in the night! For the sick, who have no one to turn the hot pillow, no one to put the taper on the stand, no one to put ice on the temple, or pour out the soothing anodyne, or utter one cheerful word—yet songs in the night! For the poor, who freeze in the winter's cold, and swelter in the summer's heat, and munch the hard crusts that bleed the sore gums, and shiver under blankets that can not any longer be patched, and tremble because rent-day is come and they may be set out on the sidewalk, and looking into the starved face of the child and seeing famine there and death there, coming home from the bakery, and saying, in the presence of the little famished ones, "Oh, my God, flour has gone up!" Yet songs in the night! Songs in the night! For the widow who goes to get the back-pay of her husband slain by the "sharp-shooters," and knows it is the last help she will have, moving out of a comfortable home in desolation, death turning back from the exhausting cough, and the pale cheek, and the lustreless eye, and refusing all relief. Yet songs in the night! Songs in the night! For the soldier in the field-hospital, no surgeon to bind up the gun-shot fracture, no water for the hot lips, no kind hand to brush away the flies from the fresh wound, no one to take the loving farewell, the groaning of others poured into his own groan, the blasphemy of others plowing up his own spirit, the condensed bitterness of dying away from home among strangers. Yet songs in the night! Songs in the night! "Ah!" said one dying soldier, "tell my mother that last night there was not one cloud between my soul and Jesus." Songs in the night! Songs in the night!

This Sabbath-day came. From the altars of ten thousand churches has smoked up the savor of sacrifice. Ministers of the Gospel preached in plain English, in broad Scotch, in flowing Italian, in harsh Choctaw. God's people assembled in Hindoo temple, and Moravian church, and Quaker meeting-house, and sailors' Bethel, and king's chapel, and high-towered cathedral. They sang, and the song floated off amidst the spice groves, or struck the icebergs, or floated off into the Western pines, or was drowned in the clamor of the great cities. Lumbermen sang it, and the factory-girls, and the children in the Sabbath-class, and the trained choirs in great assemblages. Trappers, with the same voice with which they shouted yesterday in the stag-hunt, and mariners with throats that only a few days ago sounded in the hoarse blast of the sea-hurricane, they sang it. One theme for the sermons. One burden for the song. Jesus for the invocation. Jesus for the Scripture lesson. Jesus for the baptismal font. Jesus for the sacramental cup. Jesus for the benediction. But the day has gone. It rolled away on swift wheels of light and love. Again, the churches are lighted. Tides of people again setting down the streets. Whole families coming up the church aisle. We must have one more sermon, two prayers, three songs, and one benediction. What shall we preach? What shall we read? Let it be Jesus, every body says; let it be Jesus. We must have one more song to-night. What shall it be, children? Aged men and women, what shall it be? Young men and maidens, what shall it be? If you dared to break the silence of this auditory, there would come up thousands of quick and jubilant voices, crying out, "Let it be Jesus! *Jesus!* JESUS!"

We sing his birth—the barn that sheltered him, the mother that nursed him, the cattle that fed beside him, the angels that woke up the shepherds, shaking light over the midnight hills. We sing his ministry—the tears he wiped away from the eyes of the orphans; the lame men that forgot their crutches; the damsel who from the bier bounded out into the sunlight, her locks shaking down over the flushed cheek; the hungry thousands who broke the bread as it blossomed into larger loaves—that miracle by which a boy with five loaves and two fishes became the sutler for a whole army. We sing his sorrows—his stone-bruised feet, his aching heart, his mountain loneliness, his desert hunger, his storm-pelted body, the eternity of anguish that shot through his last moments, and the immeasurable ocean of torment that heaved up against his cross in one foaming, wrathful, omnipotent surge, the sun dashed out, and the dead, shroud-wrapped, breaking open their sepulchres, and rushing out to see what was the matter. We sing his resurrection—the guard that could not keep him; the sorrow of his disciples; the clouds piling up on either side in pillared splendors as he went through, treading the pathless air, higher and higher, until he came to the foot of the throne, and all heaven kept jubilee at the return of the conqueror. Oh! is there any song more appropriate for a Sabbath night than this song of Jesus? Let the passers-by in the street hear it, let the angels of God carry it amidst the thrones. Sound it out through the darkness: Jesus the night-song, appropriate for any hour, but especially sweet, and beautiful, and blessed on a Sabbath night.

I say once more, *Christ is the everlasting song.* The very best singers sometimes get tired; the strongest throats sometimes get weary, and many who sang very sweetly do not sing now; but I hope by the grace of God we will, after a while, go up and sing the praises of Christ where we will never be weary. You know there are some songs that are especially appropriate for the home circle. They stir the soul, they start the tears, they turn the heart in on itself, and keep sounding after the tune has stopped, like some cathedral-bell which, long after the tap of the brazen tongue has ceased, keeps throbbing on the air. Well, it will be a *home song* in heaven;

all the sweeter because those who sang with us in the domestic circle on earth shall join that great harmony.

> "Jerusalem, my happy home,
> Name ever dear to me;
> When shall my labors have an end
> In joy and peace in thee?"

On earth we sang harvest songs as the wheat came into the barn, and the barracks were filled. You know there is no such time on a farm as when they get the crops in; and so in heaven it will be a harvest song on the part of those who on earth sowed in tears and reaped in joy. Lift up your heads, ye everlasting gates, and let the sheaves come in! Angels shout all through the heavens, and multitudes come down the hills crying, "*Harvest-home! harvest-home!*"

There is nothing more bewitching to one's ear than the song of sailors far out at sea, whether in day or night, as they pull away at the ropes—not much sense often in the words they utter, but the music is thrilling. So the song in heaven will be a sailor's song. They were voyagers once, and thought they could never get to shore, and before they could get things snug and trim the cyclone struck them. But now they are safe. Once they went with damaged rigging, guns of distress booming through the storm; but the pilot came aboard, and he brought them into the harbor. Now they sing of the breakers past, the light-houses that showed them where to sail, the pilot that took them through the straits, the eternal shore on which they landed.

Ay, it will be the children's song. You know very well that the vast majority of our race die in infancy, and it is estimated that sixteen thousand millions of the little ones are standing before God. When they shall rise up about the throne to sing, the millions and the millions of the little ones—ah! that will be music for you! These played in the streets of Babylon and Thebes; these plucked lilies from the foot of Olivet while Christ was preaching about them; these waded in Siloam; these were victims of Herod's massacre; these were thrown to crocodiles or into the fire; these came up from Christian homes, and these were foundlings on the city commons — children everywhere in all that land; children in the towers, children on the seas of glass, children on the battlements. Ah! if you do not like children, do not go there. They are in vast majority; and what a song when they lift it around about the throne!

The Christian singers and composers of all ages will be there to join in that song. Thomas Hastings will be there. Lowell Mason will be there. Beethoven and Mozart will be there. They who sounded the cymbals and the trumpets in the ancient temples will be there. The forty thousand harpers that stood at the ancient dedication will be there. The two hundred singers that assisted on that day will be there. Patriarchs who lived amidst threshing-floors, shepherds who watched amidst Chaldean hills, prophets who walked, with long beards and coarse apparel, pronouncing woe against ancient abominations, will meet the more recent martyrs who went up with leaping cohorts of fire; and some will speak of the Jesus of whom they prophesied, and others of the Jesus for whom they died. Oh, what a song! It came to John upon Patmos; it came to Calvin in the prison; it dropped to John Knox in the fire; and sometimes that song has come to *your* ear, perhaps, for I really do think it sometimes breaks over the battlements of heaven.

A Christian woman, the wife of a minister of the Gospel, was dying in the parsonage near the old church, where on Saturday night the choir used to assemble and rehearse for the following Sabbath, and she said, "How strangely sweet the choir rehearses to-night; they have been rehearsing there for an hour." "No," said some one about her, "the choir is not rehearsing to-night." "Yes," she said, "I know they are; I hear them sing; how very sweetly they sing!" Now it was not a choir of earth that she heard, but the choir of heaven. I think that Jesus sometimes sets ajar the door of heaven, and a passage of that rapture greets our ears. The minstrels of heaven strike such a tremendous strain, the walls of jasper can not hold it.

I wonder—and this is a question I have been asking myself all the evening—Will you sing that song? Will I sing it? Not unless our sins are pardoned, and we learn now to sing the praise of Christ, will we ever sing it there. The first great concert that I ever attended was in New York, when Julien, in the "Crystal Palace," stood before hundreds of singers and hundreds of players upon instruments. Some of you may remember that occasion; it was the first one of the kind at which I was present, and I shall never forget it. I saw that one man standing, and with the hand and foot wield that great harmony, beating the time. It was to me overwhelming. But oh, the grander scene when they shall come from the East, and from the West, and from the North, and from the South, "a great multitude that no man can number," into the temple of the skies, host beyond host, rank beyond rank, gallery above gallery, and Jesus shall stand before that great host to conduct the harmony, with his wounded hands and his wounded foot! Like the voice of many waters, like the voice of mighty thunderings, they shall cry, "Worthy is the Lamb that was slain to receive blessings, and riches, and honor, and glory, and power, world without end. Amen and Amen!" Oh, if my ear shall hear no other sweet sounds, may I hear that! If I join no other glad assemblage, may I join that.

I was reading this afternoon of the battle of Agincourt, in which Henry V. figured; and it is said after the battle was won, gloriously won, the king wanted to acknowledge the divine interposition, and he ordered the chaplain to read the Psalm of David; and when he came to the words, "Not unto us, O Lord, but unto thy name be the praise," the king dismounted, and all the cavalry dismounted, and all the great host, officers and men, threw themselves on their faces. Oh, at the story of the Saviour's love and the Saviour's deliverance, shall we not prostrate ourselves before him to-night, hosts of earth and hosts of heaven, falling upon our faces, and crying, "*Not unto us, not unto us, but unto thy name be the glory!*"

## THE WELL BY THE GATE.

"Oh that one would give me drink of the water of the well of Bethlehem, which is by the gate."—2 *Samuel* xxiii., 15.

WAR, always distressing, is especially ruinous in harvest-time. When the crops are all ready for the sickle, to have them trodden down by cavalry horses and heavy supply-trains gullying the fields, is enough to make any man's heart sick. When the last great war broke out in Europe, and France and Germany were coming into horrid collision, I rode across their golden harvests, and saw the tents pitched, and the trenches dug in the very midst of the ripe fields, the long scythe of battle sharpening to mow down harvests of men in great winrows of the dead. It was at this season of harvest that the army of the Philistines came down upon Bethlehem. Hark to the clamor of their voices, the neighing of their chargers, the blare of their trumpets, and the clash of their shields!

Let David and his men fall back! The Lord's host sometimes loses the day. But David knew where to hide. He had been brought up in that country. Boys are inquisitive, and they know all about the region where they were born and brought up. If you should go back to the old homestead, you could, with your eyes shut, find your way to the meadow, or the orchard, or the hill back of the house, with which you were familiar thirty or forty years ago. So David knew the cave of Adullam. Perhaps, in his boyhood days, he had played "hide-

and-seek" with his comrades all about the old cave; and though others might not have known it, David did. Travelers say there is only one way of getting into that cave, and that is by a very narrow path; but David was stout, and steady-headed, and steady-nerved; and so, with his three brave staff-officers, he goes along that path, finds his way into the cave, sits down, looks around at the roof and the dark passages of the mountain, feels very weary with the forced march; and water he must have, or die. I do not know but there may have been drops trickling down the side of the cavern, or that there may have been some water in the goat-skin slung to his girdle; but that was not what he wanted. He wanted a deep, full, cold drink, such as a man gets only out of an old well with moss-covered bucket. David remembered that very near that cave of Adullam there was such a well as that, a well to which he used to go in boyhood—the well of Bethlehem; and he almost imagines that he can hear the liquid plash of that well, and his parched tongue moves through his hot lips as he says, "Oh, that one would give me drink of the water of the well of Bethlehem, which is by the gate!"

It was no sooner said than done. The three brave staff-officers bound to their feet and start. Brave soldiers will take even a hint from their commander. But between them and the well lay the host of the Philistines; and what could three men do with a great army? Yet where there is a will there is a way, and, with their swords slashing this way and that, they make their path to the well. While the Philistines are amazed at the seeming fool-hardiness of these three men, and can not make up their minds exactly what it means, the three men have come to the well. They drop the bucket. They bring up the water. They pour it in the pail, and then start for the cave. "Stop them!" cry the Philistines. "Clip them with your swords! Stab them with your spears! Stop those three men!" Too late. They have got around the hill. The hot rocks are splashed with the overflowing water from the vessel as it is carried up the cliffs. The three men go along the dangerous path, and with cheeks flushed with the excitement, and all out of breath in their haste, they fling their swords, red with the skirmish, to the side of the cave, and cry out to David, "There, captain of the host, is what you wanted, a drink of the water of the well of Bethlehem, which is by the gate."

A text is of no use to me unless I can find Christ in it; and unless I can bring a Gospel out of these words that will arouse and comfort and bless, I shall wish I had never seen them; for your time would be wasted, and against my soul the dark record would be made that this day I stood before a great audience of sinning, suffering, dying men, and told them of no rescue. By the cross of the Son of God, by the throne of the eternal judgment, that shall not be! May the Lord Jesus help me to tell you the truth to-day!

As I was on the way down here this morning, I heard some one say that carrier-pigeons had sometimes letters tied under the wing, and they would fly hundreds of miles—one hundred miles in an hour—carrying a message. So I have thought I would like to have it now. Oh, heavenly Dove! bring under thy wing to-day, to my soul and to the souls of this people, some message of light, and love, and peace!

It is not an unusual thing to see people gather around a well in summer-time. The husbandman puts down his cradle at the well curb. The builder puts down his trowel. The traveler puts down his pack. Then one draws the water for all the rest, himself taking the very last. The cup is passed around, and the fires of thirst are put out; the traveler starts on his journey, and the workman takes up his burden.

My friends, we come to-day around the Gospel well. We put down our pack of burdens and our implements of toil. One man must draw the water for those who have gathered around the well. I will try and draw the water to-day; and if, after I have poured out from this living fountain for your soul, I just taste of it myself, you will not begrudge me a "drink from the water of the well of Bethlehem, which is by the gate."

This Gospel well, like the one spoken of in the text, is *a well of Bethlehem*. David had known hundreds of wells of water, but he wanted to drink from that particular one, and he thought nothing could slake his thirst like that. And unless your soul and mine can get access to the Fountain open for sin and uncleanness, we must die. That fountain is the well of Bethlehem. It was dug in the night. It was dug by the light of a lantern—the star that hung down over the manger. It was dug not at the gate of Cæsar's palaces, not in the park of a Jerusalem bargain-maker. It was dug in a barn. The camels lifted their weary heads to listen as the work went on. The shepherds, unable to sleep, because the heavens were filled with bands of music, came down to see the opening of the well. The angels of God, at the first gush of the living water, dipped their chalices of joy into it, and drank to the health of earth and heaven, as they cried, "Glory to God in the highest, and on earth peace." Sometimes in our modern barns the water is brought through the pipes of the city to the very nostrils of the horses or cattle; but this well in the Bethlehem barn was not so much for the beasts that perish as for our race; thirst-smitten, desert-traveled and simoon-struck. Oh, my soul, weary with sin, stoop down and drink to-day out of that Bethlehem well.

"As the hart panteth after the water-brooks, so my soul panteth after thee, O God." You would get a better understanding of this amidst the Adirondacks in summer-time. Here comes a swift-footed deer. The hounds are close on the track; it has leaped chasms and scaled cliffs; it is fagged out; its eyes are rolling in death; its tongue is lolling from its foaming mouth. Faster the deer, faster the dogs, until it plunges into Schroon Lake, and the hounds can follow it no farther, and it puts down its head and mouth until the nostril is clean submerged in the cool wave, and I understand it: "As the hart panteth for the water-brook, so panteth my soul after thee, O God." Oh, bring me water from that well! Little child, who hast learned of Jesus in the Sabbath-school, bring me some of that living water. Old man, who fifty years ago didst first find the well, bring me some of that water. Stranger in a strange land, who used to hear sung, amidst the Highlands of Scotland, to the tune of "Bonnie Doon," "The Star, the Star of Bethlehem," bring me some of that water. Whosoever drinketh of that water shall never thirst. "Oh, that one would give me drink of the water of the well of Bethlehem, which is by the gate."

Again, this Gospel well, like the one spoken of in the text, is *a captured well.* David remembered the time when that good water of Bethlehem was in the possession of his ancestors. His father drank there, his mother drank there. He remembered how the water tasted when he was a boy, and came up there from play. We never forget the old well we used to drink out of when we were boys or girls. There was something in it that blessed the lips and refreshed the brow better than any thing we have found since. As we think of that dear old well, the memories of the past flow into each other like crystalline drops, sun-glinted, and all the more as we remember that the hands that used to lay hold the rope, and the hearts that beat against the well-curb are still now. We never get over these reminiscences. George P. Morris, the great song-writer of this country, once said to me that his song, "Woodman, spare that Tree," was sung in a great concert-hall, and the memories of early life were so wrought upon the audience by that song that, after the singing was done, an aged man arose in the audience, overwhelmed with emotion, and said, "Sir, will you please to tell me whether the woodman really spared the tree?" We never forget the tree under which we played. We never forget the fountain at which we drank. Alas for the man who has no early memories!

David thought of that well, that boyhood well, and he wanted a drink of it, but he remembered that the Philistines had captured it. When those three men tried to come up to the well in behalf of David, they saw swords gleaming around about it. And this is true of this Gospel well. The Philistines have at times captured it.

When we come to take a full, old-fashioned drink of pardon and comfort, do not their swords of indignation and sarcasm flash? Why, the skeptics tell us that we can not come to that fountain! They say the water is not fit to drink anyhow. "If you are really thirsty now, there is the well of philosophy, there is the well of art, there is the well of science." They try to substitute, instead of our boyhood faith, a modern mixture. They say a great many beautiful things about the soul, and they try to feed our immortal hunger on rose-leaves, and mix a mint-julep of worldly stimulants, when nothing will satisfy us but "a drink of the water of the well of Bethlehem, which is at the gate." They try to starve us on husks, when the Father's banquet is ready, and the best ring is taken from the casket, and the sweetest harp is struck for the music, and the swiftest foot is already lifted for the dance. They patronize heaven and abolish hell, and try to measure eternity with their hour-glass, and the throne of the great God with their yard-stick! I abhor it. I tell you the old Gospel well is a captured well. I pray God that there may be somewhere in the elect host three anointed men, with courage enough to go forth in the strength of the omnipotent God, with the glittering swords of truth, to hew the way back again to that old well. I think the tide is turning, and that the old Gospel is to take its place again in the family, and in the university, and in the legislative hall. Men have tried worldly philosophies, and have found out that they do not give any comfort, and that they drop an arctic midnight upon the death-pillow. They fail when there is a dead child in the house; and when the soul comes to leap into the fathomless ocean of eternity, they give to the man not so much as a broken spar to cling to. Depend upon it, that well will come into our possession again, though it has been captured. If there be not three anointed men in the Lord's host with enough consecration to do the work, then the swords will leap from Jehovah's buckler, and the eternal three will descend—God the Father, God the Son, God the Holy Ghost—conquering for our dying race the way back again to "the water of the well of Bethlehem, which is by the gate." "If God be for us, who can be against us?" "If God spared not his own Son, but freely gave him up for us all, how shall he not with him also freely give us all things?" "For I am persuaded that neither height, nor depth, nor angels, nor principalities, nor powers, nor things present, nor things to come," shall take from us, into final captivity, the Gospel of my blessed Lord Jesus Christ.

Again, the Gospel well, like the one spoken of in my text, is *a well at the gate.* The traveler stops the camel to-day, and gets down and dips out of the valley of the East, some very beautiful, clear, bright water, and that is out of the very well that David longed for. Do you know that that well was at the gate, so that nobody could go into Bethlehem without going right past it? And so it is with this Gospel well—it is at the gate. It is, in the first place, at the *gate of purification.* We can not wash away our sins unless with that water. I take the responsibility of saying that there is no man, woman, or child in this house to-day that has escaped sinful defilement. Do you say it is outrageous and ungallant for me to make such a charge? Do you say, "I have never stolen—I have never blasphemed—I have never committed unchastity — I have never been guilty of murder?" I reply, you have committed a sin worse than blasphemy, worse than unchastity, worse than theft, worse than murder. We have all committed it. We have by our sin re-crucified the Lord, and *that is deicide.* And if there be any who dare to plead "not guilty" to the indictment, then the hosts of heaven will be impaneled as a jury to render a unanimous verdict against us; guilty one, guilty all. With what a slashing stroke that one passage cuts us away from all our pretensions: "There is none that doeth good—no, not one." "Oh," says some one, "all we want, all the race wants, is development." Now I want to tell you that the race develops without the Gospel into a Sodom, a Five Points, a Great Salt Lake City. It always develops downward, and never upward, except as the grace of God lays hold of it. What, then, is to become of our soul without Christ? Banishment. Disaster. But I bless my Lord Jesus Christ that there is a well at the gate of purification. For great sin, great pardon. For eighty years of transgression, an eternity of forgiveness. For crime deep as hell, an atonement high as heaven; that where sin abounded, so grace may much more abound; that as sin reigned unto death, even so may grace reign through righteousness unto eternal life by Jesus Christ our Lord. Angel of the Covenant, dip thy wing in this living fountain to-day, and wave it over this solemn assemblage, that our souls may be washed in "the water of the well of Bethlehem, which is by the gate."

Further, I remark that this well of the Gospel is *at the gate of comfort.* Do you know where David was when he uttered the words of the text? He was in the cave of Adullam. That is where some of you are now. Has the world always gone smoothly with you? Has it never pursued you with slander? Is your health always good? Have your fortunes never perished? Are your children all alive and well? Is there one dead lamb in the fold? Are you ignorant of the way to the cemetery? Have you ever heard the bell toll when it seemed as if every stroke of the iron clapper beat your heart? Are the skies as bright when you look into them as they used to be when other eyes, now closed, used to look into them? Is there some trunk or drawer in your house that you go to only on anniversary days, when there comes beating against your soul the surf of a great ocean of agony? It is the cave of Adullam! The cave of Adullam! Is there some David here whose fatherly heart wayward Absalom has broken? Is there some Abraham here who is lonely because Sarah is dead in the family-plot of Machpelah? After thirty or forty years of companionship, how hard it was for them to part! Why not have two seats in the Lord's chariot, so that both the old folks might have gone up at once? My aged mother, in her last moment, said to my father, "Father, wouldn't it be nice if we could both go together?" No, no, no. We must part. And there are wounded hearts here to-day; some have had trouble since I have been gone. I thought I would say one word of comfort to you to-day. The world can not comfort you. What can it bring you? Nothing. Nothing. The salve they try to put on your wounds will not stick. They can not, with their bungling surgery, mend the broken bones.

Zoppar the Naamathite, and Bildad the Shuhite, and

Eliphaz the Temanite, come in, and talk, and talk, and talk, but miserable comforters are they all. They can not pour light into the cave of Adullam. They can not bring a single draught of water from "the well of Bethlehem, which is by the gate." But glory be to Jesus Christ, there is comfort at the gate! There is life in the well at the gate. If you give me time, I will draw up a promise for every man, woman, and child in this house. Ay, I will do it in two minutes. I will lay hold the rope of the old well. What is *your* trouble? "Oh," you say, "I am so sick, so weary of life—ailments after ailments." I will draw you up a promise: "The inhabitant shall never say 'I am sick.'" What is *your* trouble? "Oh, it is loss of friends—bereavement," you say. I will draw you up a promise, fresh and cool, out of the well: "I am the resurrection and the life; he that believeth in me, though he were dead, yet shall he live." What is *your* trouble? You say it is the infirmities of old age. I will draw you up a promise: "Down to old age I am with thee, to hoar hairs will I carry thee." What is *your* trouble? "Oh," you say, "I have a widowed soul, and my children cry for bread." I bring up this promise: "Leave thy fatherless children —I will preserve them alive, and let thy widows trust in me." I break through the armed ranks of your sorrows to-day, and bring to your parched lips "a drink of the water of the well of Bethlehem, which is by the gate."

Again, the Gospel well is *at the gate of heaven*. I have not heard yet one single intelligent account of the future world from any body who does not believe in the Bible. They throw such a fog about the subject that I do not want to go to the skeptic's heaven, to the transcendentalist's heaven, to the worldly philosopher's heaven. I would not exchange the poorest room in your house for the finest heaven that Huxley, or Stuart Mill, or Darwin ever dreamed of. Their heaven has no Christ in it; and a heaven without Christ, though you could sweep the whole universe into it, would be a hell! Oh, they tell us there are no songs there: there are no coronations in heaven—that is all imagination. They tell us we will do there about what we do here, only on a larger scale —geometrize with clearer intellect, and with alpenstock go clambering up over the icebergs in an eternal vacation. Rather than that, I turn to my Bible, and I find John's picture of that good land—that heaven which was your lullaby in infancy—that heaven which our children in the Sabbath-school will sing about this afternoon—that heaven which has a "well at the gate."

After you have been on a long journey, and you come in, all bedusted and tired, to your home, the first thing you want is refreshing ablution; and I am glad to know that after we get through the pilgrimage of this world— the hard, dusty pilgrimage—we will find a well at the gate. In that one wash, away will go our sins and sorrows. I do not care whether cherub, or seraph, or my own departed friends in that blessed land places to my lips the cup, the touch of that cup will be life, will be heaven! I was reading of how the ancients sought for the fountain of perpetual youth. They thought if they could only find and drink out of that well, the old would become young again, the sick would be cured, and every body would have eternal juvenescence. Of course, they could not find it. *Eureka!* I have found it! "the water of the well of Bethlehem, which is by the gate."

I think we had better make a bargain with those who leave us, going out of this world from time to time, as to where we will meet them. Travelers parting appoint a place of meeting. They say, "We will meet at Rome, or we will meet at Stockholm, or Vienna, or Jerusalem, or Bethlehem." Now, when we come to stand by the death-pillow of those who are leaving us for the far land, do not let us weep as though we would never see them again, but let us, there standing, appoint a place where we will meet. Where shall it be? Shall it be on the banks of the river? No. The banks are too long. Shall it be in the temple? No; no. There is such a host there—ten thousand times ten thousand. Where shall we meet our loved ones? Let us make an appointment to meet at the well by the gate. Oh heaven! Sweet heaven! Dear heaven! Heaven, where our good friends are! Heaven, where Jesus is! Heaven! Heaven!

But while I stand here, there comes a revulsion of feeling when I look into your eyes and know there are souls here dying of thirst, notwithstanding the well at the gate. Between them and the well of heaven there is a great army of sin; and though Christ is ready to clear a way to that well for them, they will not have his love or intercession. I suppose there may be some soul in this house to-day that will never see heaven. I can not tell by any pallor of cheek or gloom of brow where such a one may sit or stand; but God knows that that one soul is lost. The grain is all gathered into barns, and it is September now; and for that soul in this house—if there be such a one—the dirge would be appropriate in two senses: "The harvest is past, the summer is ended."

But I am glad to know that you may come yet. The well is here—the well of heaven. Come: I do not care how feeble you are! Let me take hold of your arm, and steady you up to the well-curb. "Ho, every one that thirsteth, come." I would rather win one soul to Christ this morning than wear the crown of the world's dominion. Do not let any man go away and say I did not invite him. Oh, if you could only just look at my Lord once; if you could just see him full in the face; ay, if you could only do as that woman did whom I read about at the beginning of the services—just come up behind him and touch his feet—methinks you would live. In Northern New Jersey, three winters ago, three little children wandered off from home in a snow-storm. Night came on. Father and mother said, "Where are the children?" They could not be found. They started out in haste, and the news ran to the neighbors, and before morning it was said that there were hundreds of men hunting the mountains for those three children, but found them not. After a while a man imagined there was a place that had not been looked at, and he went and saw the three children. He examined their bodies. He found that the older boy had taken off his coat and wrapped it around the younger one, the baby, and then taken off his vest and put it around the other one; and there they all died, he probably the first, for he had no coat or vest. Oh, it was a touching scene when that was brought to light! I was on the ground about a week ago, and it brought the whole scene to my mind; and I thought to myself of a more melting scene than that: it is that Jesus, our elder brother, took off the robe of his royalty, and laid aside the last garment of earthly comfort, that he might wrap our poor souls from the blast. Oh, the height, and the depth, and the length, and the breadth of the love of Christ!

## CESSATION OF EXPERIMENT.

"Thou shalt see greater things than these."—*John* i., 50.

ON this, the fifth anniversary of my settlement as your pastor, I desire to tell the story of this church —a story that has never yet been told. I tell it in answer to American and European letters, so numerous that, with the aid of a secretary, I have not been able to answer them. I tell it in recognition of the goodness of God. I tell it out of justice to the men and women who sit before me; out of justice to some who have already entered upon the white-robed congregations of heaven. It is a story of escapes, deliverances, losses, self-sacrificing achievement, wild tragedy, divine help, and of world-wide sympathy, that I do not think belongs to any other church of the century. There are passages that remind me of the going of the Israelites through the Red Sea. And yet it shall not be an epic, nor a lyric, nor a dithyrambic, but only a plain pastoral.

Seated in my Philadelphia home, the "call" came from this church. The eldership deceived me in nowise. They told me it was almost an extinct church. Nineteen members were all that could be rallied to a congregational meeting to make out the "call." It was accepted, for the reason that the church was flat down; and I said to myself, "That will be just the place in which to try, on a large scale, a free church, without any established hinderances in the way." And so, putting my trust in God, and confronting the derision of some of my best personal friends at what they called a "wild undertaking," I came to this, the fairest city under the sun. Blessed be her churches! Prospered be her commerce! Christianized be all her schools!

The first summer we enlarged the old chapel, and multiplied the seating capacity in every possible way. According to the most approved style, our pew-rents went up; and as the pew-rents went up, my heart went down. The next spring the unanimous cry was for a new church, and the trustees assembled to decide what it should be. With a suppressed excitement, such as I never before or since felt, I went into a neighbor's parlor to lay before the trustees the plan of a free church. I tried to show them in that conversation that it is ungospel and unchristian to make a man's financial qualification the test of pew-holding, and to show them that we had no right to knock down, under an auctioneer's hammer, to the highest bidder, a man's chances for heaven. There was a long pause. After a while one of the brethren remarked, "I have no doubt that a church on that plan would be the highest style of Gospel church; but where would we get the money to carry on such a project?" I replied, "Put your trust in God, and depend upon the voluntary subscriptions and contributions of the people. And since my own salary may be in the way, I now here, and for all time to come, discharge you of all financial responsibility to me personally. Give me a free church, and if you can not support me, then, by pen and lecturing platform, I will take care of myself." "Well," said one of the brethren, "if the dominie believes in the plan as much as that, I think we can afford to believe in it, and

I move we have a free church"—a resolution that passed with a unanimous "Aye."

Then there came around about me a band of consecrated men and women sworn to do this work; and if I ever forget their fidelity to Christ, and their adherence to the good cause, may my tongue be forever still! The first question was to find a site for the building. Committees were appointed, and went up and down the city looking for a place, they having decided that we must have a place one hundred and fifty feet front by one hundred feet deep; and after weeks of searching, they found, within three doors of the old chapel, just the place—one hundred and fifty feet front by one hundred feet deep. Although the lot is larger now than it was then, that was the size of it then. The place was foreordained from all eternity to be the place where we should build. I was often asked, and I asked myself, "Why wasn't that lot taken?" God was keeping it for us.

The next question to be decided was, Who shall be the architect? I went to one of the prominent architects of New York, and said, "Give us a church in amphitheatrical shape." He figured on it a few weeks, and said, "An amphitheatrical building is not *churchly*." I went to another distinguished architect, and said, "Give us an amphitheatrical building, where the people can see each other's faces instead of the back of the head, and where we can all be gathered as in a great home circle, and where nothing shall be angular." He figured on it a while, and at the end of four weeks said to me that an amphitheatrical building would not be *churchly*. One day a young man came into my room, and said, "Have you decided upon an architect for the building?" I replied, "No." Said he, "Would I have any chance?" I replied, "Any man, young or old, who can give us an amphitheatrical church, where the people can all be seated in sympathy with each other, will be our architect." Then I drew out on the back of a letter, in twenty strokes, the general idea, and said, "If you can bring that out with architectural skill, you will be our man." So this plan was developed. That it was a good one, I take from the fact that there have been scores of churches since built on the same plan.

Then the trowel began to click, and the hammer to thump, and the building rose. As we were to build it for a temporary structure, to last but two years, in three months the whole affair was done; but, mark you, without having raised one dollar of contribution toward it. We depended upon the sale of the old church for the building of the new; but the purchasers of that building failed to meet their payments, and so the building came back upon our hands. Then, after the new building was done, we had to go through the work of attempting to pay for a church entirely completed, and some of you may know what tough work that is. Then we went on organizing—making hundreds of experiments in hundreds of things, because we had no precedent, no antecedent. Yet the work all the time progressed. At our very first communion in the old Tabernacle, more than ninety souls professed faith in Christ; at the second communion in the old Tabernacle, more than fifty souls; at the third communion in the old Tabernacle, more than forty souls; and that is the only way I know how to calculate the advancement of a church. Though you build a church as grand as St. Paul's, of London, and have a line of carriages, with rosetted coachmen, reaching from here to Prospect Park, I would abhor it if there were no conversions. That church is an accursed thing which knows nothing about soul-saving. Pull it down, and use its timbers and its stones for bowling-alleys and theatres. They are not so objectionable, because they pretend to be what they are; but a church which does nothing but rock souls into an eternal sleep under a gilded canopy is a gigantic hypocrisy, and defies the bolts of high heaven.

Well, the work went on. On the following summer we found that our Tabernacle was too strait for us, and so we enlarged it at an expense like building another new church. Meanwhile our church had sailed down into calm financial waters; and one December night the trustees of the church assembled to look over the affairs of the church, and they examined the income and the outgo, and saw that the next year they would have a positive surplus. They clapped their hands, and sat up very late that night talking the matter over, and they said, "This project of a free church, which some have caricatured and many have doubted, has proved to be a success." It was about eleven o'clock at night when the sexton shut the door of the old iron-clad. Alas! that was the last night of the Tabernacle. That ark would never float any more souls into glory. Its work was done. And if, when a Christian man dies, the air is full of spirits coming and going, when a Christian church is about coming to its closing moments, I think that angelic spectators move forward and backward in the scene. I think that that night the air was full of them.

When next morning, at ten o'clock, the cry of fire was lifted, it was not a hoarse uproar, but it was a voice with tears in it. I said to a man the other day, "When did you become a Christian?" He replied, "When the old Tabernacle burned. I don't cry often, I want you to understand, but I cried that morning, and I cried all day. Wasn't it awful?" O Lord Jesus! great Head of the Church! what a day that was when thy children stood before their burning altar. Some sighed. Some wrung their hands. Some fainted. Invalids with unnatural strength got up from their couches and looked out at it. It was the death-throe of a church, its departing spirit spreading abroad wings of flame—its groan, the falling timbers. Let the firemen take off their glazed hats, and twenty thousand excited spectators bow down before the catafalque of fire. Dead! Dead! Ashes to ashes!

The loss was the more complete, because it was an iron structure on which we had not been able to get adequate insurance. So we were as thoroughly rubbed out as a sponge rubs out a sum from a boy's slate at school. Then there came sympathetic letters. I never got so many letters in one day in my life as I got on the following day. And then there came practical help. One thousand dollars from Dresden, Germany, where they make pictures. Help from Sheffield, England, where they make knives; from Glasgow, Scotland, where they make steamers; from Edinburgh, where they make scholars; from Paris, where they make—revolutions; from London, where they make every thing. It was not so much the amount they gave as the way they gave it. They said they had seen the fire in Yorkshire, and in old Essex, and among the Trossacks. They told us we were prayed for among the Manchester and Birmingham operatives. You know how it was in our own city. Twenty-six churches in as many hours were offered for our occupation. They offered us their main audience-rooms; they offered us their lecture-rooms; and what they did not offer us would not be worth mentioning. The demonstration of Christian brotherhood was so magnificent, that, as soon as I could get the cinders and the tears wiped out of my eyes, I said, "Well, brethren, I am glad the thing has burned up. We only built it for two years anyhow, and it was not large enough. Now let us rise up and have a larger and a better structure."

To make the one year of our exile the more bearable, the Lord God came down with his spirit in the Academy of Music. Some people said, "You had better not go there; it is a theatre—a secular place." But we went there, and had it dedicated. We dedicated the Director's Room in that building by a prayer-meeting twice every Sabbath. We dedicated the "Greenroom" by cries of "What must I do to be saved?" We dedicated the platform by the story of a Saviour's love, and never any thing else but that, morning and night. We dedicated the boxes by men and women who rose asking for prayers. We dedicated the main audience-room by five hundred and thirteen souls professing to have found the peace of the Gospel—three hundred and seven of them connecting themselves with our church, the others going elsewhere, because we had as yet no home. And though that Academy of Music may be the scene of secular entertainments for many a year, there shall be no power in the voice of *prima donna* or in the blast of brazen instruments to drown out "St Martin's" and "Coronation," still rolling among those arches.

Meanwhile we selected a new architect—one who did

not think that an amphitheatrical building would be unchurchly; one who, after long experience in putting up some of the largest structures in England and the United States, brought all his achievements to a culmination in plans for this temple. The women—the Lord has written the record on high: I can not read it until I come up there—the women, by Fair, and by personal solicitation, raised money. The Board of Trustees brooded, after many a midnight, over the plans. The work went on, by what toil, by what hope deferred, by what anxiety, I can not tell, until on the 22d of February the veil was drawn from our eyes, and there rose before our vision this building, grander than our brightest anticipations, strong as the everlasting hills, and beautiful as a midsummer's dream; offering seating capacity to several thousand more than any Protestant church in America.

There remained but two things to be tested: Can we pay for it? Will it be occupied? The first question you answered, when, on the opening day, you put in the Lord's lap thirty-six thousand dollars, making a record for yourselves which, while it has won the admiration of Christendom, will be a page you will be glad of in the great day when Christ shall say, "Well done, good and faithful servant. Thou hast been faithful over a few things; be thou ruler over ten cities." The other question was, Will all the pews be assigned? For, mind you, though we are a free church, we are neither a mob nor a rabble. Though the pews are all free from taxation, yet they are formally assigned, that every father and mother may have their family between them; that this Sabbath they may sit where they sat last Sabbath, and next Sabbath where they sat this Sabbath; that a home feeling may be cultured; that the church may be organized, disciplined for practical Christian work, as it could not be if the pews were not assigned. We built the church so large that the trustees said, and I said, that if in one or two years we can assign all these pews to families, we shall be satisfied. The church has been open only about six weeks; yet two weeks ago we completed the assignment of all the pews—a work that would have been done the night of the opening if there had been time; and so we find that, instead of the building being too large, it is already too small. Now, if this church shall ever doubt God's goodness, or his willingness to take us straight through any righteous undertaking, then we deserve to have this building go down into the ashes of a ruin from which it shall never be resurrected, or swallowed of an earthquake that leaves not one brick or shingle behind. "Oh, give thanks unto the Lord for his goodness, for his mercy endureth forever." "Not unto us, not unto us, O Lord! but unto thy name be the glory." If God ever defended a church, if God ever led a church, if God ever blessed a church, if God ever saved a church—this is the church.

And now I demand of all those who are here to-day, and of all those to whom these words shall come, that they take this free church out of the list of experiments, and put it down in the list of accomplished facts. There are two or three things we have proved.

In the first place, we have proved that *free churches are a financial possibility.* The reason that in like undertakings, in most places, they have failed, has been because they have been on a small scale, or because they have been in a mean structure, or because they have been with poor singing, or in a repelling neighborhood. Give a free church a fair chance, and the right kind of a neighborhood, and you shall gather within its walls all classes —the rich and the poor, the cultured and the ignorant. Just the kind of a church our Lord Jesus would favor: the rich and the poor meeting together, the Lord the maker of them all. Do you know this—that nine-tenths of the pew-renting churches in this country, at the end of the year, depend upon a few rich men to come and put their hands in their pockets up to the elbow, to meet the deficit? Now I contend that that is not the way to do. Throw the whole responsibility on the people, and they will meet it. They love to be trusted. Was there ever a grander illustration of the willingness of the people of this country to support a free church than on the twenty-second of February? Mind you, it was in the midst of great financial depression. Mind you, it was like the building of three churches in three years—the first Tabernacle built in 1871; the enlargement of that structure (which was almost like erecting another building, for expense) in 1872; then this structure in the early part of 1874. Do you believe that a church conducted on any other principle could have roused up enough sympathy to be able to build three churches in a little over three years? I trow not.

Oh, we were tempted, again and again, to go back to the old plan! I was offered, as some of you know, twenty thousand dollars per year salary, if I would allow or consent to the selling of the pews in the old Tabernacle; but we had consecrated ourselves to the work of building a free church, and we do not want any rest from it until we rest in Greenwood, the pleasant bed where I have a great many good friends sleeping this morning.

We proved another thing, and that is, that *a free church can be made attractive to the refined and the cultured.* The stereotyped objection, all over the world, to a free church has been, "You break down the barriers of society, and then the cultured and the refined will not come into such a place." We have put the falsehood upon that objection to a free church. There is not anywhere—there is not in any church in this land or in England—more educated men and women, more professional men, more lawyers, doctors, artists, teachers, more men who can make an intelligent public address upon every question of finance, politics, morals, and religion; so that when a man introduces his family in this Christian association, he introduces them into the highest style of refinement. I have wandered up and down the world—and I suppose I have seen as much of it as any man of my age—and I now say that it is my highest ambition to have my own children worthy of the Christian, elevated society in which I have here introduced them.

Again, we have proved that *the people will come to receive a literal and unvarnished* Gospel. The impression is abroad that you must fix up the Gospel to suit the age, instead of fixing up the age to suit the Gospel; and the young men coming out of our theological seminaries have the impression that they must palliate the prejudices of society, and must cover over the natural rottenness of the human heart, and that they must tell men what very clever people they are, and that they only need to be pressed in a little one way, and pulled out a little the other way, and then they will be all right. And they say, "All you want is development." Is it? Development! You might as well go to a man bent double with the cramps of Asiatic cholera, and tell him that all he wants is development. It is a lie. He needs to have his disease killed, so that he may get well. Until our heart is changed by the grace of God, it is scabbed and ulcerous with a great leprosy; and it is not development we want, but it is the cure of an eating, loathsome, blasting, damning leprosy. Our whole nature throughout, and throughout, and throughout wrong, needs to be made over and over, and over again. I wish that every word of that passage could come down with five tons' weight of emphasis—"Except a man be born again, he can not see the kingdom of God;" though he had given one hundred thousand dollars to religious institutions, though he never used a bad word in his life, though he paid all his debts, though he lived on the tip-top round of respectability—"Except a man be born again, he can not see the kingdom of God." But so little do we hear about this doctrine of regeneration in this day, that it is almost considered indelicate for a man to read in a public assemblage the words of Christ to Nicodemus about the new birth. And as to there being any hell, if we make any allusion to that, it must be with exquisite circumlocution, as "the place of high temperature," or "the world insalubrious," or, as a minister recently called it, "the great elsewhere!" I say to the young men who are studying for the ministry—and there are thirty connected with this congregation—if you have any idea that it is necessary to preach an emasculated Gospel in order to get people to come and hear it, you make a vast mistake. An eminent minister of New York said to me some time ago, "I have a very large audience, but they are all Christians. I can not get the worldly people to come in and listen to me. I hear that a good many worldly people come to hear you. You must preach some very strange thing. What did you preach about yesterday?" "Well," I replied, "I preached yesterday morning on 'Seek ye the Lord while he may be found;' and in the evening I preached about 'Strive to enter in at the strait gate.'" Said he, "Is that all?" "Yes," I replied, "that is all." Oh, my friends, there is *a judgment-seat in every man's heart*, which tells him that the Bible is true; and if it be true, the wicked and the righteous can not go to the same place. So I say, Young men who are entering the ministry, if you really want a fresh theme, if you really want a novel theme to preach about, preach the old Gospel. Do not preach about "development"—that is hackneyed. Do not preach about the Darwinian theory of the origin of our race—that is worn out. But if you want something new, really new—so new that tens of thousands of people in this day do not know any thing about it—then give them "Repentance" in the morning, and "Faith" at night; and in order to variety, next Sabbath give them "Faith" in the morning, and "Repentance" at night.

I believe that within the next twenty years there will be an earthquake amidst the American and English pulpits, and that those which have adhered to the old Gospel will stand, and that those which have preached any thing else will go down. Paul cries out, with great emphasis, "If any one, though he be an angel from heaven, preach any other Gospel, let him be accursed."

Where is Theodore Parker's pulpit to-day? He was the most fascinating man I ever heard—a mighty man; but he denied the divinity of Christ, and denied the inspiration of the Scriptures. Where is his pulpit to-day? Boston tried to patch it up and prop it up; but when Theodore Parker died, his pulpit died with him. Where is the pulpit of Edward Irving, the most brilliant man that ever stood in the pulpit of England? He forsook the simplicity of his father's faith, and when Edward Irving died, his pulpit died with him. But while those men were preaching, each in his day, the one in Boston and the other in London, there were self-sacrificing men in our Western wilderness preaching Jesus and the resurrection. They died of the malaria from the canebrakes; but what became of their pulpit? It multiplied into five thousand other pulpits, and the song for which Bishop Asbury, and George Reynolds, and Jacob Kruber gave the pitch is still humming amidst the beechwoods beyond the bluffs of the Mississippi.

Now this church has been gathered and built as an exponent of a literal Gospel. So it shall stand. That the Lord has approved our plan in the past, I have only to state that eight hundred and ninety-two souls have connected themselves with this church through these five years; while by letters from all parts of this land, and from England, Scotland, Ireland, Australia, and the islands of the sea, we have an intimation that through your prayers, and the help that you have been able to give your pastor, thousands of souls have been brought into the kingdom of Christ. The old Gospel is the power of God and the wisdom of God unto salvation.

But now five years are gone. God has closed the fifth volume, never to be opened until the fiery fingers of the judgment shall open it, amidst a flying heaven and a burning earth. During those five years, a good many have gone out from us into the eternal world. Some of them, I fear, went unprepared. It is absurd for a man to preach a sermon in which he implies that all the dead are happy. Some of those who went out from us during the past five years into the eternal world gave no evidence of repentance. There was in their last struggle a look of terror about the face that I did not like. They mentioned, in their last moments, the name of father, or mother, or wife, or child, but they did not mention the name of Jesus—

"Jesus, the name high over all
In hell, and earth, and sky."

They did not speak of him. I could not sleep nights, asking myself the question, "Was it my fault? Did I give them fair warning?" "God have mercy upon their soul," would be an appropriate prayer this morning—if it were not too late!

But oh, how many of our friends, during these five years, have gone away in Christian peacefulness! The evening came on them with the soft step of the dew. There was sobbing in the room, and there were wailings that made the heart ache, and cries of "What will we do without father?" "How lonely the world will be without mother!" "Speak, my darling, once more! Do you know me? Say, my child, do you know me?"

Ah! no wonder they made no response. How could they take your hand when Christ had it in both of his? How could they hear your voice when the heavenly escort, come to fetch them home, were in full chant? How could they see you in the turned-down light of the sick-room, when the morning of heaven was surging in upon their soul at full tide? See! see! there are angels in the room. Oh, those dying looks, those enchanted faces, those closing expostulations! If I could, this morning, bring those five years of Christian death-bed triumphs before you, you would spring to your feet shouting the glory; and those radiant ones who have gone up from your homes would seem moving up and down again through these very aisles, and you would see their brows garlanded with joy, and their necks jeweled with light; and as they looked upon you, their countenances sympathetic for your loneliness, you would want to die too, so as to be with them. Do not cry! Do not cry! Parents, you will get back your child. Sorrowful orphans, you will see father again—you will see mother again. God will wipe away all tears from your eyes.

During these five years, thirty-two of our members have gone out of life, and they all went away in the sunrise. Blessed be God! I knew them here, and I will know them better there.

And now, as a church, we put out into a future unknown, so far as particulars are concerned; but we know one thing about it: "Thou shalt see greater things than these." We have only just built the fort out of which we are going to fire upon the Lord's enemies. We have only just planted the stake from which we are going to swing out in the offing the Gospel net. We really believe that, where we have had hundreds brought to God, we will have thousands. We mean to pray the church through. To God be the glory for the past! In God is our hope for the future. You and I may die—that will not have any thing to do with the cause. The cause will go on. The sorrowful will be comforted. The tempted will be delivered. The dead will be raised. There are going to be larger harvest-homes, and stronger doxologies, and more jubilant hallelujahs.

Oh, men and women! impenitent, committed to my charge, how can I give you up? If there be any power in prayer, in tears, in heart-breaking solicitations, you must come in. Oh, fire-crowned Sinai, unlimber now thy batteries! Oh, quaking Calvary, now plead thy love! Oh, Day of Judgment, now unsheathe thy glory! Oh, Heaven, display thy thrones! Oh, pit, flash forth thy terrors! And amidst the rising, and the falling, and the quaking, and the wailing, and the shouting, and the praying, as one billow of an aroused sea has been known to pitch a steamer with a thousand passengers high and dry upon the beach, so now this moment, with one great surge of penitence and prayer, let all this audience be landed on the shore of eternal safety.

My heart overflows with emotion when I think that I have another pastoral year less of work to do. I am not tired. God has been very good to me all these years. Notwithstanding the work I have been called to do here in this church, and in the Lay College, and in the editorial chair—a combined work that many supposed and prophesied would crush me—I have never had a day of real sickness in my life, and a headache is to me unknown, save as some of my good friends, with their hands on their hot temples, have described it. God has been very good to me. I ascribe this health and prosperity first to God, and then to the two facts that I have a very good home, and a congregation who give me no annoyance. They are in sympathy with me and my work. If any of them do not like me, I have been too stupid to find it out. I thank you for all your forbearances toward me. I thank you for all the generosity with which you have met my worldly necessities. Above all, I thank you for the prayers that in public and private you have offered for me and mine. I hope to live and die with you. It is my highest ambition to be your servant for Jesus sake. And when it is time for me to rest, then I want to be carried out through these very streets by the men who sit before me to-day. Their arms are good and strong, and they will know how to let me gently down into the last sleep. Many of them are my children in the Gospel. They were good to me while I lived. I would not be afraid to trust myself in their arms when I am dead. And then, one by one, you will come out to the same silent neighborhood; and when the morning of the resurrection dawns, in its holy light we will wake up together, and as I cry, "Are you all here?" you will know my voice, for you have heard it so often, and you will answer, "All here!"

"I believe in the communion of saints and the life everlasting. Amen."

THE END.

www.ingramcontent.com/pod-product-compliance
Lightning Source LLC
Chambersburg PA
CBHW032142010526
44111CB00035B/859